FIVE PERSPECTIVES ON TEACHING

Mapping a Plurality of the Good

Second Edition

Center for Graduate Studies
West Coast University
Los Angeles, CA

Cover: **Inukshuk – Vancouver, Canada**

The cover shows an *Inukshuk* statue created by artisan Alvin Kanak from the North West Territories in 1987 as a gift for the World Expo in Vancouver. The traditional meaning of the *Inukshuk* is "Someone was here" or "You are on the right path." As such, *Inukshuk* are used by the Inuit for communication and survival.

Cover photo by:

Anne Taylor (photo)
Steve Pinney (concept)

FIVE PERSPECTIVES ON TEACHING

Mapping a Plurality of the Good

Second Edition

Daniel D. Pratt
Dave Smulders
and
Associates

Krieger Publishing Company
Malabar, Florida
2016

Original Edition 2016

Printed and Published by
KRIEGER PUBLISHING COMPANY
KRIEGER DRIVE
MALABAR, FLORIDA 32950

Copyright © 2016 by Krieger Publishing Company

Library of Congress Cataloging-in-Publication Data

Pratt, Daniel D., 1942-
  Five perspectives on teaching : mapping a plurality of the good / Daniel D. Pratt, Dave Smulders, & Associates. — Second edition.
     pages cm
  Includes bibliographical references and index.
  ISBN 978-1-57524-319-1 (alk. paper)
  1. Adult education—Cross-cultural studies. 2. Teaching—Cross-cultural studies. 3. College teaching—Cross cultural studies. 4. Adult learning—Cross-cultural studies. I. Title.
  LC5219.P73 2015
  371.102—dc23

                                        2015008250

10 9 8 7 6 5 4 3 2

Contents

SECTION III

Dedication

In memory of John B. Collins

With enthusiasm and without limit,

John gave of his intellect and his time.

He cared enough to ask all the right questions.

John was, quite simply,

the quintessential academic

and a rare friend.

He will be missed more than words can say.

Foreword

One of the great pleasures of reading this book in its first edition was the way that teaching was complexified. By that I mean the way that Dan Pratt and his team explicitly and repeatedly challenged the oversimplification of teaching into a unitary set of 'best practices' that could be identified and then applied across multiple and very different contexts. The contextuality of teaching was a strong theme in the first edition and over the years it has been interesting to see Dan and his colleagues develop and refine the five orientations they laid out in the 1998 edition, presenting updated findings and instruments at numerous international conferences. Indeed, for their work on one of these instruments—the *Teaching Perspectives Inventory* profiled in chapter 11—Dan and John Collins were recognized by the American Association for Adult and Continuing Education who awarded them the 2012 *Imogene Okes Award for Outstanding Research in Adult Education*.

The authorial team has changed for this second edition, although Ric Arseneau remains from the first edition. This allows for an updating, expansion and reframing of the five perspectives through fresh eyes. The second edition also benefits from the contributions of Michelle Riedlinger, a colleague who teaches academic writing. But what I perhaps appreciate most about this second edition is that it repeatedly acknowledges that many of us draw on different perspectives at different times. If teaching is about helping something as complex as learning then it surely implements the Ignation notion of *Tantum Quantum*—that context constantly alters how a practice is put into effect.

Yet, at the core of a teacher's work is a teacher's being. I cannot abandon my core convictions, erase all the experiences that are constitutive of my identity, nor become somebody else. Within the course of a weekend seminar or workshop I will probably spend some time teaching specific content, mentoring learners, demonstrating how skills should be practiced, brainstorming social change strategies, and trying to democratize the classroom. Though these tasks seem to cross perspectives they are all enacted by me, Stephen Brookfield, informed by my most basic convictions; for example, my belief that the most important pedagogic knowledge I need to do good work is a constant awareness of how people are experiencing their learning, or my belief that I must always try to model whatever I'm asking learners to do.

So how I teach at any moment on any day is strongly influenced by the purposes I'm trying to achieve and what I know about the people I'm working with. Some things do hold constant; but exactly what I'll do, and the way I'll do it, varies with local circumstances. When I find myself in practice, some particular event—a provocative and disturbing question or a student's body language—may change radically the way I'm teaching in that particular moment. The constancy across those circumstances is my commitment to democratic classrooms and people's right to be treated with compassion and respect. Thus, variations in my teaching are built upon a foundational commitment that holds true across contexts and circumstances. It is, therefore, not what I do, but why I do it, that is central to understanding my perspective on teaching.

Consequently, the book asserts that people do not simply choose between different perspectives, as if they were choosing which color jacket to wear today or which item to order off a menu. How we teach is, at least partly, a function of who we are. I will never lose my conviction that classrooms should be democratized wherever and whenever possible. I will always believe that students' preferences and needs should be responded to, even if I disagree strongly with them. I will die believing that people need to be treated compassionately and respectfully, even as I struggle with learners who I personally dislike for their bigotry, myopia, ego-aggrandizement and refusal to shut up.

I love this book because I see myself in its pages and because it acknowledges the rich complexity of teaching. I also admire enormously the consistent integrity, compassion and rigor that it's chief author—Dan Pratt—brings to all his projects. Dan, it's been a privilege to count myself as a colleague of yours for the past 35 years.

Stephen Brookfield
John Ireland Endowed Chair,
University of St. Thomas,
Minneapolis-St. Paul

SECTION I

Section I provides an overview to the framework which guided the original research, and the basic structure of five perspectives on teaching that emerged from that research.

Chapter 1 introduces a general model of teaching, with five elements and three relationships. This model formed the backbone of the observations and interviews from which the five perspectives emerged. It is the conceptual framework through which teaching was examined and from which perspectives emerged.

Chapter 2 looks at indicators of commitment that helped define perspectives on teaching: beliefs, intentions and actions (including assessment and teaching strategies).

Chapter 3 introduces each perspective as a complex lens through which teachers view the elements and relationships within the general model of teaching. Section I, therefore, provides a conceptual platform that should help you interpret the more visceral descriptions of each perspective in Section II.

CHAPTER 1
The Research Lens

Daniel D. Pratt

SEEKING A PLURALITY OF THE GOOD

Increasingly, teachers at every level and in every context are being asked to articulate and reflect upon their approach to teaching. They do so for many reasons—some more benign (e.g., as part of a workshop) and others more critical (e.g., as part of an evaluation). Few within the education community, whether educating youth or adults, argue against this movement. Most simply presume it is a worthy and appropriate task, assuming perhaps that it will provide better understanding and more equitable judgment of teaching (Pratt, 2005).

At the same time, there has been a move to adopt a single, dominant view of effective teaching, usually one that is 'learner-centered' and based on a constructivist view of knowledge and learning. In other words, teachers are asked to reflect on who they are and how they teach, but with an implied message that that reflection should conform to some preconceived notion of a 'good' teacher (Pratt, 2002).

In part, the argument for this move is a reaction against teacher-centered instruction that has dominated much of education, particularly adult and higher education, for much of the past century. Yet, to argue for a singularity of good in teaching while also asking people to reflect on their teaching implies a false promise of opportunity to be different from the dominant view of teaching (Pratt, 2005). It also contradicts a mounting body of evidence that effective teaching depends on context (Pratt, Harris, & Collins, 2009; Pratt, Sadownik, & Jarvis-Selinger, 2012), discipline or field of practice (Shulman, 2005), and culture (Tweed & Lehman, 2002). Clearly, one size does not fit all.

Despite the evidence, many adult educators assume that andragogy[1] represents the best way to teach adults, especially when adult education is compared to youth education. Yet, we know there are many effective adult educators who do not see themselves as andragogical "facilitators." For some this is due to their personality and preferences for teaching in a more directive style. Others may have no choice, due to the nature of what they teach (e.g., safety procedures in a hospital or for exiting an airplane in an emergency). For other adult educators, the role of facilitator might be at odds with their cultural traditions for a teacher as, for example, in the case of a Chinese master teaching Tai Chi to Westerners. In addition to these challenges, there is an additional question as to whether the role of andragogical facilitator reproduces existing forms of power that give privileges to some people over others. In any case, there is good reason to question, rather than accept, the assumption that there is one best way to teach adults.

Indeed, the mounting evidence strongly suggests that there is no basis for assuming a single, universally best approach to teaching adults. Both the philosophical and empirical evidence argues against it. What is needed instead is a plurality of perspectives on teaching that recognize and respect a diversity of teachers, learners, content, context, ideals, and purposes. Adult and higher education are pluralistic in people and purpose, in content and in context, and should, therefore, be pluralistic in regard to what is considered effective teaching. Such diversity compels us to acknowledge a plurality of the good in teaching.

A GENERAL MODEL

While this plurality must be acknowledged, we must also recognize the impasse that would result if we had no way of identifying essential differences between perspectives. One way to accommodate a plurality of the good, while also identifying the fundamental ways in which they differ, is to construct a conceptual model. Such a

---

[1] Andragogy is "the science and art of teaching adults" (Knowles, 1980). It is built upon two central, defining attributes: First, a conception of learners as self-directed and autonomous; and second, a conception of the role of teacher as facilitator of learning rather than presenter of content.

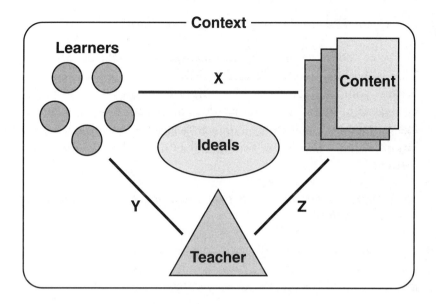

Figure 1.1 A general model of teahing

model, developed for the initial research that lead to this book, is presented in A General Model of Teaching (Figure 1.1).

The model contains five elements (teacher, learners, content, context, and ideals) and three relationships (lines X, Y, and Z). The easiest way to understand how the model works is for you to think about your own answers to these questions:

Teacher: What is the primary role of a teacher?

As you imagine yourself as a teacher, what is your role and responsibility? What are you to do? As a teacher, what do learners expect of you? If your teaching is being evaluated, what would the evaluators expect of your role and responsibility? How might your role differ from teachers you have had?

Learners: Who are your learners?

What do they bring to the learning situation that might influence their learning or your teaching? What do you want to know about them? Why do you want to know that? What will be their role in relation to what you want them to learn?

Content: What do you want people to learn?

What do you want people to learn in your field or discipline? Why is that important? What might be difficult about learning that? Within your subject area, what might learners resist or be less motivated to learn? Is there an order or structure to your content that is important to learning it or teaching it? Are there concepts or key principles that must be learned before other things can be learned?

Context: Does the context in which you teach influence how you teach?

If so, how does it influence your teaching? How does it influence what people learn and how they learn? What is it about context that controls or predetermines your approach to teaching?

Ideals: What ideals or values influence your teaching?

What ideals or values guide your teaching? Why are those important? If your teaching were to be evaluated, would it be important for the evaluators to understand and appreciate those ideals? Why?

In our original research, each element served as a potential focus for interviewing respondents about their perspectives on teaching. Some teachers more readily talked about their learners, while others were more interested in talking about subject matter or content. Most people were quite willing and able to talk about each of the elements, although with different degrees of clarity and commitment, with the exception of the element of ideals. It seems that most respondents held their ideals implicitly, as taken-for-granted values, rather than explicitly as well-articulated statements. However, teachers holding a Social Reform Perspective were an exception to this (see Chapter 8).

Relationships between Elements

The relationships between elements provided another avenue for understanding respondents' views of teaching (lines X, Y, and Z in Figure 1.1).

In the research it was clear that people imagined different ways of engaging learners in the content, but they also held different assumptions about what learners brought that influenced their learning of that content. And most of our respondents held strong beliefs about assessing what people knew or learned related to the content. Thus, issues related to engagement, prior knowledge, motivation, and assessment are implied in line X in the general model.

Line Y is about the relationship between a teacher and the learners. As you can imagine, people preferred different kinds of relationships with learners, ranging from close, almost *in loco parentis* relationships, to indifferent or nonexistent relationships. Each of those, and all relationships in between, was justified in terms of the teacher's beliefs. Thus, we remained open to the possibility that a host of reasons and traditions was at play in understanding the relationship between teacher and learners.

Finally, line Z represented beliefs about what teachers must know in order to teach their discipline or field of practice. This is referred to as the teacher's 'content credibility' and speaks to assumptions and beliefs about the amount and type of knowledge one must have to be an effective teacher. Again, there was wide variation in what our respondents said about the knowledge one must have to be a teacher, ranging from advanced degrees and/or extensive experience as a practitioner to simply being able to facilitate discussion among people. We were, once again, aware that what people were telling us was in part a reflection of their own training and enculturation into cultural traditions and communities of practice.

Again, reflect on your own views and think about how you would answer these questions:

Line X: Engagement, prior knowledge, motivation, and assessment.

What do you do to engage learners in the content? What prior knowledge or beliefs do they bring with them that influence their learning of your content? How do you use that in your teaching? Describe your students' motivation, in relation to learning what you teach. How do you 'hook' that motivation? How do you assess what people have learned? How do you use assessment to help people learn what you want them to learn?

Line Y: Teacher's relationship with the learners.

What can students expect from you? What do you expect of them? Describe a learner that was challenging for you. Why was that person/situation challenging? How did you deal with that?

Line Z: Assumptions about content credibility

What training or background is essential to teaching what you teach? What is important for you to know or be able to do? How do you establish your content credibility or expertise with students? How do you deal with a question that you can't answer? What do you do when people challenge the utility or relevance of what you are teaching?

Once again in the research, educators said that not all the relationships were equally significant for them. Some were more meaningful, others less so. Not one of the 253 people studied in the original study held all the elements and relationships as equally important. This opened the possibility that perspectives might be anchored in different combinations of elements and relationships. Indeed, their comments revealed that teachers were committed to a particular blend of elements and relationships. A further analysis of those commitments led, in turn, to an understanding of the indicators of commitments: people's beliefs, intentions, and actions (Figure 1.2).

COMMITMENTS IN TEACHING

Return, for a moment, to the General Model of Teaching (Figure 1.1). As a conceptual framework the model simply identifies elements and relationships that may be important in teaching. It does not suggest relative importance or significance; no element or relationship is pictured as more dominant than others. Yet, the fundamental difference between perspectives rests upon the belief that some elements (and relationships) are more important than others. That is, educators show greater or lesser commitment to some elements than others when talking about their teaching.

Commitment is defined here as a sense of duty, responsibility, obligation, or even loyalty associated with one or more elements within the General Model of Teaching. It is revealed through the way a person teaches (actions, including teaching strategies and

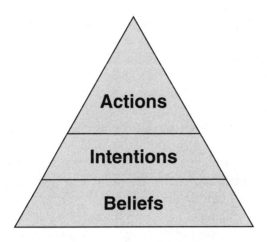

Figure 1.2 Indicators of commitment

forms of assessment), what a person is trying to accomplish (intentions), how a person assesses what people have learned, and statements of why those actions, intentions, and forms of assessment are reasonable, important, or justifiable (beliefs) (Figure 1.2). Commitment is, thus, pivotal for understanding perspectives on teaching.

As mentioned above, a teacher's commitment is usually directed more toward one or two elements than others; it is prominent while teachers plan, conduct, evaluate, and reflect upon their teaching. This does not mean they have no regard for the other elements; rather, some elements are more noticeable in teachers' thinking and tend to be the focal point for clarifying their intentions and beliefs related to teaching.

Commitment to a particular element was the focus of respondents' comments in the original research. Those committed to an element (e.g., content, learners, context) spoke vividly about it. To give you an idea of how commitment to an element sharpens a teacher's awareness of it, four elements are represented here, with some elaboration from respondents in the original research.

Learners

Many of the teachers we have studied reveal themselves to be learner-focused in their commitment. When reflecting on what went well or what they might do differently, these educators focused their reflection and comments on their learners. For example, when asked, 'What are you trying to accomplish?' some teachers spoke about helping students gain confidence in their ability to learn a particular content or subject matter. This was especially true if the subject matter had a reputation for being difficult. One woman, teaching science to non-science majors, spoke of wanting to change students' beliefs about science, but she also wanted to change students' beliefs about their ability to learn science. She was a dedicated scientist, but in her teaching she was equally committed to helping students feel confident about learning science.

For some teachers, especially those in adult basic education, intentions were focused on helping people overcome previous failures. They wanted students to know that they cared, deeply, about them. As one teacher said,

> I would like my students to think I cared about them. I cared about their learning and I cared about the quality of their work. Most of all, I hope they would believe that they could make a difference in their lives. Why? Because I think these are the best things I can possibly do as a teacher, is care about my students and have them learn to respect themselves.

Still others focused on the learner's intellectual development or clinical reasoning. They talked about helping people learn to think critically, to solve problems, or to go beyond the obvious and probe the content for its deeper meaning or significance. As one physics teacher at an Oregon community college put it, "I want to teach more about less; I want to help people think, not just about physics, but about the physical world around them." In that statement he was making content the servant of thinking and rejecting institutional pressures to cover the syllabus.

In each case, the subject of these teachers' conversations, and the focus of their commitment, was the learner, not the content. The content was a means; the learner was the end. This is not uncommon in adult and higher education, which has a long history of attracting teachers whose primary commitment is to their students. From adult basic education to graduate school, many of those involved in the teaching of adults think first about the learners as they plan, conduct, evaluate, and reflect on their teaching.

Content

Some teachers felt a strong commitment to their content (also called discipline, profession, trade, or field of practice). A great many of the teachers in higher education were committed to the discipline or content area they taught. They felt passionately about chemistry, forestry, nursing, or literature and they turned to that content when addressing the question, 'What are you trying to accomplish?' Watching them teach, one could see their enthusiasm; it was apparent they had strong feelings about their subject matter. Further, they expected learners to be committed to that subject matter or discipline. As one teacher of anatomy said, 'I love anatomy! And I hope my students do too.'

We saw a similar dedication in the training of service industry and trades personnel. For example, the director of training for Sheraton Hotels in Singapore expressed a strong sense of responsibility toward the hospitality industry. However, his commitment was not to the industry, per se, but to a particular kind of excellence as defined by his hotel. The Sheraton staff and management prided themselves on setting standards of service and training that went beyond industry standards. They felt, as do many who are committed to content, that education and training should be concerned most of all with building an accurate and sufficient foundation of knowledge so as to support high standards of achievement or professional practice.

Context

Other teachers were equally clear about their commitment to context, that is, the need to locate learning in authentic contexts of practice and social relations. They could not imagine significant learning taking place apart from real life and the place where learning was to be applied. Of course, there are many kinds of context— cultural, historical, political, geographical, organizational, and so forth. However, here context refers to the physical and social environment where people learn.

I first became aware of people's strong feelings about context while working with Aboriginal Canadians in the Yukon Territory of Canada. The most powerful and important teachers in the communities were the elders. They embodied much of what younger people were expected to learn about life in the North including a range of skills and values. Whether the content was storytelling, hunting and trapping, or sorting out social conflicts, people learned alongside someone more experienced within a community of people that was interdependent. Learners watched, listened, and gradually participated in the social community of working and living together. Life and learning were one; context was the place where living and learning coincided.

However, it wasn't just Aboriginal Canadians who expressed this sentiment. Instructors in the trades, managers, physicians, nurses, and coaches also questioned learning that didn't happen on the job or in the field of play. Knowledge and skill were understood to be socially situated, that is, located in the practices and social exchanges of working and living alongside others in communities of practice. (Wenger, 1998; 2006) They, like the elders of the north, saw context as the critical element for meaningful learning. Some went so far as to say that context was, quite simply, the most powerful teacher of all.

Ideals

Perhaps most emphatic of all were those who defined their teaching in terms of an ideal, principle, or core value. These people believed, for example, that teaching ought to be governed by a commitment to justice or equality, or the need to redress power imbalances within society. Their commitment was to a set of clearly articulated values or ideals rather than to content, learners, or context. One woman, teaching automotive maintenance for women, was very clear that her agenda was to help women bring about social change that would redress the imbalance of power affecting employment and advancement in the automotive industry based on gender. This principle was more important than the individuals in her classes. Her commitment was clearly to changing society, not just to the immediate skill development of women attending her classes.

SUMMARY

The diversity of learners, content, context, and ideals in adult and higher education suggests that any meaningful examination of teaching needs to address the nature of a teacher's commitment if it is to make any meaningful, lasting change in the person's teaching. The General Model of Teaching presented here identifies elements that pointed to forms of commitment, expressed in terms of actions, intentions, and beliefs. How these actually coalesce into the five perspectives presented in this book will be detailed in subsequent chapters.

Perspectives, then, govern what we do as teachers and why we think such actions are worthy or justified. They are indicated by commitment toward one, or more, of the elements and relationships within the General Model of Teaching and expressed through actions, intentions, and beliefs related to those elements. The five perspectives presented in this book are not the only perspectives on teaching; I make no such claim. Yet, they are a faithful representation of the views of more than 250 adult educators in the original studies and hundreds of thousands that have completed the Teaching Perspectives Inventory since then.

In closing this chapter, let me spell out several propositions that emerged from the research and guided the writing of this book.

Proposition 1: There is no single, universal, best perspective on teaching.

Most books, and evaluators of teaching, would have us believe there is an agreed upon view of how best to teach adults. This volume rests on a different assumption, one that values a pluralistic view of teaching and a diversity of commitments and perspectives.

Proposition 2: Perspectives are neither good nor bad.

Each perspective holds the potential for good and for poor teaching. In our research we saw examples of various qualities of teaching in each of the five perspectives. Therefore, it's important to remember that holding a particular perspective does not predict the quality of someone's teaching.

Proposition 3: Approaches to teaching are guided by individuals' dominant and back-up perspectives on teaching.

Guiding perspectives, in turn, are manifest through the following: beliefs about knowledge, learning, and appropriate roles, responsibilities, and relationships for instructors of adults; intentions about what a teacher is trying to accomplish through teaching; and strategic actions and forms of assessment.

> *Proposition 4: Some educational beliefs are more central to one's being than others and, therefore, are less open to change.*

Some of our beliefs are so rooted in core values that they represent long-held and significant aspects of who we are and how we see ourselves in relation to the world. With these deep-rooted beliefs, we sometimes assume that our values should be everyone's values. At the other end of the spectrum we may hold beliefs that are more peripheral than central to our image of self-as-teacher and, therefore, more open to challenge and change.

> *Proposition 5: Improvements in instruction can focus on actions (e.g., improving lectures, developing assessments), intentions (e.g., clarifying exactly what you want people to learn), or beliefs (e.g., articulating what you believe most influences learning).*

Many readers might wonder if it's possible to improve their teaching without receiving direct feedback on our teaching or the effects of our teaching. It's an important question, and the answer is "yes." An increasing body of research suggests we can improve our teaching through reflection, especially if that reflection considers the underlying beliefs and intentions that guide our teaching (e.g., Dall'alba, 2009; Trowler & Cooper, 2002). In fact, it is difficult to imagine significant growth in teaching without reflecting on what you are trying to accomplish, how you go about it, and why you think that is important. As mentioned in the second proposition, teaching is guided by an interrelated set of actions, intentions, and beliefs. Therefore, reflection MUST go beyond actions, to include one's intentions and beliefs.

> *Proposition 6: Development as a teacher can mean improving current educational practices or it can mean challenging fundamental beliefs about instruction or learning.*

Faculty or staff development programs often focus on helping people improve what they routinely do as teachers, for example, learning how to give better lectures, conduct more effective discussion groups, develop better means of assessment, and so on. However, there is another important way in which we develop as instructors and that is through critically reflecting on what we believe about teaching and learning. One of the authors in adult education literature who has greatly affected my work is Jack Mezirow, now retired from Teachers' College, Columbia University. He has written extensively on a form of learning called "perspective transformation." This form of learning addresses the fundamental ways in which we see ourselves in relation to others and in relation to our work. This is another avenue of growth or development for teachers. Perspective transformation doesn't happen often, and when it does, it rarely comes quickly. But when we experience this form of learning it is truly profound; it affects every aspect of teaching because it involves a change in the belief structures that we hold close to our core being and which normally go unchallenged.

Proposition 7: Perspectives can be measured and profiled.

Perspectives on teaching were initially discovered through extensive interviews and observations. Now individuals can simply go to: www.TeachingPerspectives.com (that's one word) and receive a graphic profile of their orientation to teaching. The web site is freely available and individuals are invited to take the Teaching Perspectives Inventory (TPI) multiple times if they wish to track their development over time. However, it's important when taking the TPI to focus on one and only ONE teaching setting and group of learners. If you take the TPI a second or third time, you may change focus by considering a different teaching situation.

The TPI can also be used to understand how your students see you as 'teacher'. After students have had sufficient time with you to know you as a teacher, ask them to fill out the TPI 'about you' (entering your email address, instead of their own). You will get their collective views of your teaching—anonymously. You may then want to have a conversation with them about their profiles of your teaching compared to your own profile. If you do this, it's important to assure students that their responses will be anonymous. Alternatively, you might start your class by having people fill out the TPI on a teacher that was memorable to them—but using a pseudonym rather than the person's name. Again, you could have them enter your email, rather than their own, which would result in you receiving their 'memorable teacher' profiles anonymously. This would provide grist for a discussion early on about what kind of teaching has worked well for people in the past. It also sets the stage for having them fill out the TPI on your teaching.

REFERENCES

Dall'alba, G. (2009). Learning professional ways of being: Ambiguities of becoming. *Educational Philosophy and Theory*, 41, 34-45.

Knowles, M. (1980). *The modern practice of adult education: From pedagogy to andragogy*. Edgewood Cliff, NJ: Prentice Hall Regents.

Pratt, D. D. (2005). Personal Philosophies of Teaching: A false promise? *ACADEME, American Association of University Professors*, 91(1), 32-36, January-February.

Pratt, D. D., Harris, P., & Collins, J.B. (2009). The power of one: Looking beyond the teacher in clinical instruction. *Medical Teacher*, 31(2), 133-137.

Pratt, D. D., Sadownik, L., Jarvis-Selinger, S. (2012). Pedagogical BIASes and clinical teaching in medicine. English, L. M. (Ed.), *Health and Adult Learning*. University of Toronto Press, 273-296.

Shulman, L. (2005). Signature pedagogies in the professions. *Daedalus*, 134(3), 52-59.

Tweed, R. G., & Lehman, D. R. (2002). Learning considered within a cultural context: Confucian and Socratic approaches, *American Psychologist*, 57(2), 89-99.

Trowler, P. & Cooper, A. (2002). Teaching and learning regimes: Implicit theories and recurrent practices in the enhancement of teaching and learning through educational development programmes. *Higher Education Research & Development*, 21, 221-240.

Wenger, E. (1998). *Communities of practice: Learning, meaning and identity*. Cambridge, University of Cambridge Press.

Wenger, E. (2006) *Communities of practice: A brief introduction*. Retrieved January 16, 2012, from http://ewenger.com/theory/index.htm

CHAPTER 2
Indicators of Commitment

Daniel D. Pratt

ACTIONS, INTENTIONS, AND BELIEFS

A number of years ago, I attended a 3-day workshop on teaching. Twenty-five people, from widely different subject areas came together with a common desire to be better teachers. Some taught university students; others taught people from the community. Still others taught patients and worked in homes or at bedsides. We represented a wide range of disciplines and experience. Some were there as a condition of recent employment; others were there out of choice. No one was there because their teaching had been judged problematic.

Over the 3-day weekend we learned how to write behavioral objectives, sequence content, give lectures, write different levels of questions, conduct a discussion, and plan for assessment of learning. All of this was done within a supportive and well-structured environment. The instructors were enthusiastic and well prepared; clearly, this program had been delivered many times before, in several parts of the country. Yet, some thing seemed fundamentally wrong.

A few days after the workshop I had time to reflect on it all. We had been led through a particular view of teaching, composed of a set of skills that were assumed to apply regardless of our learners, content, context, or personal preferences and beliefs. Not once had we been introduced to an alternative view or asked what we thought effective teaching might mean in the context of our work. There was no mention of beliefs or values, or even any possibility that we might have different notions of

17

what it meant to teach, to learn, or to know something. In-
stead, we were given a set of generic skills that were assumed
to be appropriate across disciplines, contexts, learners, and
even cultures. Effective teaching had been reduced to a formu-
laic set of teaching techniques and skills, most of which could
be captured on videotape for review and further practice. There
were two implicit messages in this workshop: First, there was
only one legitimate view of teaching; second, it didn't matter
what, where, or whom you were teaching, these were the es-
sential skills.

This experience is not uncommon. Many people characterize
teaching as a set of generic skills or techniques to be mastered. The
assumption is that if teachers have sufficient content knowledge, all
they need to learn is a predetermined set of skills to be on the road
to effective teaching. Teaching is thus conceived of as a politically
neutral, skilled performance—setting objectives, leading discussions,
giving lectures, asking questions, providing feedback, and so forth.
Any values, beliefs, and commitments embedded in those actions,
go unexamined. Effectiveness is equated with doing these things
with a degree of skill; the more skilled the performance, the better
the teaching.

This view is evidenced by the proliferation of manuals and
texts focusing on teaching techniques. As a consequence, when first
asked to think about different perspectives on teaching, people often confuse technique with perspective: "Sometimes I teach according to one perspective; other times I take a different perspective. It
all depends on the situation." What they are saying is that they vary
their approach or use of techniques depending on the situation. They
may even change their intent or purpose, along with the approach
they take, depending on the circumstances. The terminology might
change, but the implication is the same—teaching is understood in
terms of a flexible set of actions and intentions, sometimes modified according to the situation. Beliefs and values are assumed to
play a minor role, if any, in teaching.

But, as shown in the last chapter, beliefs and values are not
insignificant; they are fundamental. They are the submerged "bulk
of the teaching iceberg" upon which any particular strategy or intention rests. To look only at what is visible (i.e., actions) is to miss

the difference between techniques and perspectives. Perspectives are composed of three "indicators of commitment" that can be made visible: actions, intentions, and beliefs. This chapter considers each of these in turn.

ACTIONS

How do you routinely prepare for an instructional session? Do you have a routine for starting or ending a session? If I observed your teaching, what would I see you doing; what would I see the learners doing? How do you assess whether students have learned? What type of feedback do you provide your students? What is 'typical' of your teaching? What do you do well, as a teacher? What do you want to learn to do better?

First attempts at improving teaching often focus on actions—the strategies, techniques, and forms of assessment we use to engage people in content. As you can see from the questions above, they are the most concrete and accessible aspect of a perspective on teaching. We might work on improving our lectures, leading discussions, asking questioning, setting objectives, or developing means of assessing learning. These are the ways in which we activate our intentions and beliefs. It is what we do to help people learn. In adult and higher education we refer to these as techniques. Within schooling for children and youth they are called methods. In both cases, we are talking about strategic activities that are meant to help people learn—a means of helping them engage in meaningful ways with content or procedures to be learned.

Regardless of their perspective on teaching, instructors use a variety of strategic actions to help people learn. The choice of strategies usually depends on what they want to accomplish and how familiar or comfortable they are with the approach. It might also depend on the amount of time available. For example, in a 1-hour class that I teach at my university, I might use a 20-minute lecture, followed by small group discussions, and then reconvene the whole class for a debriefing of the small group activity, linking their discussion to my initial lecture. Throughout the hour, I intersperse comments with questions to probe people's learning and further engage them in particular aspects of the content. Before the close of the hour I ask people to write one 'take-home' message from the session and one question they would like addressed the next time we meet.

For those of you who have taught, this is not an unusual sequence of events; in fact, it is recommended that we vary the stimulus, or the learning activity, every 30 minutes or so, usually by switching instructional strategies to engage people more actively in what we want them to learn. *Strategies, then, are activities that engage learners with the content and facilitate learning.* Effective teachers use multiple strategies, sometimes changing as often as every 20-30 minutes, in an attempt to actively engage learners in the content. Similarly, assessment can also be used strategically to engage learners. For example, see Chapter 4 for information on 'test-enhanced learning'.

Certainly, all teacher's actions, including strategies and assessment approaches, are important to understanding any view of teaching. Yet, unless we understand what a person is trying to accomplish (intentions) and why they think that is important or reasonable (beliefs) we are in no position to judge the effectiveness of their actions. Consequently, it is also unlikely we will have any meaningful way to help them improve their teaching.

INTENTIONS

What are you trying to accomplish? What would you say is the essential purpose of your course, program, rotation, workshop, etc.? Do you have a clear sense of purpose and intention that guides your instruction? What is your role and responsibility in achieving that intention or sense of purpose?

Intentionality is the driver of teaching. Without a clear sense of purpose, we would have no way of judging the effects of our actions or the quality of our teaching. Indeed, I would go so far as to say that, as teachers, we cannot be any better than our intentions inspire us to be. Intentions are, therefore, crucial to understanding, evaluating, and improving teaching.

Objectives vs. Intentions

Within much of adult and higher education, instructional objectives are equated with instructional intent. It is assumed that an effective teacher should be able to specify what the learner will be able to do at the end of a teaching session. Instructional objectives, it is argued, accomplish three things: 1) they articulate the goals of a curriculum so that colleagues and learners can compare what is expected across different courses or programs; 2) once clearly stated, objectives facilitate the selection and organization of content; and 3) if objectives are clearly specified, they make it possible to assess learning and evaluate the effectiveness of teaching. For many, this may appear to be a rational and convincing argument for writing instructional objectives as a means of clarifying instructional intent.

However, objectives are not the same as instructional intent. Objectives are statements that indicate what specific behavior will stand as evidence of learning. They are usually written in behavioral form; that is, they use verbs to clearly indicate what kind of behavioral change would be accepted as evidence of learning. The implication is that learning outcomes must be both predictable and observable. While this may be true for some intentions, not all intentions for learning outcomes can be behaviorally specified (see list below).

Furthermore, even when trained to write objectives, many educators do not use them. In our research, teachers seldom mentioned using behavioral objectives. Here are some of the reasons they gave for not using instructional objectives:

*   Learning within complicated environments (e.g., emergency medicine) was so complex as to require an exhaustive number of objectives.
*   The nature of the content or subject (e.g., creative writing) was trivialized if reduced to behavioral indicators.
*   It was impossible to predict with any accuracy the most important forms of learning that would result from their teaching (e.g., developing compassion toward patients).
*   It was feared that objectives could inadvertently cause learners to take a superficial approach to learning, that is, they would simply learn to fulfill the objectives (e.g., pretending to work in teams).
*   The most important learning was situated in contexts of application and, therefore, it was difficult to specify in advance what might be the best evidence of learning (e.g., attitudinal changes toward safe driving).

- Objectives were thought to restrict a teacher's ability to be flexible and responsive to the dynamic nature of teaching and the complex mix of learners (e.g., retraining for the workforce).

Thus, although objectives may be useful to some teachers as a means of stating their expectations for learners, they are not as useful in determining a teacher's sense of commitment and perspective on teaching. In fact, teachers studied in the original research, for the most part, found it difficult to use objectives as a means of indicating what they were trying to accomplish, yet they had no difficulty articulating their intent. They quite readily answered the question, "What are you trying to accomplish?" with responses that were natural, easily expressed, and coherent. They had an agenda, a game plan, or a set of aspirations. Further, it was apparent that they planned for, and reflected on, their teaching using intentions, not instructional objectives.

Intentions Are (Part of) Commitment

Intentions are general statements of the instructor's agenda or overall sense of purpose. They are an indication of a teacher's commitment. Whereas objectives are specific and may be distant from a teacher's sense of commitment and purpose, intentions are held with intensity and conviction. For example, a teacher of literacy talked about her intentions and aims in the following terms:

> As an advocate of feminist, antiracist pedagogy, I want to develop a sense of community in which speaking, listening, reading, and writing [are] not limited to school, but will spill over into the larger community . . . Their [the students] ability to liberate themselves from illiteracy and related social oppression depends on changing individual and group ways of thinking [as well as] opening the doors of public institutions previously considered as inaccessible . . . [this is part of] wanting to promote attitudinal growth leading to social change . . . it is an educator's moral obligation to contest ideological presumptions that inscribe systemic inequities.

As you can see, her intentions are an important indicator of her commitment and very likely an essential part of her perspective on teaching. In another, less strident example, an instructor teaching a course on evaluation said her intention was to provide people with sufficient knowledge about evaluation theory and practice so that they had a choice of approaches when conducting evaluations. She held this intention with clarity and conviction; it was quick to come forth in our conversation and clear in its articulation. This clarity of intent allowed her to be flexible in the attainment of that intention. She was able to adjust the course as she went along, to take advantage of unanticipated turns and events in the journey. Furthermore, evidence of the students' attainment of this intent manifested in ways she couldn't have predicted. For example, one student told her about attending a presentation on evaluation that was clearly representative of only one approach, and how meaningful it was to be able to ask about other possible views and approaches to evaluation.

It is also apparent that intentions are an extension of commitment; teachers feel passionate and firm in their statements of intent. This is not the case with objectives. In over 40 years of teaching, I can't recall anyone speaking passionately about an instructional objective! Not only is it a distant and fractured representation of intent, it is also expressed in a form that doesn't feel natural to most teachers. The behavioral straightjacket of objectives is not at all like the flexible and passionate robe of intent displayed by educators in our initial studies. Intentions, therefore, are clearly more than a collection of objectives. *They are an enthusiastic statement of commitment and an indication of one's role and responsibility.* Intentions give direction and justification to actions, and are an essential part of understanding someone's perspective on teaching.

However, they too are only part of the architecture of commitment. Although intentions are a more direct statement of commitment than actions, there is a third, less visible but more powerful, indicator—beliefs.

BELIEFS

When students/learners are having difficulty, what do you do; why do you do that (what is your rationale for doing that)? What characterizes highly effective teaching in your area/discipline/field? What is the most important thing that you have learned about effective teaching? How have you changed, as a teacher, over the years? What do you want people to take from your teaching; and why is that important? What is learning; and how do you know when someone has learned what you are teaching? Can you think of a motto or metaphor that guides you in your teaching?

Beliefs are a critical aspect of commitment in teaching. Yet, they are the most abstract and least accessible aspect of a person's perspective on teaching because they usually go unstated. Every teacher tacitly holds beliefs or assumptions about learning, knowledge, and the role of a teacher. But very few think about them or go so far as to name them. As such, our beliefs are held with varying degrees of clarity, confidence, and centrality. Some are vague and implicit; others are clear and readily explained. Some are held tentatively; others are considered incontestable. Some are marginal to the way a person thinks; others are central and even dominant.

The measure of centrality of a belief is not necessarily a matter of logic or rationality but, more often, the extent to which the belief itself is not in question. When a belief is held without question it acts as arbiter in determining whether our actions, our intentions, or even other beliefs are reasonable and acceptable. Most teachers are able to accommodate a variety of changes in circumstances—including changes in what they teach, whom they teach, and under what conditions—as long as those changes do not challenge their core beliefs, e.g., those most central to their taken-for-granted assumptions and values.

Beliefs, therefore, represent the most stable and least flexible aspect of a person's perspective on teaching.

Beliefs regarding knowledge and learning are, usually, the most central of all beliefs related to teaching. Our beliefs about knowledge, for example, influence our rendering of the material we teach and what we will accept as evidence that people have learned that material. Our beliefs about learning determine how we will engage people in that knowledge and what roles and responsibilities we will assume as teachers. Yet, what is meant by knowledge and learning is usually taken for granted. It is either assumed that educators are in agreement on what they mean, or that these concepts are not

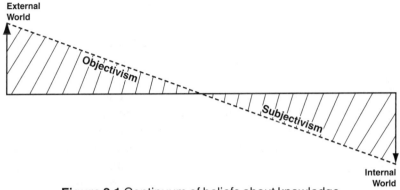

Figure 2.1 Continuum of beliefs about knowledge

particularly relevant to the question of how to teach. It is impossible to adequately understand someone's perspective on teaching without understanding the underlying personal beliefs about knowledge and learning that buttress intentions and actions.

Beliefs about Knowledge

It is not possible to talk about teaching without, at least implicitly, adopting some belief about knowledge or "personal epistemology." Yet, as Candy noted decades ago, "When authors advocate a particular approach to teaching (or learning), only rarely do they make explicit their view of what constitutes valid knowledge, or how it is created, shared, or reproduced" (1991, p. 262). Though not surprising, this neglect must be addressed if we are going to make a reasonable case for perspectives on teaching.

There are two fundamentally different views of knowledge that inform perspectives on teaching. One conceives of knowledge as existing independent of the learner (objectivist); the other conceives of knowledge as something that is personally, socially, and contextually constructed by the learner (subjectivist). Objectivist views are based on a logic of discovery; subjectivist view are based on a logic of interpretation. They are presented here as the ends of a continuum of personal beliefs about knowledge. Although I will discuss them as bipolar opposites, they are more accurately represented as a continuum (Figure 2.1), suggesting that not everyone is completely objectivist or subjectivist in their beliefs about knowledge.

Objectivism

One of the most basic beliefs of an objectivist view is that people can rationally come to know the world as it really is; the facts of the world are essentially there to be accurately described or discovered. The object, therefore, of teaching is to provide a literal account of what the world is like. Viewing the world from this perspective can tempt us into believing that it is not a perspective at all, that it is simply how the world really is. Scott and Usher (1999), writing about educational research, point out the seductive nature of this perspective in seeming to be so evidently true from a common sense point of view.

> How obvious it seems . . . that the world exists independently of us; that the measure of truth should be its correspondence with reality; that we should be able to delimit knowledge and separate the valid from the invalid; and that, given the success of science, the scientific method should be the guarantee of validity and the road to truth. (p. 16)

They sum up their observations about realism overlaid by positivism in three propositions: 1) reality is self-evidently available, 2) science is free of its own cultural confusions, and 3) knowledge is produced by means of immutable methods (p. 14).

From this view, knowledge, or what people learn, exists independent of their knowing it; learner and content are distinctly separate entities. Indeed, objectivism posits that basic theories, principles, and rules that govern our lives and world exist quite separately from our experience of them; knowledge about the world exists "out there," waiting to be discovered. And, because it is assumed there is an external world out there waiting to be discovered, only questions pertaining to that "real world" are truly scientific. Other questions, such as those concerning morality and aesthetics, fall outside the realm of legitimate scientific inquiry (Guba & Lincoln, 1994). This is the classic subject-object dualism wherein knower (learner) and knowledge (content) are believed to be separate.

From an objectivist point of view, truth is a matter of the "goodness of fit," or correspondence, between observation and description. Therefore, whether one is a scientist, journalist, teacher, or a citizen testifying at a trial, observations are expected to be neutral and represent no particular interests or purposes; descriptions, likewise, are to be objective or detached reports of what happened. To demonstrate one knows a subject, body of knowledge, or way of doing something, one must accurately describe it or reproduce it. A statement is true when it corresponds to reality and false when it does not. In other words, truth is a matter of the accuracy of reproduction (in language or action) of reality as judged by some authority.

Competence and authority are highly correlated to how much expert knowledge one possesses. The more one has knowledge or expertise validated through experience, observation, and experimentation, the more competent one is judged to be and the more authority one holds over those who wish to have that knowledge.

Therefore, to be a teacher one must be an expert in the content area. Further, one must hold and present that content objectively. Objective knowledge is that which is not distorted due to the influence of particular interests and values. The opposite, from an objectivist point of view, is subjective knowledge, which by definition (within this conception of knowledge) is distorted through the bias of values and personal interests or interpretation. From an objectivist point of view, facts and values can and should be kept separate.

There is within objectivism another, slightly softer, belief about the separation of facts and values. It acknowledges that they are not actually separate, but interdependent. Yet claims of objectivity may still be achieved as long as values are allowed to dictate problems (what we examine) but not prejudge solutions (what we find). Therefore, we may allow that values will influence what we decide to teach, but we must guard against values distorting the content or influencing our decisions as to whether the content has been correctly learned.

Subjectivism

Subjectivism represents quite different beliefs about knowledge and truth. From this point of view, reality is understood to be pluralistic and plastic—pluralistic in the sense that any reality is expressible in a variety of symbolic and linguistic systems (e.g., societies and cultures); and plastic in the sense that reality is stretched and shaped to fit the purposes and intentions of the people involved (Schwandt, 1994). Knowledge and truth are dependent upon what individuals bring to the moment of perception. As such, knowledge and truth are created, not discovered; and the world is only knowable through people's interpretations of it. Subjectivism is, therefore, a fundamentally different way to view knowledge. As Kneebone states, "When your field of study is people, not molecules, there are many different versions of reality and many different ways of knowing. It all depends on points of view . . . " (p. 516).

As with any social activity, teaching "is a constructed reality, the product of the meanings people give to their interactions with others . . ." (Smith, 1989, p. 8). Imagine, for example, a stump of a tree or a large post that was seen by different people in the dark of night. The first, a young man arriving late for an appointment, thought it was his friend patiently waiting for him; second, a young person walking home from a scary movie, was certain it was something to be feared; and third, a police officer thinking it might be a suspect that he had been looking for. But all the time it was the stump of a tree or simply a post. From a subjectivist point of view, we see the world through our experience; that which we have inside of us is projected onto the world we perceive. Therefore, knowledge is neither a copy nor a mirror of some external reality but, rather, a construction of the individual experiencing it. From this point of view, people (learners) do not merely respond to the world; they impose meaning and value upon it and interpret it in ways that fit, or make sense to them.

Rather than look for correspondence with the outside world, subjectivists looks for correspondence with the inner world, the observer's particular interests, prior knowledge, purposes, and values. Suddenly the criterion of detachment makes no sense. Why would one want to be detached from one's prior knowledge or purposes for observing in the first place? Thus, to subjectivists, it is not the action that is important as much as the meaning of the action, to both the actor and the observer. To them, prior knowledge, experience, and intentions infuse actions with meaning.

Knowledge, from a subjectivist perspective, is personally constructed, socially mediated, and inherently situational. Our perception and interpretation of the world are intimately tied to our language, our experience, and our ways of thinking and valuing. From this point of view, we can never know the world as it is because our perceptions are shaped by our experience. Nor can we detach our experience from the purposes and values that bring us to that experience. Whereas the motto of objectivism might be "seeing is believing," the motto of subjectivism might be "what is seen depends on what is believed." Therefore, to subjectivists, the absolute separation of mind and world, observer and observed, subject and object, or even learner and content must be rejected.

So, how do subjectivists see objectivity? To them, objectivity means consensual agreement between observers, rather than detachment from an observer's place, purpose, or values. The process of arriving at truth is not one of striving for a correspondence between observation and description, but one of negotiation about the meaning of observations. Subjectivists assume that we all observe the world from a particular place of interest and purpose. Therefore, truth is based on the "goodness of fit" between various interpretations, not on the reproduction of a static observation, faithfully described. This is true for subjectivists in all concerns about truth whether it involves deciding someone's guilt or innocence, or evaluating teaching. Subjectivists ask different questions about truth: How believable is the interpretation; how widely held is this interpretation; how well does it agree with the interpretation of others that might have more experience or knowledge; and how did they arrive at this interpretation?

Indeed, this view of knowledge holds that one cannot observe in any reproducible way without a conceptual or theoretical framework. There can be no value-free observations; what counts as data, that is, what we then report from our observations, is influenced by the interests, purposes, and social practices of those doing the observing. This is similar to the Cree and Ojibwa belief that "to tell the truth" means "I will tell it as I know it," which allows for each observer to tell a different version of what happened. Through this process, truth is arrived at not by seeking correspondence, but by seeking consensus; not by looking for a perfect match, but by finding a reasonable fit; not by assuming detachment but by assuming commitment. Truth, therefore, is relative rather than absolute; it depends upon time and place, purpose and interests.

Conceptions of Learning

Both objectivists and subjectivists agree that learning is the primary aim of all teaching. Yet, teachers (and learners) differ in their beliefs about what it means to learn, and what influences that learning. Some of the most influential research on beliefs about learning was done in Sweden where university students were asked, "What does it mean, to learn? What do you actually mean by learning?" (Saljo, 1988). Saljo's work was subsequently replicated with a number of adults studying at the Open University of Britain. The results consistently showed that people held one of six different conceptions of learning. All conceptions represent a belief that learning means a change in something. However, they differ most significantly in their belief about what changes. They are presented here, slightly modified from the original research, in order to illustrate the relationship between beliefs about knowledge and beliefs about learning.

Quantitative Changes in Knowledge

The first two conceptions of learning rest upon a belief that learning is a change in the amount of knowledge or skill one has. These are additive conceptions of learning because they portray learning as a process of expanding a person's existing store of knowledge or improving performance; all learning is therefore to be built upon a platform of what already exists. Yet, there is no suggestion that a person's existing knowledge might interact with the new knowledge; new knowledge is simply added to, or mapped upon, old knowledge.

1.   *Learning is an increase in knowledge.*

People holding this conception think of learning as an increase in the amount of information they can recall. They liken it to filling a container with discrete items; information or knowledge need not be related to anything. An increase in the quantity of information, therefore, signifies learning.

2.   *Learning is memorization, usually for recall or recognition on tests.*

Here, as with the previous conception, there is an assumption of learning equating to an increase in the amount of information one has. However, the purpose for learning is related to testing. Knowledge resides in the authority of the text or teacher, and is to be transferred from that authority to the learner. Learning has occurred when the learner can accurately reproduce the content to the satisfaction of the authority (e.g., teacher).

These two conceptions of learning are based on an objectivist epistemology, sometimes referred to as a received view of knowledge. The content to be taught (and learned) is thought of as an accumulated body of facts, principles, rules, theories, and procedures that have been verified through experience, observation, and experimentation. Authorities, such as teachers, are assumed to have more experience with the content and, therefore, to have accumulated a greater body of knowledge which can then be passed on to learners. Thus, these conceptions tacitly assume that learners will be the receivers and teachers the transmitters of knowledge.

These conceptions reify authority as text and/or teacher, and rest on a received view of knowledge. Learning is the accurate and efficient reproduction of knowledge (information, procedures, skills, attitudes, etc.) in a form that resembles the knowledge of their texts and/or teachers.

This is not an uncommon understanding of learning. Much of formal education is directed toward a nonproblematic, additive view of learning, that is, one which either increases how much someone knows, or fine-tunes knowledge or skill to increase a person's speed or efficiency in retrieving the information.

Bridging Conceptions

The third and fourth conceptions of learning are something of a bridge between the views on quantitative and qualitative changes in knowledge or skill understood as learning. The third conception is still anchored in a belief that learning is a process of adding greater amounts of knowledge or proficiency of performance, but it assumes that knowledge is only useful to the extent it can be applied in a practical setting, as opposed to memorized for tests. The dominant belief about knowledge behind such a view is still objectivist: knowledge is believed to exist "out there" and is to be reproduced by the learner in forms that resemble the knowledge of those more experienced or more knowledgeable. However, learning, in this conception, adds the crucial dimension of **application** to existing ways of knowing and acting.

3.   *Learning is the acquisition of information and procedures to be used or applied in practice.*

The difference between this conception and the preceding two is in the assumption of application, and consequently, the kind of knowledge that is valued. Knowledge that is immediately applicable is seen to be more valid. Learning is a process of acquiring such knowledge as is necessary and appropriate to practical applications. A sense of purpose, beyond testing is, in this conception, an integral part of learning. The learner is placed in a slightly more interactive role with knowledge, making judgments about what is useful content. However, the context of application is now an important aspect of learning and teaching.

As in the first two conceptions, learning is associated with the accumulation and application of knowledge; that knowledge is received without challenge or modification. New learning, as before, is mapped onto the learner's existing cognitive structures and accepted in forms represented by an authority. Furthermore, learning relies on the unquestioning acceptance of both the knowledge and the authority of teachers and texts; there is little or no assumption of authority by the learner to alter the knowledge before it is applied. However, an important difference between this conception and the previous two is the emergence of context into the meaning of learning.

4.   *Learning is believed to be dependent on context; that is, what is learned is determined, in part, by the context in which it is learned and applied.*

This fourth conception of learning brings context more explicitly into the mix of learning, specifically into the transfer of learning. No longer is learning a stable entity, easily transferred from sites of acquisition to sites of application. Rather, it is something that is contextually focused and dependent. Thus, learning is context specific, that is, what is learned is a product of the context in which it was learned. Therefore, it is not so easy to take that learning into a new or different context. This influence of context on learning is often talked about as the *context specificity* of learning. A medical educator in the Netherlands explains it this way:

> In medical education, the new centrality of context caused quite a stir. Context specificity was discovered more or less concurrently in research of expertise in medical problem solving and

in psychometrics. Problem-solving ability was no longer conceptualized as a stable entity. Quite the opposite in fact, it was context specific in the extreme, depending crucially on experts' and learners' idiosyncratic experiences . . . The findings from expertise research and psychometrics were replicated in virtually all areas of medical education. Even generic skills, such as professionalism, communication, team performance and leadership proved context specific. (van der Vlueten, 2014).

Context now becomes vitally important when teaching and learning for application. Transfer of learning cannot be taken for granted. You can learn how to keep score in a baseball game, but that's not going to help you keep score in a hockey game. Thus, as my colleague, Kevin Eva so aptly concluded, "context specificity is a profoundly general phenomenon" (2003).

Qualitative Changes in Knowledge

In the final two conceptions of learning, there is a clear shift from objectivism to subjectivism regarding the underlying beliefs about knowledge. In these conceptions, learning is understood to be an interpretive process, not an additive one. Learning means making sense out of something, not just accumulating information. Conceptions four and five move the learner from a position of passive, unquestioning acceptance of knowledge and authority, to active interpretation and interrogation of content in an effort to "make knowledge their own." The learner now enters the picture as an active agent, shaping both the process and product of learning.

5.   *Learning is the abstraction of meaning.*

In this view there is a significant shift away from satisfying an external authority by reproducing content as taught, to reconstructing it in ways that are personally meaningful to the learners. Learners move from the background to the foreground as they extract meaning based on what they already know. They have become active interpreters, rather than passive receivers, of what is learned.

6.   *Learning is a complex interpretive process aimed at understanding reality and self as co-determinant.*

This belief about learning emphasizes the interdependent relationships between individual, social, historical, and cultural ways of knowing. Individual learners are situated within a constellation of values and contextual factors that influence both the process and product of learning. From within this view, the meaning of any subject matter is dependent upon cultural, historical, and personal factors. For example, when learners are asked to critically reflect on the relationship between gender and learning, if they hold this conception of learning, they must consider the social, cultural, and historical meanings of such concepts as "girl," "boy," "woman," "man," and a range of other designations such as lesbian, gay, bisexual, transgendered, and queer or questioning. Therefore, the interpretive process (learning) involves the complex interaction of individual, social, cultural, and historical factors.

With conceptions five and six, learning is more than simply mapping knowledge onto existing structures. It involves the learner in actively making, or revising, cognitive maps into which knowledge and experience can fit. Furthermore, it is the learner who constructs the cognitive map that is learned, not the teacher; the person has now entered the process of learning as an arbiter of meaning. In these conceptions, trying to replicate an authority's interpretation of knowledge, or performing exactly like a teacher, is understood to be impossible; instead, learning necessitates an interpretation of the content, not a reproduction of it. Therefore, the object of learning has shifted from the content, per se, to the ways in which learners construe or understand the content. Learning is, thus, understood to involve a dynamic relationship between purpose, context, and person.

As you can see, the two major views of learning, quantitative and qualitative, are highly related to the two major views of knowledge, objectivism and subjectivism, (Figure 2.2).

Quantitative views of learning position the learner in the background, as a receiver of objective knowledge. Knowledge is believed to exist independent of the learner; therefore, teaching is a matter of efficiently moving it from outside to inside. Once that process is complete, the learner either (a) knows more or (b) performs better; the test of learning in these conceptions is the ability to reproduce the knowledge of the authorities in more accurate and efficient forms. Learners are positioned as receivers of knowledge from authorities.

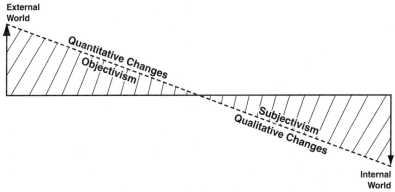

Figure 2.2 Conceptions of knowledge and learning

Qualitative views of learning position the learner squarely in the foreground, with content subject to the learner's interpretation. Knowledge, or what is learned, is understood to be influenced by the purposes, values, and interests of the learner, within cultural and historical contexts. Teaching and learning, therefore, are subjective processes involving the negotiation of meaning. Conceptions three and four are a bridge between the two views of knowledge, suggesting a transition from objectivism to subjectivism.

Some readers might disparage conceptions one and two, thinking they cannot possibly represent an informed view of learning. Indeed, we might assume that all teachers should hold beliefs about learning that resemble conceptions five and six. Yet, even if we could agree that some of these views of learning are more appropriate than others, we must acknowledge that learners come with their own beliefs about what constitutes learning. Curiously, it is learners' beliefs, even more than the beliefs of their teachers, which significantly influence the approach they take to learning as well as what they ultimately learn.

`What is most important, for our purposes, is to recognize the interrelationship between personal epistemologies and conceptions of learning. Each of these is part of an elaborate and coherent system of beliefs that forms a perspective on teaching. Our beliefs about knowledge and learning are part of a larger system of beliefs and intentions that have significant implications for how we understand the process of teaching and the purposes of education. For example, if we understand learning as a quantitative increase in knowledge, we would very likely teach our content and evaluate students' learning quite differently than someone who believes learning means examining what we know from several different points of view. Consequently, our assumptions about appropriate roles and responsibilities would also be quite different.

The problem is that most of us go about teaching without articulating what we believe or why we do what we do as teachers. Yet, based on over 40 years of teaching, I am convinced that all teachers act within a tacit system of personal intentions and beliefs about what is to be learned, how and why it should be learned, and what their role and responsibility will be in that process. As we gain experience, we should be able to articulate those intentions and beliefs, and there should be more agreement between all three—actions, intentions, and beliefs.

I do not mean to imply that there will always be a consistent and logical relationship between actions, intentions, and beliefs. Indeed, I suspect that this is often not the case. Teachers in higher education, for example, often believe their courses are developing critical thinking in learners. Yet, many of them teach in ways that discourage these noble aims; their actions are inconsistent with their espoused intentions and beliefs. As a result, some of the best work in faculty development today is attempting to help professors bring their actions in line with their intentions and beliefs (Kember, 1997; Kreber, 2002).

When it is well articulated, this interrelated web of actions, intentions, and beliefs ultimately forms the backbone for a sense of commitment in teaching. In turn, commitment forms the basis for a point of view or perspective on what teaching means and how it should be carried out. The next chapter moves from evidence and indicators of commitment to their broader consequences, that is, five qualitatively different perspectives on teaching.

REFERENCES

Candy, P. C. (1991). *Self-direction for lifelong learning: A comprehensive guide to theory and practice.* San Francisco: Jossey-Bass.

Eva, K. W. (2003) On the generality of specificity. *Medical Education,* vol. 37, pp. 587–8.

Guba, E. G., and Lincoln, Y. S. (1994). Competing paradigms in qualitative research. In N. K. Denzin & Y. S. Lincoln (Eds.), *Handbook of qualitative research* (pp. 105-117). Thousand Oaks, CA: Sage Publications, Inc.

Kember, D. (1997). A reconceptualisation of the research into university academics' conceptions of teaching. *Learning and Instruction*, vol. 7, no. 3, September, pp. 255-275, Pergamon Press. Kneebone, R. (2002). Total internal reflection: an essay on paradigms. *Medical Education*, 36, 514-18.

Kneebone, R. (2002). Total internal reflection: an essay on paradigms. *Medical Education*, 36, 514-518.

Kreber, C. (2002). Teaching excellence, teaching expertise, and the scholarship of teaching. *Innovative Higher Education*, vol. 27, no. 1, pp. 5-23.

Saljo, R. (1988). Learning in educational settings: Methods of inquiry. In P. Ramsden, (Ed.), *Improving learning: New perspectives* (pp. 32-48). London: Kogan Page, Ltd.

Schwandt, T. A. (1994). Constructivist, interpretivist approaches to human inquiry. In N. K. Denzin & Y. S. Lincoln (Eds.), *Hand book of qualitative research* (pp. 118-137). Thousand Oaks, CA: Sage Publications, Inc.

Scott, D., & Usher, R. (1999). *Researching education: Data, methods, and theory in educational enquiry*. London and New York: Cassell.

Smith, J. (1989). *The nature of social and educational inquiry: Empiricism versus interpretation*. New Jersey: Ablex Publishing Company.

van der Vlueten, Cees P. M. (2014). When I say ... context specificity, *Medical Education*, vol. 48, no. 3, pp. 234-235.

CHAPTER 3
Alternative Frames of Understanding

What the mind does not know, the eyes cannot see.

Daniel D. Pratt

INTRODUCTION TO FIVE PERSPECTIVES

You are biased.

It is a simple enough assertion that is as close to fact as anything one might express in three words or less.

I am biased.

This is neither absolutely good nor absolutely bad. It is merely an unavoidable reality that we all bring our own past experiences to bear on our understanding and interpretation of new information. (Eva, 2008)

When people ask, "What's your perspective on this?" what are they asking? Chances are, they are asking where you stand on an issue: What is your view, outlook, position, or stance? Can you put into words your commitments—your thoughts and beliefs related to a specific issue? They might just as well have asked, "What is your own bias on this?" for each perspective is really a particular point of view, biased in some way that may or may not be obvious to you. It depends on what you believe and what vested interests are most important to you.

When we speak of a perspective on teaching, we are speaking of much the same thing: an interrelated set of beliefs and intentions that give direction and justification for our actions (which include our teaching strategies and assessment approaches). Thus, although perspectives are enacted through actions, they are far more than the activities or teaching techniques used by teachers. They are a lens through which we view the world of teaching and learning. We may not be aware of our perspective because it is something we look through, rather than at, when teaching. As we shall see in later chapters, our perspective on teaching becomes the object of our attention only when we reflect upon our beliefs, intentions, and actions and their interrelationships.

For the most part, each person's initial perspective on teaching is received without question or challenge. It is the result of years of being a learner, in the home, at school, in the community, on sports teams, and in a thousand other moments responding to someone teaching us. While being taught and while watching others learn, we form impressions about what teachers do, what learners do, and how the process of teaching works and how it doesn't work.

Eventually, a set of conceptions related to learning and teaching evolves within an individual and is carried forward until it is challenged, perhaps because it no longer works, or because an alternative perspective emerges and seems to make better sense.

But until we change a perspective consciously, how does it operate? How does it affect what we see and do? The German philosopher Nietzsche claimed that it is a fiction to assume we can take a pure, objective stance toward knowing anything. Knowing from such a posture requires,

> . . . an eye [that is] turned in no particular direction, in which the active and interpreting forces, through which alone seeing becomes seeing something . . . these always demand of the eye an absurdity and a nonsense. There is only a perspective seeing, only a perspective "knowing"; and the more affects we allow to speak about one thing, the more eyes, different eyes, we use to observe one thing, the more complete will our "concept" of this thing, our "objectivity", be. (Nietzsche, 1969, p. 119)

The same is true for perspectives on teaching. If we are familiar with only one perspective on teaching, it will dominate our perception and interpretation of all that goes on, yet remain hidden from our view. Just as our own culture is invisible to us, until we travel or live in another culture, other ways of thinking about teaching are invisible to us if we know only one perspective on teaching. Thus, if we want to understand our own view of teaching, we must first see the broader landscape of perspectives on teaching. By contrasting our perspective with other perspectives, we begin to see how we are similar to, and different from other teachers we know. And we begin the process of moving from thinking there is one best way of teaching, to recognizing that there is a plurality of the good in teaching.

The account of the teaching workshop presented at the beginning of Chapter 2 illustrated an implicit denial of alternative ways of thinking about teaching and, consequently, a denial of any such thing as a perspective on teaching. That is, the workshop portrayed a singular and dominant view of teaching, characterized by generic skills and behavioral objectives, devoid of variation in context, content, learners, beliefs, and commitment. Knowledge, learning, and our teacher roles could only be interpreted within the dominant, but invisible, perspective; alternative views did not seem to exist.

What happens, then, when we behave as though all teachers share the same perspective and acknowledge the same criteria for effective teaching? What are the consequences and why does it matter? We go there next.

PERSPECTIVE AS JUDGMENT

Each perspective on teaching involves a complex web of actions, intentions, and beliefs; and each, in turn, creates its own criteria for judging or evaluating right and wrong, true and false, effective and ineffective, appropriate and inappropriate. Perspectives determine our roles and idealized self-images as teachers as well as the basis for reflecting on practice. When you talk with another educator who believes as you do, there is an immediacy of communication and the feeling of being understood. However, just the opposite holds true when there are disagreements between people holding different perspectives on teaching. It is as if each is from a different culture, where values and meanings are different.

This commonality or disparity in perspective becomes even more apparent and significant when one's teaching is being evaluated. Evaluation of your teaching makes more sense and is less disturbing when done by someone from the same perspective as your own. It is easier to understand and agree upon criteria and judgments of what is "effective" when like minds negotiate these things. On the other hand, evaluations that cross perspectives can be problematic, to say the least.

For example, when my teaching was being evaluated for promotion, the evaluation process called for two colleagues to review my teaching syllabus and observe at least three consecutive hours of instruction. Here's what happened during and following one colleague's observation of my teaching:

It was a three-hour class in the late afternoon with about twenty students. The topic was a comparison of different cultural understandings of 'learning'. When the class was over, my colleague suggested that he and I meet for a cup of coffee in the coming week to discuss his observations. I readily agreed, thinking this would be a good chance to talk about teaching with a respected colleague.

We met at a small café on campus where we could have a quiet conversation. The setting was congenial; the conversation not quite so agreeable. My colleague opened with this question: "Dan, do you think your students are getting their money's worth?" I was so taken off balance, I could hardly reply. It seemed more like an accusation than a question.

I was stunned. Everything I had experienced to that point suggested my teaching was not only adequate but, in some regards, exemplary. I was so shocked I could only ask, "What do you mean?" The response was, "Well, you didn't answer their questions; they asked several questions and you just turned the questions back to the group. In fact, they left that evening with more questions than answers. I expect you know the answers to their questions and they deserve answers."

I had carefully considered my approach to this class and this topic and believed firmly in three things: first, that my students brought with them prior knowledge, opinions, and values that would influence their understanding of alternative views of learning. Second, I believed that students would need to explore their own experiences of learning alongside contrasting experiences if they were to appreciate views that were markedly different from their own. And finally, I believed there were no correct 'answers', as suggested by my colleague. Rather, there were different ways of understanding learning and that those differences were deeply embedded in the cultural heritage my students brought to the conversation. Thus, my strategy was to: (1) open a conversation that began with their experience; (2) locate that experience in cultural and historical contexts; (3) invite opinions but challenge people to give evidence and/ or rational arguments in support of those opinions; and (4) avoid giving single-perspective 'answers' to important questions about cultural variations in our understanding of learning.

I'm not sure my colleague accepted this as sufficient reason for doing what he thought was 'short-changing' my students. Nonetheless, I knew that my students understood this strategy because we talked about it. They knew why I would ask a question, in response to a question. The rules of engagement in my class had been discussed and agreed-upon well before my colleague arrived. Students understood the rationale behind my strategic approach in our class. However, in a moment that held high-stakes for my career, what mattered more was the contrast between my beliefs and those of my colleague about learning and about appropriate roles for a teacher.

No amount of explaining would answer this charge. Two very different perspectives on teaching were about to collide. It was an instance of what the sociologist, Kenneth Burke (1935), wrote when he said, "A way of seeing is also a way of not seeing." I held the view that graduate seminars were a forum for exploration and inquiry; my colleague was of the opinion that the role of a professor was to provide information, not questions; to act as authority, not co-learner. It was as if we were speaking past each other while discussing the same episode. Unfortunately, one person was in a more powerful position than the other. Evaluation presents problems of power imbalance, which conflicting perspectives can exacerbate.

As I mentioned earlier, perspectives are enacted through techniques, but they are far more than simply the actions or techniques of teaching. In the example just given, the disagreement went well beyond the issue of lecturing versus questioning. It included different conceptions of knowledge, learning, teaching and the very purposes of graduate school. In other words, each of us brought to this transaction a set of meanings and values that "framed" the events in particular ways. What my colleague's mind did not know, his eyes could not see.

Each of our personal "frames" consisted of a set of interrelated conceptions. From within each of our perspectives, our conclusions made sense. Each of us could have written an evaluation of the teaching and justified conclusions on the basis of his observations.

Each evaluation would have been internally consistent, that is, co-herent and logical, based upon the ways in which key elements and processes were interpreted. Internal consistency is quite natural in long-held perspectives. But the two reviews would have been sub-stantively different.

A similar process may have happened to you if you have ever left your home culture to travel or work in another culture. Back home, your understanding of what's done is intact and solid; your worldview is internally coherent and logical. And yet, walking around that first street, encountering that first social situation in a market square, a restaurant, a post office, or navigating traffic, you realize that your logic is not their logic. At the moment of that real-ization, that which was invisible and taken for granted becomes vis-ible and becomes the object of awareness and open to scrutiny and examination for the first time.

A number of years ago, I was getting ready to teach my first course in Hong Kong. As you can imagine, I was excited to learn about Hong Kong and shared that excitement with a friend. To my surprise, she dismissed this as naïve and said that I would very likely learn more about Canada than about Hong Kong. I dismissed that, thinking that she really didn't understand what I had said. But, after 10 years of teaching there I believe she was right; I learned a great deal more about my own culture than I did about the culture of Hong Kong. I had a basis of comparison and, for the first time, my own culture was visible to me.

In much the same way, perspectives on teaching are cultural views of teaching and learning, powerful but largely invisible frames of reference through which all of us make meaning of our worlds. They limit our perceptions in much the same way; until we encoun-ter a basis for comparison, our own assumptions remain invisible. It isn't possible to forget our perspective, any more than it's possible to forget our cultural upbringing; but it is possible to engage mean-ingfully with new perspectives.

ACCEPTING VS. ADOPTING NEW PERSPECTIVES

Just as it's quite common to judge a new cultural experience on the basis of our own logic, it's also quite common to judge another's teaching in terms of one's own perspective. This is especially true within institutions where evaluation of teaching crosses disciplin-ary or programmatic boundaries (e.g., colleges and universities). In such instances, evaluation focuses on the technical or skill-based activities of the teacher, more than any underlying beliefs or intentionality. It is assumed that effective teaching is relatively similar regardless of variations in context, learners, content, and teachers. This approach is justified on the assumption it is more objective and, therefore, more impartial. It may be more expedient, but it is neither objective nor impartial.

This doesn't mean people have to adopt another's perspective before they can evaluate their teaching. People can learn about other perspectives without adopting them. It is much like the distinction between acculturation (learning about a culture) and enculturation (adopting a culture). To learn about a culture is to understand its norms, traditions, language, values, and ways of relating; to be enculturated is to internalize those norms, traditions, and language as a way of building a sense of self, identity, and membership in the social groups of that culture.

In much the same manner, we can learn about other perspectives on teaching, and acknowledge their appropriateness for other people and circumstances, without taking them on as our own. That is, we can learn about a different perspective, without adopting that perspective. This is the most common result of reading a book on teaching. Most people find ways to confirm what they already believe rather than change the more central beliefs they hold regarding teaching.

The remainder of this chapter will introduce five perspectives on teaching that came from interviews and observations with over 250 people teaching adults a variety of subjects, in a variety of contexts (Pratt, 1992a). Their experience represents years of decisions, reflections, and refinement of actions, intentions, and beliefs. It is impossible to capture the richness of that diversity, particularly the cultural and social nuances that are not easily understood by outsiders such as myself. Each perspective will be explained in more depth in Sections II and III.

INTRODUCING FIVE PERSPECTIVES ON TEACHING

Before reading about alternative perspectives, go online and take the Teaching Perspectives Inventory (TPI) at: www.Teaching Perspectives.com as a way of exploring your own perspectives. As you take the TPI, stay focused on one subject area (content) and group of learners. For example, if you teach different levels of students, with different subject matter and under different circumstances, choose one of those teaching situations—a group of learners, a subject area, and a context—and stay focused on that throughout the TPI. This will give you a more accurate read on your teaching perspective. You can subsequently, of course, take it again, focusing on a different teaching situation. If you take it more than once, compare your results and notice where there are similarities and differences in the two 'profiles' of your teaching. It is important that you do this before reading about other perspectives if you want to have some indication of what you believe before exploring other beliefs about teaching.

Pause now and go to: www.TeachingPerspectives.com

The rest of this chapter assumes that you have taken the TPI and you have seen your profile. From here the chapter introduces you to the five perspectives, briefly, before taking you into the more detailed explanations in the next section of the book. Remember, no perspective is universally 'better' than any other; each is best suited to specific people, aims, values, and contexts. However, since they represent contrasting and sometimes competing views of teaching and learning, people inevitably value some perspectives more than others. It would be inappropriate and invalid, therefore, for anyone to say that all five perspectives are equally representative of their teaching.

Yet, while people tend to prefer one perspective more than others, they also have some measure of commitment to more than their preferred perspective. In examining the TPI profiles for 100,000 educators from more than 100 countries (Collins & Pratt, 2011), the vast majority held one of these perspectives as their dominant view of teaching with one or two additional 'back-up' perspectives, allowing them to accommodate changes in learners, content, and context across a variety of educational circumstances.

A Transmission Perspective: Managing Knowledge

Community College Math Instructor

> *My job is twofold: First, I have a lot of people that have to learn this math so they can go on to something else, whether*

it's some application of it or the next course in the required mathematics program. For both groups, I need to be really clear about the sequence of what comes next and what they need now. I mean, math really is quite simple, if it's presented clearly and you do each day's work. So, I need to be clear about what it is they need to learn and then be sure they do the assignments. If I do that, they should have no trouble when they go on from my class to the next one. The second part of my job, as a math teacher, is to represent math as a discipline. I love math. I really do! And if I didn't like math, they [the students] wouldn't like it either. So I let my enthusiasm show. I like it, in part, because it's beautiful. How many things in this world are so straightforward and organized? So, I try to show people that math isn't the "baddy" that everyone says it is. They don't need to be afraid of it. I did it, and I'm no Einstein.

Obstetrics and Gynaecology Physician

As a clinical preceptor for gynaecology residents, I offer a 4-week elective in lower genital tract disease. The residents' early specialty training is primarily hospital based. Consequently, junior residents do not have a lot of exposure to patients presenting with nonurgent gynaecology problems in an office setting. It is critical that residents learn the basic knowledge and skills required to manage this type of patient. Unfortunately, residents typically arrive on my service with very little background knowledge about these diseases and essentially no practical experience. To facilitate the residents' learning of this content area I have taken the following steps:

1. *Residents are provided with a set of learning objectives that outline the knowledge and skills that are needed to manage patients. Residents are provided with a standard textbook and a binder of supplemental articles that I expect them to read during the rotation. One afternoon per week is set aside as 'protected time' for the residents to do this reading.*

2. *I make a point of scheduling a variety of different patients into the clinics so that residents are exposed to a range of disease conditions.*

3. *I meet with the residents once a week to answer any questions they have about what they are learning and to test them on their knowledge of the material.*

4. *At the end of the rotation I give the residents a formal written exam. In addition I elicit their formal feedback of the rotation and ask them to identify ways that the rotation could be improved.*

    Most residents learn a great deal during this rotation and find it a rewarding experience as they see their knowledge and skills improving. (Pratt et al., 2012).

This is, perhaps, the most "traditional" and long-standing perspective on teaching. It is based on the belief that a relatively stable body of knowledge and/or procedures can be efficiently transmitted to learners. The primary focus is on efficient and accurate delivery of that body of knowledge to learners. Thus, teachers with this as their dominant perspective feel obliged to adequately cover the content, regardless of time constraints. The dominant elements are the teacher and the content; and the dominant relationship between elements is represented by line Z (content credibility), that is, the teacher's concern for and authority over that which is to be learned (Figure 3.1).

The arrow's path and direction illustrate the instructional process, which has first regard for accurate and adequate representation and efficient presentation of content. Notice that the process arrow goes through the content to the learners, suggesting the name of this perspective, that is, the transmission or delivery of content from teacher (or other resources) to learners. The primary responsibility of a transmission-oriented teacher, therefore, is to present the content and then help learners accurately reproduce that same content in its authorized and accurate forms.

With this rather substantial respect for the content, teachers are expected to be an "expert" in what they teach. Good teachers are expected to be knowledgeable in their subject areas and, if they are practitioners, they should be experienced in their fields. They are expected to know their content well enough to answer most questions, provide multiple examples, give clear and detailed explanations, and specify with authority and precision just what people are

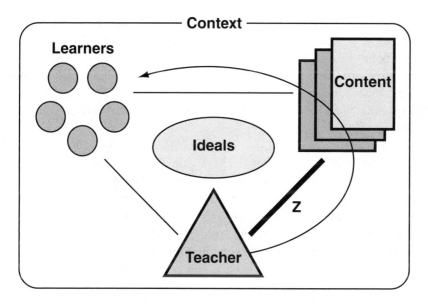

Figure 3.1 A Transmission Perspective

expected to learn. Therefore, content credibility (line Z) is of paramount importance.

Compared to other perspectives, this one is primarily "content-centered" with an emphasis on what the teacher does in the process of teaching and how well the content has been planned, organized, represented, and delivered. Transmission Perspective teachers are often concerned about adequately covering the content within constraints, such as a limited amount of time. They also speak about the coordination of their material or course with other parts of a program or curriculum, thus, implying assumptions they hold about the hierarchical nature of the knowledge they teach. That is, what they teach depends upon what has come before and, in turn, forms a necessary basis for the mastery of subsequent courses and content.

People holding a dominant Transmission Perspective usually teach well-defined content, that is, material where there is clear agreement about right answers and where new content fits hierarchically into or upon prior knowledge. This kind of knowledge can then be managed and presented in a step-by-step fashion. Well-defined content includes such topics as safety procedures, plumbing, grammar, math, electronics, military training, anatomy, most competency-based programs, and a number of operating protocols in the airline industry, computing science, and surgery. However, this perspective is not limited to those teaching well-defined content areas. Some cultures also stress this perspective and do so with the highest regard for teachers and their role in passing on to the next generation particular ways of knowing and being (Pratt, 1991; 1992b; Pratt & Nesbit, 2000).

No matter what the content, teachers from this perspective either find or impose structure on their subject matter. In fact, it is not a difficult task for transmission teachers to regard most content areas as well defined. This is especially so when basic concepts or techniques are introduced through formal presentations, then applied in practice, and finally built upon step-by-step as a subject matter becomes increasingly complex and its application more variable. Thus, most often it is not the content itself that determines how it is taught, but the teacher.

If you have had a negative experience with teachers from this perspective, it likely conjures up images of conceptions one and two of learning in Chapter 2: Learning as an increase in knowledge; and learning as memorization, usually for recall or recognition on tests. Indeed, many teachers from this perspective believe learning is a matter of accumulating a body of information and reproducing it on tests or assignments. This received view of knowledge, and reproductive view of learning, typifies much of what has been found in research on conceptions of teaching in higher education (e.g., Akerlind, 2003; Fox, 1983; Ho, Watkins, & Kelly, 2001; Kember, 1997; Kember & Gow, 1994; Kember & Kwan, 2000; Prosser & Trigwell, 1999; Prosser, Trigwell, & Taylor, 1994; Samuelowicz & Bain, 1992; Trigwell & Prosser, 2004). Furthermore, the work of Gow and Kember suggests that this perspective is associated with surface approaches to learning (Gow & Kember, 1993; Kember & Gow, 1994). This evidence, along with the experience of many readers, might lead one to conclude that all teaching within the Transmission Perspective results in rather superficial learning. Yet, it is my contention that this is the result of the perspective's implementation, rather than its underlying orientation. There are too many examples of effective teaching that fall within the Transmission Perspective to say it is categorically and unequivocally ineffective. As presented in Chapter 4, the Transmission Perspective can be an exciting, engaging, and effective source of learning.

An Apprenticeship Perspective: Modeling Ways of Being

Carpentry Instructor

For me, teaching means helping this guy [his apprentice] get beyond the stuff they taught him at school and learn how to work a job. There's a big difference between nailing 2 x 4s in a class project and working with a bunch of guys on a construction site that are never sure about the next job . . . There's more to carpentry than pounding nails . . . I mean, first of all, I have to be good at this, not just talk about it [carpentry]. There's no way I could teach him if I wasn't a pretty good carpenter myself. But it's more than that. I mean, this is a way of life, not just a job. Sure, I have to know what he can do and what he can't do. When he started he couldn't do much of anything besides the most basic stuff. And that's what you do when you start. It's not exciting work but it has to be done . . . Now, he's doing more than hauling stuff up to us on the scaffolding; he's actually doing most of what we do. But still, there's so much more, you know?

Orthopaedic Surgeon

I'm a surgeon and I have a variety of learners working with me in the operating room, some as inexperienced as third year medical students. I am often asked if I think medical students can actually do anything useful in the OR. Yes, I think so. They can help prepare and position the patients; they can learn about establishing a sterile field; and they can be involved in the post-op orders and care of the patient. Initially I tell them about the medical history of the patient. Then I briefly describe the procedure that we will be performing and what they can do in the operating room. In the OR, I introduce the student to the operating team and demonstrate how to prep the patient and set up for the operation. Students can be helpful, but you can't assume that they intuitively know what it takes to be a good assistant. This is part of what needs to be demonstrated and explained. The operating room can be an intimidating place for medical students, so it is important to make them feel that they have a functional role in the operation and are not a 'third wheel.' (Pratt et al., 2012).

While the Transmission Perspective is the stereotypical view of teachers in classrooms, the Apprenticeship Perspective represents a long-standing view of teaching outside classrooms. Within this perspective, teaching is a process of socializing learners into a specific community. By community, I mean a group of people with a common sense of purpose, shared repertoire of practices, and clearly defined roles, suggesting levels of authority, responsibility, and identity (Wenger 1998; 2006). Community can refer to a family, a trade or vocation, a profession, one of the marital arts, or even a cultural grouping. In each of these communities the process of socialization results from intensive, diversified, and prolonged participation in the work and social relations of the community.

The dominant elements in the General Model of Teaching are the teacher, content, and context. However, in this perspective the content and teacher are fused as one, signifying the inseparability of teacher and content, within context (Figure 3.2). Here, teachers teach who they are, as much as what they know or can do (Palmer, 1998).

In this perspective, teachers are expected to embody the knowledge and values of their community of practice. They are an extension of the values and knowledge as lived or practiced within that community. What they know (and wish to teach) cannot be learned in any authentic way if it is abstracted or removed from the place of its application, that is, its context. In a very real sense, context is both the object of what is to be learned and the agent of people's learning. People with this as their dominant perspective understand that, very often, context IS the teacher.

Therefore, what one learns, and can then do, is defined by the context and situation of the moment. Learning something in one context for application in another can be fraught with problems, as was mentioned in Chapter 2 when discussing context specificity. Practicing soccer drills is not the same as playing in an important game; learning to do math problems from a textbook is not the same as figuring out which groceries to buy with a limited amount of money; and practicing first aid in the classroom is not the same as applying what you know at the scene of an accident.

Furthermore, from this perspective what we learn is not only influenced by the context in which we learn, it is also given meaning by that context. That is, we are dependent upon similar cues, from the context, to retrieve and use that knowledge. An everyday

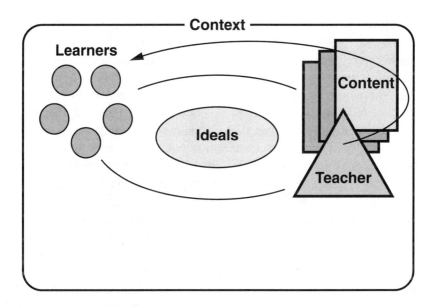

Figure 3.2 An Apprenticeship Perspective

example of the situated and indexed nature of knowledge comes from recognizing people and knowing who they are within the context of knowing them. Outside the usual context of our local neighborhood we may recognize the grocery clerk as someone we know but can't quite place. We know she is familiar, but can't remember who she is because she is out of context, not indexed (Arseneau, 1994, p. 34).

A convincing example of this argument comes from the director of a self-defense program for women, called Model Mugging. The program is based on the principle that one must practice self-defense under conditions that come as close as possible to the real thing. It was started by a woman who was attacked and raped, even though she had earned a third degree black belt in karate. When she most needed them, her considerable skills in self-defense were nearly useless. Why? Because she had trained in contexts devoid of the flood of emotions that accompanies a real attack. She had practiced and learned a great deal about self-defense in the dojo, or training center, but when confronted with the shock and fear of a real attack, she froze. Something was terribly wrong with the way in which she learned self-defense, that it was so completely unavailable when she most needed it.

Lave & Wenger (1991), Wenger (1998), and Sfard (1998) emphasize the power of particular forms of participation in learning. Their central message is that learning is more than a cognitive process of acquisition; it is also a social process of participation. However, the nature of participation is critical if learners are to make the most of learning in contexts of practice. Simply being in a context of practice does not assure that students will learn those practices. They must participate at a level that is within their zone of proximal development (Vygotsky, 1978), a level at which they are challenged, but capable. And the nature of their participation must be legitimate, that is, it must be part of the authentic practices of the community. Therefore, when learners are immersed in a complex environment, such as a professional kitchen or a busy medical clinic, they need guidance and assistance if they are to participate at an appropriate level. The central task of a teacher within the Apprenticeship Perspective, therefore, is to teach to the learners' zone of proximal development, that is, the distance between what learners can do on there own and what they can do under the guidance of a more experienced teacher or in collaboration with more capable peers.

Finally, this view of teaching is committed to learning a role and identity as well as a set of skills or body of knowledge (Jarvis-Selinger et al., 2012). Learning is directed as much at learning to be someone, as learning to do or know something. Through guided practice, and success on real tasks, this perspective professes that people begin to believe they have a legitimate role in relation to others, whether as a negotiator, a member of a soccer team, a responsible and capable shopper, or a first-aid attendant.

Chapter 5 will give more details. For now, it is enough to know that this view of teaching is fundamentally committed to locating learning within contexts that are as authentic as possible. In that context, one learns not just a set of skills or body of knowledge, but what it means to be a competent practitioner. Consequently, learning is about more than the acquisition of knowledge and skills; it is also about learning through participation and in the process becoming a legitimate member of a community (Sfard, 1998). As members of that community, teachers try to move learners from the periphery to more central roles, from low risk to high risk procedures, and from simple to complex ways of understanding, in an attempt to have learners take on ways of thinking and problem solving that are necessary for membership in a community of practice (Wenger, 1998).

A Developmental Perspective: Cultivating Ways of Thinking

Developmental Psychologist (education)

I am a developmental psychologist by training but my role is as an instructor in a teacher education program. Traditionally I teach child and adolescent development to individuals who are going to become elementary and secondary school teachers. My courses are not the only psychology courses these students may have completed, but one of the differences is that in a professional teacher education program, these courses are designed to be more practical. Given that there is a variety in the types of learners who come into a teacher education program, one of the first tasks for me, as their teacher, is to understand their 'frames of reference'. Are they a parent with school-aged children? Do they have younger siblings? Have they worked as a sports coach or volunteered with youth? Knowing this is important to me because it provides a frame of reference to know what to teach, how to teach, and where to begin. It also helps me to draw out practical examples from their personal experiences which I think makes learning meaningful. I have lots of examples from my experience teaching in secondary classrooms, but their stories help personalize what we're learning. It also helps them change the way they think about various school-aged groups—so things like 'break negative stereotypes' of concepts like "teenager" is a goal. One of my challenges is that you could do a graduate level degree on child and adolescent development (I know, I have) but if you don't know where they are coming from and what they need and how to change their thinking the course could quickly become overloaded with information. My hope is that by being in one of my courses, I can change the way teachers think about developmental psychology and they also come away with a practical understanding that will fit well with their future professional aspirations.

General Practitioner (medicine)

> *I am a family doctor, working in a rural area. For about 3 months each year, I have medical students or residents working in my clinic. For the most part, I really enjoy having them around. They keep me sharp and it's exciting to see the next generation coming along* .

> *With the students, most of what I do is at a pretty basic level. They need to use their basic science learning while also learning to take a history and do a physical exam. But even then, it's not straight forward, because it involves making adjustments to different patients. They generally need structure—not a script, but a structure—for thinking about how a chief complaint can lead to a differential diagnosis. So I give them a structure that was given to me. It involves seven things that can help them gather information related to the presenting problem: location, quality, severity, chronology, setting, aggravating or alleviating factors, and manifestations. They can't yet focus their information gathering toward a differential diagnosis, because they don't comprehend the big picture. They've not seen enough patients yet. Everything looks important to them.*

> *With the residents it's different. My goal is similar, that is, to help them learn how to make a good differential diagnosis and come up with an appropriate treatment plan. But they don't need the formulaic structure that students need; they need to see a wide range of patients and learn to reframe a chief complaint (e.g., pain for last 24 hours) into more general categories of presenting problems (e.g., acute onset of pain). They need to build a repertoire of clinical cases. The vast majority of what I see, in the course of a day, is stuff I've seen before. I don't mean that I rush past any patient's chief complaint. But experience does count. I want to help residents build that kind of clinical experience. (Pratt et al., 2012).*

This is the dominant perspective throughout much of education in North America today (Ambrose et al., 2011). It is based on a psychological view of learning wherein learners are assumed to have developed their own personal cognitive map to guide their interpretation of the world. As learners encounter new information or situations, they first try using their existing map. If that doesn't quite work they are confronted with a dissonant situation where they must either revise their map or reject it and construct a new one. Either way, prior knowledge and ways of thinking form the basis of each learner's approach to new content and provide a window into their thinking.

It is this process of constantly revising one's understanding that gives this perspective its focus. Learners are perceived to be in a state of balance or equilibrium as long as their cognitive map fits the intellectual terrain. When they are confronted with new information that doesn't fit, it causes a moment of imbalance or disequilibrium until they can either dismiss the new information or revise their cognitive map. Thus, the teacher's role is to challenge and disturb that equilibrium. Learners then attempt to reestablish their equilibrium by reconstructing their understanding.

Within this perspective, content moves to the background and learners come to the foreground, making it a "learner-centered" philosophy of teaching (Figure 3.3).

Whereas commitment in Transmission and Apprenticeship Perspectives centered on authentic forms of representing the content, here commitment is about helping learners develop more complex or critical ways of thinking within a specific domain of knowledge and practice that resemble expert thinking or problem solving. Thus, learning is not simply a process of adding more to what is already there; it is, at least initially, a search for meaning and an attempt to link the new with the familiar. But ultimately it is a qualitative change in both understanding and thinking. The teacher's task, therefore, is to help learners think like experts in a discipline, profession, vocation, or craft. Threshold concepts—core ideas that are essential to opening up a new and previously inaccessible way of thinking about something—are now the means, rather than the end, and are used to establish and develop preferred ways of thinking or reasoning (Meyer, 2010).

Learning is, therefore, the process of revising or replacing previous ways of thinking, acting, or believing. The product of learning is the emergence of new or enhanced understanding and cognitive structures. Stated somewhat differently, learning is a change in the quality of one's thinking rather than a change in the quantity of one's knowledge.

Effective developmental teachers, therefore, must be able to build bridges between learners' present ways of thinking and more

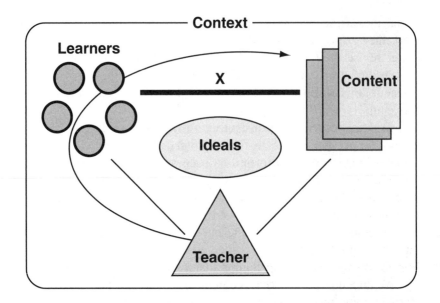

Figure 3.3 A Developmental Perspective

desirable ways of thinking within a discipline or area of practice. Bridging between these two forms of knowledge means teachers must be able to identify and then reconstruct essential concepts in language and at levels of meaning that can be understood by learners. In addition, learners' conceptions of knowledge and ways of thinking must be respected as legitimate, though incomplete, ways of knowing. Thus, instead of working to pass along information or "get information across," these teachers try to introduce learners to the "essence" of their content in ways that engage what they already know and expand their ways of knowing (Bain, 2004).

Within this perspective, effective teachers explore their learners' current conceptions of content and then challenge those conceptions to help learners move to more sophisticated levels of thinking and reasoning. This is not always easy. A common tendency for beginning teachers within this perspective is to fall back into the role of "expert" and provide more answers than challenging questions. But perhaps the most difficult challenge for teachers in this perspective is to develop means of assessing learning that are congruent with the beliefs and intentions of this perspective. While teachers may be able to bridge from a learner's prior knowledge to more desirable ways of understanding and thinking, they may not be able to develop tests, assignments, and means of assessment that allow learners to demonstrate how their thinking has changed to more resemble that of a professional.

As you might have already guessed, teachers holding this as their dominant perspective on teaching have a profound respect for learners' prior knowledge. Indeed, they take that as the starting point for their work, proceeding from the known (learners' prior knowledge) to the unknown (more sophisticated forms of understanding and thinking). In this perspective, teaching is a process of adapting the teacher's knowledge to the learners' level of understanding. This is a significant shift from more traditional, especially transmission, perspectives on teaching. Chapter 6 sets out seven guiding principles, the first of which is that prior knowledge is the key to learning. From this principle, the chapter moves on to explain how a teacher can activate prior knowledge so learners can bridge between new content and what they already know.

A Nurturing Perspective: Facilitating Personal Agency

Outdoor Recreation Instructor

Most people, at least here in the West, think outdoor recreation means developing some kind of skills. For example, in kayaking that would mean boat-handling skills, pre-trip planning and management skills, understanding tides and river currents, or any other tasks that focus on the activity of kayaking. The essence of my work, and of recreation in general, is the development of a person's sense of well-being. Not just their physical well-being, but their whole being. I try to provide physical, intellectual, and emotional challenges to people; that means I have to attend to their whole being, not just to their physical ability or their physical accomplishments.

Pathology Instructor

As a pathologist, every day I take care of hundreds of patients whom I never see. I am responsible for interpreting their blood tests correctly and quickly, diagnosing their bone marrow biopsies, and ensuring that their transfusions are safe. Our medical school creates hundreds of new physicians every year, and as a teacher I help each of them care for patients whom I will never meet. Every time these physicians see a patient with abnormal bleeding, every time they encounter a complete blood count or a coagulation result, they will approach these problems with the tools I have given them. Their patients are, in a way, my patients too.

I make it a point to get to 'connect' with each of my students. To connect with my students, I work very hard to understand what they already know—how much, or how little. It is all very well to have learning objectives and exit competencies, to know where the students have to finish their educational journey, but even the clearest map is useless if where you are right now is a mystery. Knowing where to start, which amounts to having 'educational empathy', is sometimes challenging: clearly, any medical school class with artists and writers sitting next to nurses and Ph.D. scientists is bound to have wide variations in background knowledge. I make a real effort to find where the students are, to know what they know, and to guide each of them to their destination – challenging and supporting them along the way (Pratt et al., 2012).

Philosophically, the Nurturing Perspective has been the most prevalent view of teaching for adult educators within North America for at least 30 years, as represented in the work of Malcolm Knowles (1980, 1984, 1986). Yet, it is not confined to the cultural norms of the United States and Canada. The original research for this study found variations of this perspective throughout much of Asia, as well as the United States and Canada.

As with each perspective, this one is characterized by a fundamental belief about what influences learning and gives direction to teaching. In the Transmission Perspective it is the belief that effective teaching depends, first and foremost, on the content expertise of the teacher; with the Apprenticeship Perspective it is the belief that learning must be located in authentic social situations related to the application of knowledge; with the Developmental Perspective it is the belief that prior knowledge and ways of thinking are the essential determinants of what people will subsequently learn. In the Nurturing Perspective, it is the belief that learning is most affected by a learner's self-concept and self-efficacy. That is, learners

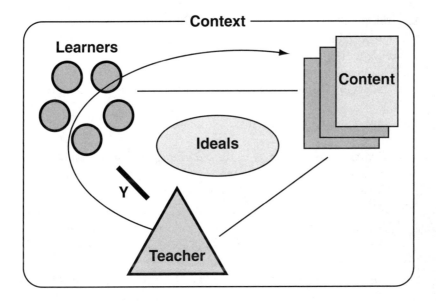

Figure 3.4 A Nurturing Perspective

must be confident that they can learn the material and that learning the material and skills will be useful and relevant to their lives. Thus, in Figure 3.4, the dominant elements are the teacher, the learner, and importantly, the relationship (line Y) between them (e.g., Bates et al, 2013).

A nurturing relationship need not be permissive or possessive. It is, in its own way, professional and demanding, characterized by a high degree of reciprocal trust and respect, and always seeks a balance between caring and challenging. Caring means empathizing with learners while providing support and encouragement as they attempt to learn; challenging means holding to expectations that require effort, but are achievable, and meaningful for learners.

The goal, from this perspective, is to help people become more confident and self-sufficient learners. To achieve this, learners must not only be successful, they must also attribute success to their own effort and ability, rather than the benevolence of their teacher or the serendipity of circumstance. This perspective is, therefore, fundamentally concerned with the development of each learner's concept of self as learner. Thus, once again, content becomes a means rather than an end. It is the means through which individuals achieve certain goals and, more importantly, learn that they are capable and self-reliant learners. From this perspective, a learner's self-esteem must never be sacrificed on the altar of academic standards or achievement.

A Social Reform Perspective: Seeking a Better Society

Automotive Repair Instructor

Teaching, for me, is more about changing society than repairing cars. When these women are wrestling with a wrench that's heavy and trying to reach down into the engine, I want them to think about why it's so difficult. It's not accidental that the wrench is heavy and the bolt a long reach away. Who do they think designed the tools and the engine? Who were they intended for? What does that say about being a mechanic? Or even repairing your own car? That kind of discrimination is what I'm out to change. Sure, I want them to be able to maintain their car; I don't want them dependent on someone else for that. But, my teaching is just as much about changing society as it is about repairing cars. If they can keep their car running but have no idea they've been systematically excluded from certain occupations. . . what's the point?

Trauma Surgeon

Recently, a woman was brought to the emergency department, unconscious and in serious condition. Her car had been hit by another car. The driver of the other car was also brought to emergency with a number of injuries. He was conscious but disoriented. The woman survived the night, but was comatose and had a poor prognosis. The man was treated for a number of non-fatal orthopedic injuries, but kept over night in hospital for observation and monitoring. The next day, at morning case conference, I presented this case and asked the residents how they would discuss each patient's condition with their respective families. After some discussion, I added information given to me by the officers that attended the scene: the man had been drinking and had a number of driving while impaired charges. On this occasion, he was impaired and had been driving with out a license. I asked the residents if this would affect their discussion with each patient's family. Most felt it would not. I then asked the residents where their responsibility as health care providers ends. Does it end with the death of the woman? Does it end with the discharge of patients? Some of them were really engaged in the discussion; others were not at all convinced that their responsibility extended beyond the care of the injuries incurred. I believe that physicians need to see how individual health and mortality are part of more complex societal issues—in this case the relationship between alcohol and driving. As physicians, we often see the tragic end result of society's illnesses. I think we have a responsibility to advocate for changes that will improve the bigger picture of health (Pratt et al., 2012)

This view of teaching has been prominent in adult education for some time, most notably in movements that espouse a clear and articulate vision for social justice. However, commitment to social change ranges from feminist movements to fundamentalist religious movements. In all cases, the social reform perspective is distinctive for the presence of a well-articulated ideal or set of principles that are linked to an explicit vision of a better society. Each ideal is based on a core or central system of beliefs, usually derived from an ethical code (such as the sanctity of human rights), a religious doctrine (such as the sanctity of God's law), or a political or social ideal (such as the need to redistribute power and privilege in society).

Every teacher represents an underlying "political" stance toward what is considered normal, tolerable or desirable and the role of education in relation to that. In turn, one's ideology gives rise to ideals, that is, one's conception of "the good" or "the just." Yet, many teachers persist in their claim they are neutral in terms of their ideals and ideology. They deny that their content and the way they teach that content represent particular interests and exclude others. This is not the case with social reform teachers. In the Social Reform Perspective, ideals emerge from an ambiguous and covert position of influence (as in the other four perspectives) to occupy a clear and prominent place of significance in teaching.

The dominance of ideals overshadows all other elements within the General Model of Teaching (Chapter 1). Emphasis is on social, cultural, political, or moral imperatives that determine, to a great extent, how each of the other elements and relationships is under-

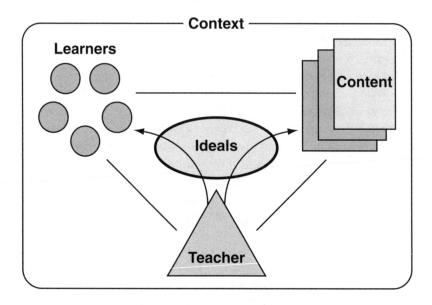

Figure 3.5 A Social Reform Perspective

stood. The focus of commitment, and therefore of teaching, shifts from micro to macro concerns, from finding better technologies of instruction, ways of knowing, and means of facilitating cognitive or personal development, to issues of a moral or political nature. Learners and content are secondary to a broader agenda as the commitment and agenda shift focus from the individual to the collective. This perspective becomes challenging to learners when differing ideals blind the teacher or make him indifferent to anything about his learners. Ideological change at any cost can have serious learning consequences on students.

No single ideology characterizes this perspective; consequently, there is no unifying view of knowledge, learning, or learners; for some social reform educators these aspects of teaching can differ based on context, learners, and subject matter. Within this perspective, there are multiple views of knowledge, ranging from objectivist views based on the immutable truth of God's word, to subjectivist views based on the need to understand what it means to have choice over matters concerning one's own body. For example, one individual, teaching in the People's Republic of China, spoke of how he was guided by the Communist Party's teachings regarding obedience to authority and the need to maintain harmony and order in society. For him, these were "first principles," necessary for China and for himself. Another person, a woman teaching other women in a work reentry program in Canada, expressed the view that knowledge and authority were socially constructed and relative, and, as part of the learning process, were to be challenged.

One fundamental difference between perspectives can be found in the nature of the means and ends of each perspective. The nature of the ends they seek, and the means to those ends, depend on the beliefs that comprise them. As you read Chapter 8 notice that within the Social Reform Perspective the ends (goals) of the other perspectives (e.g., mastering content, moving from the periphery to more active and central roles in a community of practice, developing ways of thinking, and enhancing self-efficacy) become the means toward the accomplishment of social changes beyond the bounds of the participants and learning environment. Thus, while Social Reform teachers may be pleased with their students' learning, it is not sufficient: they must have an impact on society to accomplish their teaching mission. That is the end, and all else the means, by which they seek to achieve their teaching goals.

CLOSING THOUGHTS

Ideally, this volume would present accounts of the perspectives layered with dimensions of the cultural nuances and the myriad applications that made the evidence of these five patterns so striking (Chapters 1 and 2). But the publication and linguistic constraints of the book, and the desire for authored chapters by colleagues whom I could regularly consult have resulted in a North American bias for the detailed contextual descriptions of the perspectives. Section II provides a more detailed and contextual description for each of the five perspectives.

Finally, if you haven't yet done it, you may want to take the *Teaching Perspectives Inventory* (TPI). The TPI is freely available at: www.TeachingPerspectives.com and yields a 'profile' that graphically presents your scores on each of the five perspectives and suggests which ones are dominant, back-up, and recessive. Several additional documents are available at that site, including a guide to help interpret your profile. By the fall of 2014, more than 300,000 people, from 105 countries had taken the TPI. In chapter 11, John Collins and I will give you some indication of how different disciplines and professions compare, based on data from teachers with five or more years of experience teaching in their respective discipline or profession (Chapter 11). There is also a video clip available on the TPI web site, wherein I demonstrate how to interpret a TPI profile.

REFERENCES

Akerlind, G. S. (2003). Growing and developing as a university teacher – variation in meaning. *Studies in Higher Education*, 28(4),   375-390.

Ambrose, S. A., Bridges, M. W., DiPietro, M., Lovett, M. C., and Norman, M. K. (2010). *How Learning Works: Research-based principles for smart teaching*. San Francisco: Josey-Bass.

Arseneau, R. (1994). *A study of the impact of a resident teacher education program on teaching self-efficacy, beliefs about teaching, and self-reported teaching behaviours*. Unpublished master's thesis, The University of British Columbia, Vancouver, Canada.

Bates J, Konkin J, Suddards C, Dobson S, Pratt DD (2013). Student perceptions of assessment and feedback in longitudinal inte= grated clerkships, *Medical Education*. 47 (4), 362-374.

Burke, K. (1935). *Permanence and Change*, as cited in, T.W. Crusius, *Kenneth Burke and the Conversation after Philosophy*, University of Southern Illinois Press, 1999, p. 133.

Eva, K. W. (2008). On the limits of systematicity, *Medical Education*, 42, 852-53.

Fox, D. (1983). Personal theories of teaching. *Studies in Higher Education*, 8(2), 151-163.

Gow, L., & Kember, D. (1993). Conceptions of teaching and their relationship to student learning. *British Journal of Educational Psychology*, 63, 20-33.

Ho, A., Watkins, D., & Kelly, M. (2001). The conceptual change approach to improving teaching and learning: An evaluation of a Hong Kong staff development programme. *Higher Education*, 42, 143-169.

Jarvis-Selinger, S,, Pratt D. D., Regehr, G. (2012). Competency is Not Enough: Integrating identity formation into the medical education discourse, *Academic Medicine*, 87 (9), 1185–1190.

Kember, D. (1997). A reconceptualization of the research into university academics' conceptions of teaching. *Learning and Instruction*, 7(3), 255-275.

Kember, D., & Gow, L. (1994). Orientations to teaching and their effect on the quality of student learning. *Journal of Higher Education*, 65(1), 58-74.

Kember, D. & Kwan, K-P. (2000). Lecturers' approaches to teaching and their relationship to conceptions of good teaching. *Instructional Science* 28, 469-490.

Knowles, M. S. (1980). *The modern practice of adult education: From pedagogy to andragogy*. Chicago: Association Press, Follett Publishing Co.

Knowles, M. S. (1986). *Using learning contracts: Practical approaches to individualizing and structuring learning*. San Francisco: Jossey-Bass.

Knowles, M. S., & Associates (1984). *Andragogy in action*. San Francisco: Jossey-Bass.

Meyer, J. H. F. (2010). Helping our students: Learning, metalearning, and threshold concepts, in J. Christensen Hughes & J. Mighty (Eds.) *Taking Stock: Research n Teaching and Learning in Higher Education, Queen's Policy Studies Series*, London, Ont: McGill-Queen's University Press.

Nietzsche, F. (1969). *On the genealogy of morals* (W. Kaufman & R. J. Hollingdale, Trans.). New York: Vintage Books.

Pratt, D. D. (1991). Conceptions of self within China and the United States. *International Journal of Intercultural Relations* (USA) 15 (3), 285-310.

Pratt, D. D. (1992a). Conceptions of teaching. *Adult Education Quarterly*, 42 (4), 203-220.

Pratt, D. D. (1992b). Chinese conceptions of learning and teaching: A Westerner's attempt at understanding. *International Journal of Lifelong Education* (UK) 11 (4), 301-319.

Pratt, D. D. (2002). Good teaching: One size fits all? In Jovita Ross-Gordon (Ed.) *An Up-date on Teaching Theory*, San Francisco: Jossey-Bass.

Pratt, D. D. and Nesbit, T. (2000). Cultures and discourses of teaching. In Arthur Wilson and Elizabeth Hayes (Eds.). *Handbook of Adult and Continuing Education*. San Francisco: Jossey-Bass.

Pratt, D. D., Arseneau, R., Collins, J. B. (2001). Theoretical Foundations: Reconsidering 'good teaching' across the continuum of medical education. *The Journal of Continuing Education in the Health Professions*, 21 (2), .

Prosser, M., Trigwell, K., & Taylor, P. (1994). A phenomenographic study of academics' conceptions of science learning and teaching. *Learning and Instruction*, 4, 217-231.

Prosser, M., & Trigwell, K. (1999). *Understanding learning and teaching: The experience in higher education.* Buckingham, United Kingdom: Society for Research into Higher Education and Open University Press.

Samuelowicz, K., & Bain, J. D. (1992). Conceptions of teaching held by academic teachers. *Higher Education*, 24, 93-111.

Sfard, A. (1998). On two metaphors for learning and the dangers of choosing just one. *Educational Researcher*, 27(2), 4-13.

Trigwell, K., & Prosser, M. (2004). Development and use of the Approaches to Teaching Inventory. *Educational Psychology Review*, 16(4), 409-424.

Vygotsky, L. (1978). *Mind in society: The development of higher psychological processes.* Cambridge MA: Harvard University Press.

Wenger, E. (1998). *Communities of practice: Learning, meaning and identity.* Cambridge, University of Cambridge Press.

Wenger, E. (2006) *Communities of practice: A brief introduction.* Retrieved from http://ewenger.com/theory/index.htm.

SECTION II

Section II presents a glimpse of the richness of detail and emotion that was evident during the original research. Each chapter features a colleague who responded to our request to write from within a perspective about their philosophy and approach to teaching. These individuals were asked to tell their stories, to represent their views on teaching, in a way that would be faithful to the original research, while also revealing their own personal beliefs and commitments.

Our writing team met several times across three years (2011-2014) discussing how this 2nd edition should differ from the 1st edition and providing feedback to each other on multiple drafts of chapters. In the final months, we asked a 'third party', Michelle Riedlinger, to read several of the chapters and provide her thoughts as she read our work. Michelle teaches academic writing at another university and had not read the first edition of this book. Thus, she came to our work much like others might for the first time. Her feedback helped clarify our collective writing, while holding true to the voice of each author.

Each chapter in Section II is a personal elaboration of one perspective, as if the authors were asked, "What does it mean, to teach from this perspective; and what characterizes effective teaching from that perspective?" Thus, each chapter in this Section represents a 'mirror' for readers to look into and see if they find an image of themselves. Of course, as mentioned before, readers may see reflections of their beliefs and commitments in more than one perspective, as did the authors who wrote these chapters.

In Section III, Dan Pratt and Dave Smulders return to present an analysis of the perspectives, provide a means for profiling your own teaching, and address the difficult matter of evaluating teaching while respecting the plurality of the good you are about to encounter in the next five chapters.

CHAPTER 4
The Transmission Perspective

Daniel D. Pratt and Sandra Jarvis Selinger

INTRODUCTION

It was a very traditional lecture theatre that seated at least 200 of my classmates from Education. The course was compulsory, meant to introduce aspiring teachers to the world of education and schooling. I was near the back of the room and could barely see the podium. We waited only a few moments before the professor entered from an underground tunnel that ended at a door just behind the podium. We expected another 'boring talking head' tucked in behind a podium and droning on for an hour. But as she began you could feel this was going to be different.

First off, she didn't dim the lights, but kept everything in the lecture hall bright. Secondly, she moved around the entire 200-seat lecture theatre, never anchoring herself behind the podium. As she moved up and down the long sets of stairs on each side of the room, she continued to project her voice to the entire class, but her eyes spoke to those closest to her. She expertly transformed this impersonal lecture hall into an intimate setting. She was talking 'with us' not 'at us', and her delivery only confirmed her passion for education. She used her own experience to bring educational theories to life. She recounted stories of her students to help us understand what social-emotional development looked like in school-aged children. She invited us to think about our own experience as learners, that we might better understand the relationship between cognition, emotion and learning.

She was a maestro of her content, and it was impossible not to be swept up in her enthusiasm and passion for this material. (Sandra Jarvis-Selinger)

Most readers will have experience with a teacher who has demonstrated characteristics of the Transmission Perspective. Some of it good (as above); some of it, not so good. Unfortunately, the 'not-so-good' examples are often the most memorable. Some teachers equate talking with teaching: "I told them; ergo, they should have learned it." They do not represent the kind of teaching we want to celebrate in this chapter. We want to disrupt the negative images of this perspective and replace them with images like the one above. When done well, this approach to teaching can spark students' interest in a subject or content area.

Effective, however, means that every act of teaching should spring from a concern for student learning (Bain 2004). And student learning depends upon student engagement. Yet, we know from studying hundreds of teachers that represent this perspective, they sometimes have tendencies that run counter to actively engaging learners, such as:

- 'Covering the material' without giving an organizing framework
- Overloading learners with information (too much; too fast)
- Equating talking with teaching
- Seeing every question as an opportunity to talk more

Each of these tendencies comes from a desire to teach content, which can be good. But they can also be symptomatic of not attending to the central premise of this book: What is learned is more important than what is taught. In other words, we want to avoid the tendency to be so attentive to our content that we forget about engaging learners.

Because the number one challenge for teachers holding a Transmission Perspective is the engagement of learners, we have built this chapter around three keys to engagement to help focus on engaging learners, while holding strong to a commitment to content:

1.   Foster active, rather than passive, engagement.

2.   Avoid cognitive overload.

3. Use advance organizers.

Each key to engagement addresses one or more of the common challenges to effective teaching within the Transmission Perspective.

THREE KEYS TO ENGAGEMENT

The first 'key' highlights the difference between 'active' and 'passive' engagement of learners, which we will illustrate with two true stories. The second key highlights an important difference between teachers and learners, that is, the ability to process content-related information. Again, using personal examples we will illustrate how to avoid cognitive overload. The third key provides three ways to use advance organizers to increase active engagement. Collectively, the three keys to engagement have helped us increase learning and long-term retention of the content we want people to learn.

Key No. 1: Foster active, rather than passive, engagement

Active and passive engagement are related to intrinsic and extrinsic motivation respectively. Thus, intrinsic motivation is key to active engagement. Let's begin by looking more closely at what intrinsic motivation looks like in educational settings and what activates it.

Learners are intrinsically motivated when they: (1) see the relevance in what they are learning; and (2) have confidence in their ability to learn the material. For example, Deci & Ryan (1991) have shown that learners were actively engaged when two conditions were present: (1) the goal or purpose for learning was meaningful to them; and (2) they perceived that goal to be achievable. They contrasted that with learning the same material for testing purposes. There was still purpose and possibly self-confidence in students that they could learn the material. Indeed, they successfully learned the material for testing, but then forgot it because they were not actively interpreting and integrating it. When testing marks an endpoint for learning, rather than a strategy for learning, the motivation is extrinsic to the person and what is learned is soon forgotten.

Of course, some very high-stakes tests can be powerful motivators. But, as powerful as they are, the learning that results too often fades after testing. Deci and Ryan are convincing in their argument that intrinsic motivation equates with active engagement whereas extrinsic motivation more often equates with passive engagement. In this chapter, and throughout the book, we equate active engagement with intrinsic motivation, that is, the perception by learners that the material is relevant and that they have the ability to learn it in its authorized form(s).

The opening vignette is one memorable example of how a teacher from a Transmission Perspective, in a large lecture theatre, was able to personally engage her students and make the material relevant and memorable. But let's look at another example from Sandra that was memorable, for the wrong reasons.

Early in my career as an educator in a School of Medicine, I was asked to give a lecture to the medical residents on the im_ portance of teaching. Since medical residents work alongside and teach undergraduate medical students, the administration felt that we should be promoting residents-as-teachers. This lecture was delivered to approximately 150 residents from a variety of medical specialties (surgery, family practice, psychiatry, internal medicine, etc.).

Having trained to be a secondary school teacher and having been in many teaching roles from kindergarten to graduate education courses, I have a passion for learning to teach. I wanted everyone to know what I knew and I couldn't wait to present all that I had learned about teaching. This was my first mistake.

As well, not having a lot of experience with large lecture theatres, I planned a talk that was overloaded with information and 'under filled' with student activity. I just didn't know how to engage 150 people who seemed to be sitting miles away from me. That was my second mistake.

Finally, what I also failed to realize was that the audience didn't share my passion. This was a group of people who were training to be physicians and saw little or no value in taking time out of their schedule to hear about how important it is to be a teacher. Strike three—I bombed.

You can imagine the scene: I wanted to be out of there as fast as I could; the residents wanted to leave even faster. That was the longest hour of my life. I felt I had to finish, which I did, but with none of my usual passion. My regret was how this would affect the residents' opinion of teaching and their opinion of educators like me in the future.

Contrast this with an unexpected success story. This time Sandra was asked to give a similar talk in a similar lecture format to a similar group of people; only this time instead of individuals training to be physicians, she was speaking to experienced physician-educators who train residents and medical students.

I was to present at 'grand rounds,' a monthly series of lectures attended by practicing surgeons who also teach residents at various hospitals. So I was facing the same issues as before, coupled with the fact that the traditional topics for grand rounds (e.g., new surgical techniques) were very different from the topic of my educational talk.

Reflecting on my earlier 'bomb', I decided to change one fundamental thing—my PowerPoint presentation. I reworked my slides to remove all the bullet points, layered them with pictures and single words or a single phrase in an effort to make it more conversational and engaging, rather than the usual pedagogical crutch of having most everything that I would say on slides.

I also planned to leave about 10 minutes for questions at the end. I didn't want to leave more time than that because, honestly, I was nervous about their reaction to my talk. I was still extremely uncertain that what I felt was important would be important to them.

Early in the presentation they seemed to be listening, but I couldn't tell if my material was 'engaging' them. They were silent, polite, but I had no idea if they were cognitively with me. I thought I might be losing the audience again.

Then, a funny thing happened. This was a one-hour lecture. But less than 20 minutes into my talk, I realized that I was about two slides away from the end. How could this have happened? The thing I failed to realize was that when I revised my slides to be less text heavy I had also inadvertently reduced my script (i.e., my speaking role) that was meant to accompany those slides.

We have all been given advice about total number of slides in a talk or seen what "death by powerpoint" can look like—"What? He had 82 slides for a 60 minute presentation!" Well, as much as that may be a reasonable exclamation, at that moment I wished I had 82 slides! By minute 20, my one-hour talk would be done! I began to panic (internally), while simultaneously trying to talk slower and not show my panic. It wasn't going to work. I was going to bomb again.

But in that moment of panic I did the only thing I could do—I asked them a question. I was surreptitiously looking around for the exit, wondering how much sweat was showing. And then an unlikely thing happened—a community-based surgeon said "I don't understand why we are talking about teaching, I don't teach, I practice surgery". Although this was reminiscent of the perceived response to my previous lecture, the comment turned out to be the perfect segue into a lively debate about whether surgeons teach. To make a long story short, the rest of the 40 minutes was a talk-show style session, where I facilitated questions, provided direction for who would speak next and generally stayed out of the debate.

Much to my delight, I had provided the group with just enough information to prompt a lively, substantive discussion about their work and the critical roles and responsibilities that come with being a surgeon educator. The subsequent feedback I received only confirmed for me that the session had been a great success. By handing over control of the content, people were able to participate on their own terms and make substantive contributions. It was the first response that both threatened me and rescued me: Someone was honest and brave enough to raise a fundamental question to which everyone in the room could contribute.

As a footnote, the debate ended with a great majority of the group arguing that a surgeon can't get through a day without teaching patients, students, families, colleagues, and others. So not only did I get them engaged in this session, but we also resolved a contentious issue and came to what I believe is an important take-home message: teaching was a critical part of their job.

This story is a reminder that teachers coming from a Transmission Perspective do not need to relinquish their commitment to content or their responsibility to present it as clearly and sufficiently as possible. But they may need to reposition their knowledge to find a balance between delivering it (which is all right) and inviting learners into a conversation about that content. That's what the teacher in the opening scenario was doing. It's also what Sandra discovered, albeit accidentally under the panic of running out of content in a high-stakes teaching situation. When planning her session, Sandra didn't feel confident opening up the presentation to facilitated discussion but was 'forced' to when she ran out of material.

The Transmission Perspective is often the default for instructors who don't feel confident that they can effectively engage their audience with the material. It might be because they don't know the material well or they anticipate hostility—or both. In this situation, Sandra began by presenting information that she knew well. She didn't expect that it would evoke a hidden, but critical, question: Are they teachers or are they surgeons? When it did, she took advantage of the unexpected situation and shifted her audience from being passive receivers to being active participants. For the rest of the time she was with them, her content knowledge was selectively called out in response to their comments and questions, rather than being predetermined and delivered. In other words, a fundamental or 'big question' (Bain, 2004) engaged them in a conversation about teaching. It doesn't get much better! We'll say more about Bain's 'big questions' as a form of engagement later in this chapter.

Despite the general focus on content, it is simplistic (and wrong) to equate the Transmission Perspective with lecturing. This would presume that a perspective is revealed directly from a choice of instructional methods. Nonetheless, this may be the place where most of us can recall teaching episodes that did not go well. For example, have you ever walked out of a teaching session knowing that your learners didn't connect with your content? Sometimes you feel it in the midst of teaching; other times it's upon reflection that the 'I think I lost them' feeling comes to mind. Large lectures may be the place where this happens most. It is certainly one of the venues in which we have to be most intentional about shifting from having a passive audience to having actively engaged learners.

Much of the literature on teaching adults promotes the idea of moving learners away from being just an audience into becoming participants (e.g., Ambrose et al., 2010; Azer, 2009; Bowman, 2000; Brown & Race, 2002; Burkill et al., 2008; Ernest & Colthorpe, 2007; Jones 2007; Nasmith & Steinert, 2001; Race, 2005). Among those works, four books are particularly good: Ambrose and colleagues (2010) have collected their experience from years of faculty development and derived seven principles that can be used to engage learners. Their book is practical and shows how even a text can be engaging. Bowman (2000) offers a concise, practical guide to actively engaging learners. Each 'chapter' or idea is presented in very brief form—often just two pages. Each speaks to the title of her work - how to avoid "Death by Lecture". Race (2005) is an award-winning teacher in the UK who has written several books on learning and teaching in further education. Chapter 5 of his 2005 book is filled with practical ideas that can be used to engage learners in large classes. The fourth is Ken Bain's book, *What the Best College Teachers Do* (2004). This is, quite simply, one of the best research-based books on teaching in higher education that we've ever seen. It is filled with stories and evidence about truly exceptional teachers in seventeen different disciplines. His findings and recommendations are not limited to a Transmission Perspective on teaching, but they are certainly relevant to this Perspective.

One of the most prolific and convincing authors is Eric Mazur from Harvard University. He has studied his own teaching and written extensively on this topic. As of this writing, there are several YouTube videos of him demonstrating and explaining how he engages students in physics classes at Harvard. Here are current titles of some of the more interesting ones, without the URLs as those may change over time:

• Eric Mazur shows interactive teaching

- Eric Mazur on stopping time
- Eric Mazur, confessions of a converted lecturer
- Why you can pass tests and still fail in the real world

Finally, engagement can also come from an unexpected source —testing. As noted earlier, testing can produce passive engagement if students are simply studying for testing as the end point of learning. Although teachers have long known that assessment drives learning, the reality is that when students study primarily for tests, learning is actually subordinated to assessment. They learn what they expect will be on the test. When the tests are 'high-stakes' examinations, e.g., for certification or licensing, students rightfully build an economy of time, focusing exclusively on what they believe will be assessed. This is due, in part, to competing demands on their time, such as a crowded curriculum, parenting responsibilities and/or paid work. Clearly, most testing today is not an opportunity for learning. Fortunately, there is a way to make testing an opportunity for learning that lasts—it's called Test-Enhanced Learning (Brown, Roediger & McDaniel, 2014).

Testing can be more engaging and more productive of long-term retention if it is 'assessment for learning' rather than 'assessment of learning'. There is a great deal of research to support this claim and much of it comes from the research lab of Henry Roediger and colleagues at Washington University Memory Lab, St. Louis, Missouri. Their work, known as Test-Enhanced Learning, has been replicated in the basic sciences and medical education (e.g., Karpicke & Roediger, 2008; Klionskky, 2004; Larsen, Butler, & Roediger, 2008; and Wood 2009). This body of work tells us that frequent testing, with feedback on results, is a powerful form of active engagement for learning. While the research is readily available and accessible, two excellent summaries have been written in the *New York Times* (Belluck, Jan. 20, 2011; Roediger, July 20, 2014). Drawing on work published in the journal *Science*, Belluck explains why taking a test is not just a passive mechanism for assessing how much people know. It actually helps people learn, and it works better than a number of other study strategies, to help them accurately recall that same material a week later. Roediger goes further and explains how to structure tests and use them to best effect for improving understanding and long-term retention of material. Both authors stress the need to make tests low-stakes or no-stakes, that is, changing the way we think about testing—not as a form of assessment, but as a means of helping people learn.

Repeated studying, without feedback on the product of that studying, is a form of passive engagement. But testing can be a form of active engagement. It is 'active' engagement because **retrieval** is the central mechanism that strengthens the pathways in the brain to that which is learned (Brown, Roediger & McDaniel, 2014). When learners recall the material they refresh their memory of it in ways that make it 'their own'. Testing in this way also represents a method for organizing or "chunking" information for learners. This means they can then more accurately recall it a week or even six months later (Larsen, Butler, & Roediger, 2013). For this to work, testing should be repeated frequently, spaced over time, and focused on assessment for learning, not assessment of learning. Testing should require effort by students to recall the material and it should provide feedback on their answers. Finally, this form of engagement should replace the exclusive use of popular study strategies that have been shown to be of little or no utility for long-term retention and transfer of learning, such as highlighting, rereading, and summarizing (Dunlosky et al., 2013).

Yet, even with this further aspect of active engagement, referred to in the beginning of this section, we can unwittingly interfere with active engagement by overloading our learners with too much, too fast, or at too high a level. That's what our second key to engagement is all about.

Key No. 2: Avoid cognitive overload

Teachers that are inclined toward a Transmission Perspective have to be wary of three interrelated problems: first, the feeling that we have to 'cover' a lot of material (it's all so very important and interesting); second, the tendency to assume that if the material is self-evident to us, it should be self-evident to our learners; and third, a deep sense of duty to our content (which compels us to cover it all). In the Transmission Perspective, our content can be our worst enemy.

In most cases more is not better. Novice learners are constrained not only by the limits of working memory (like all of us) but also because they need to use more of it to interpret, organize, and make sense of new information. Figure 4.1 shows the differ-

Active & Spare Capacity

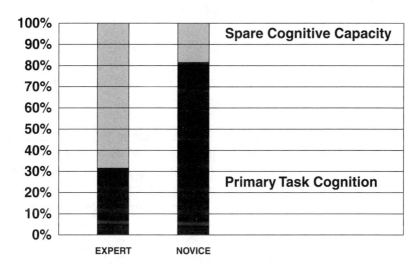

Figure 4.1 Cognitive capacity in experts and novices

ence between an expert and a novice in their active and spare cognitive capacity during a teaching moment. When talking about their subject, instructors have a lot of spare cognitive capacity with which to consider their next point, reflect on how things are going, and even attend to the back of the room. They know where the lecture is going, what is most important, and how it all fits together. In other words, they already have the big picture in mind.

The situation is quite different for learners. They are trying to understand each part of the lecture (or reading) as it is delivered. This is difficult, especially if they have little or no background in the subject. Their minds shuttle back-and-forth between what was just said, how that relates to what they already know and how everything is supposed to fit together. But unless they already know something about the topic, they have no way of assembling the pieces into a meaningful whole.

Beginning teachers approach their new role with enthusiasm and excitement, hoping to help others discover the excitement of their discipline or field. But they have forgotten how their content looks through the eyes of a novice, or to the student that is required to take this particular course. For example, novice teachers mistakenly believe that the importance and relevance of their content will be obvious to students. The reality is not quite so hopeful. Concepts and connections that are self-evident to the teacher can be obscure and confusing to learners. They miss the obvious. They don't know where to begin, can't pick out what's important, and often don't see the thread of reasoning that makes it meaningful. Learners are limited by what they already know (or don't know). It's as if they are in a foreign land, without the local language, trying to find a restroom or subway station. The signposts don't mean anything yet.

Because cognitive overload occurs faster in beginners than in experienced learners it can be difficult for a teacher to estimate how much can be presented, at what pace, and at what point learners are likely to experience cognitive overload. To resolve this dilemma, instructors need to plan and teach from a novice's point of view.

For example, imagine that you have to teach a procedure to novices in your profession. You may have performed this procedure dozens or even hundreds of times. By now it will be nearly automatic and the number of steps seemingly quite small. But for the novice, the procedure can appear complex, involving many seemingly separate steps. Using a medical education example, inserting a central line[1] to an experienced physician is seen as four to six integrated steps. For a novice it can be as many as forty separate steps. The novice's working memory is taxed beyond capacity trying to remember all those discreet steps. Add to the sheer number of steps the realization that they have to do this with great care or they will injure the patient. All the while, the novice is under the watchful eye of an experienced doctor, adding the emotional stress of being evaluated. Cognitive overload just went through the roof!

Experienced musicians face this same problem when they teach beginners. Here's how one musician and teacher described the process:

When a youngster chooses to begin playing a musical instrument, usually sixth grade in the Albuquerque Public Schools,

---

[1] In medicine, a central line is a long, thin, flexible tube placed into a large vein in the neck, chest or groin and is used to give medication, fluids, nutrients, or blood products over a long period of time, usually several weeks or more.

here is one possible sequence of events that might evolve. Typically the musical component I choose to teach first is rhythm. This involves the understanding of note values, the reading of rhythmic notation, and the clapping of simple rhythmic exercises. Next, usually in about two weeks, the students choose an instrument and are taught basic instrumental pedagogy for good tone production. This includes the appropriate use and amount of air pressure, proper embouchure (lip and jaw muscles) for wind instruments and proper stick handling for mallets and non-pitched percussion instruments. At this point, I begin teaching melodic notation and show how this relates to the specific instrument the student is playing. Articulation (tonguing and slurring of notes), accents and use of dynamics are gradually incorporated. Throughout the whole process students must be encouraged to be conscientious of blend, balance, intonation, and its relationship to the entire ensemble. In other words "are you the most or least important part of the music here?"

The goal is to have all these skills meld to become fluid and natural—all the while keeping the students' excitement and joy of music. My favorite method for this is with the introduction of familiar tunes that are appropriate for the student's level. This is essential for their sense of accomplishment and motivation to continue. This entire process generally begins in elementary school and carries throughout middle school, high school and the university level. Learning musical skills takes many hours of practice, repetition, and reinforcement. It is a life-long endeavor. (Thomas Martin, *New Mexico Music Educators Association Hall of Fame Award 2002).*

But there's another challenge not obvious in the above example. Think back to when you were a student and when you were asked to read something new, something totally new, in preparation for the next class. Here's how one student recounts her first reading of something on transformative learning theory:

We were assigned a book by Jack Mezirow—a man I knew nothing about. I knew his name and that's about all. But I was keen, so I jumped into the text thinking this was going to be interest-

ing. Somewhere about the second or third page, I realized I had no idea what I had just read. Although I had read it, I didn't understand it.

So I started over, this time with a highlighter. As I read, I highlighted everything I thought was important. By the end of the fifth page, I had highlighted about half of what was in those five pages. I really had no idea what was important and what was not—and I still didn't understand what I had read.

We were told this book was important, so I tried another strategy: I started over again, this time making marginal notes. But about the fifth or sixth page, I had a new dilemma—although my notes were more selective than my highlighting, everything I wrote was simply repeating the words in the text. I wasn't able to paraphrase or question or summarize anything I'd read. I still didn't get it!

By the time I got to the end of the first chapter, I was totally frustrated. I had some idea what this was about, or at least I thought I did, but when I tried telling my friend about it, I couldn't explain what it was about or why it was so 'important'. In other words, I had read the chapter, more than once, through my highlighting and margin notes, as I tried to be an active learner. But had no idea what it was all about. What worried me more was that we were only on the first chapter. I seriously thought I should consider dropping the course.

This experience is not unusual. In fact, it is quite common for students enrolled in graduate programs in adult education coming from another discipline or profession as they encounter different language, different concepts, and—again, all too often—other students that seem to understand the reading when they do not.

What's going on there? And how does it relate to cognitive overload? Again, it has to do with those three interrelated problems mentioned at the beginning of this section, specifically, the tendency to assume that because the material is clear and meaningful to us, it should be clear and meaningful to our learners. We understand not only the individual pieces, but how each piece contributes to the larger picture. The longer we have been teaching or doing something, the more our understanding and performance of it have be-

come habit, automated, and self-evident to us. Even long, complicated procedures have been chunked into a few easily executed
steps. To make matters worse, we very likely have forgotten what it
was like to learn this material or these procedures for the first time.

In contrast, novices are still struggling with each new concept
or procedural step as separate and unconnected to the larger picture. Learners quite commonly say that they cannot understand the
structure of their teacher's lecture or demonstration. That's because
they have no meaningful framework for listening, observing, interpreting and organizing new information. Without a sense of the
whole, the parts remain just that—separate parts. As a result, they
have a difficult time deciding what is important and what is not
important. However, when given something to help them interpret
new information and something to which it is related, cognitive load
is reduced, learning is enhanced, and retention is improved. This
invites the third key to engagement, something called 'advance organizers' (Ausubel, 1968).

Key No. 3: Use advance organizers

Learners in every discipline and at every stage of their training
benefit from having something to link old information with new,
and to interpret and organize new information. Ausubel (1968) called
these *advance organizers*. Advance organizers are general and comprehensive concepts, questions, or issues placed early in an instructional session or course to help learners understand and organize
material that follows. Bain (2004) found these to be defining features of highly effective teachers across seventeen disciplines. They
continue to be a foundation for effective teaching from preschool
through graduate training and every aspect of adult education.

There are many forms of advance organizers, but three that are
particularly useful within the Transmission Perspective are conceptual frameworks, big questions, and threshold concepts.

Conceptual Frameworks

Conceptual frameworks are a way to think about something
(Bordage, 2009); they are also a lattice on which to hang new information. Used as advance organizers, conceptual frameworks can
provide a condensed picture of what we want people to learn or
reconsider. They specify important concepts and relationships be-

tween those concepts. A great deal of our common, everyday life is organized around frameworks for thinking and/or navigating. For example, the local grocery store (or supermarket) is organized in such a way that when you enter you have a general sense of where different products are located. Produce will be on one side of the store, with meat and fish in a different part of the store. There is a predictable consistency such that even new stores are easily navigated if we are familiar with the general framework.

The General Model of Teaching in Chapter 3 is another example of such a framework (or model). While it is a relatively simple visual model, it gains in complexity and meaning as we explain the elements and the relationship amongst those elements. Not only does it give a snapshot for thinking about teaching, it can be used to illustrate differences between perspectives on teaching. Thus, it is also a conceptual framework for understanding each of the five perspectives on teaching. It can also be used as a conceptual framework for studying or researching your own teaching or the teaching of others (e.g., Hopkins, 2014; Jarvis et al., 2010).

Let's look at another example. This time Sandra was teaching an undergraduate course in childhood development for students training to be elementary teachers. There is a vast amount of information on childhood development. Psychologists, psychiatrists, physicians, sociologists, and educators devote entire careers to investigating every aspect of child development. Sandra was expected to reduce this volume of material to the essence of what teachers might need; and she was expected to do that within one undergraduate course. She was now confronted with a couple of critical issues: first, her sense of duty to the content and what should be kept as well as what could be dropped; second, a framework for presenting the material that could be easily learned and recalled. Here's how she thought about this dilemma:

> *I truly believed that my course was the only child development course these future teachers were going to have. Therefore, I had to teach them everything I knew about child development. What helped me acknowledge and then move away from this overwhelming sense of duty was a moment's reflection on two things: first, that it was impossible to actually teach everything I knew about child development in one course; and second, they didn't really need all that. In other words, I had to realign my thinking by reflecting on why my students*

needed this content: they were going to be elementary teachers, not psychologists. So authentically understanding the students' points of view meant I had to ask myself: how much do teachers need to know about child development? This helped me cut down on the information load and focus on what might be essential for elementary teachers. I needed to move away from "I have to teach them everything", to "I have to teach them what they can use and give them an approach to continue to build their knowledge after my course ends".

Sandra's resolution of the tension between duty to content and responsibility to learners was based on the rule of parsimony: simple frameworks (or theories) are preferred to overly complex frameworks, all else being equal. Her intention changed from 'teach them everything I can about child development' to 'teach them a useful and memorable framework related to child development.'

This is not unusual. Many Transmission-oriented teachers have likely experienced a situation in which they were expected to teach future practitioners something important to their work, but condensed into one course or even one session. Sandra explains how she resolved this situation for her students and for herself:

I have, many times in my career, been guilty of cognitive overload. But because I had taught this course for a few years already, I was able to build on my past experience to improve my teaching. In this particular instance, I designed the 12-week course around three major themes: head (cognitive development), heart (social development), and hand (physical development). I used those words (and images) over and over again across all the areas of child development. I structured questions throughout the course to help students think, "Is this about a head issue? A heart issue? Or a hand issue?" It reduced the amount of information I needed to present and provided a simple and memorable organizing framework, which helped (during most weeks) to guard against cognitive overload.

This also proved to be an effective way to structure the course during the planning phase. Being able to review content and figure out where it fit into the head/heart/hand model helped me decide what to include in the course. It also worked in terms of 'educational real estate'. In other words the calendar

*math worked. Three major organizing topics divided into 12
weeks made each area four weeks long. That real estate math
also gave me a strong framework to guard against feeling
they needed to learn everything I knew about child development.*

*Besides aiding in planning, my head/heart/hand approach also
helped students organize and remember what they learned. This
simple reoccurring imagery and language gave them 'hooks'
for understanding and remembering new concepts. It gave them
ways to relate and connect seemingly disparate pieces of information together. The feedback from my students was extremely
positive. They began to adopt that kind of framework approach
in other things they learned about. One student told me, for
example, that in another educational systems course he created a policy/pennies/people approach, as a means of asking
whether adopting a change in the school system related to policy
(i.e., the district or school level), pennies (i.e., the cost) or
people (i.e., individuals resistance to change). Using a framework helped him explain his content to others; and it helped
them remember it.*

This not only helped student teachers build a foundation for
understanding the children they would be teaching, it also contrib-
uted to more positive teaching evaluations for Sandra. However,
she admits to occasionally falling again into the cognitive overload
deep end. As Sandra's example illustrates, one of the Transmission
teacher's tasks is to constantly manage what information to share
with the learners. Cognitive overload may simply be the result of
adding more content over time, but we have to recognize that when
something is added, something else has to be removed so as to not
overload the students' capacity for new information.

Learners can process more information and recall it with greater
ease and accuracy when given frameworks for organizing and remembering. But another way to help them become actively engaged
involves what Ken Bain calls 'big questions'.

Big Questions

Too often in teaching, we focus on the details of our subject
rather than standing above those details to engage students with the

questions, problems, and challenges that motivate us. In doing so, our students never see the breathtaking vistas and mysteries of our field. One way of engaging students is to introduce contentious issues, puzzling problems, or 'big questions' first, so that the details of a course can attach to those more engaging issues, puzzles, or questions. For brevity, we will focus on big questions.

Big questions help people learn by giving them something to hold onto, something to return to, something to help them interpret and make sense of new ideas. Big questions give people new ways of thinking or believing. Such questions cannot be answered by going to the web. They need to be pondered and studied, usually in the company of more experienced people, that is, teachers. Such questions are anchors that students return to time and again as they read, listen, discuss, and prepare for assessments (Bain 2004).

Bain's work, from which we got the idea of big questions, was guided by two 'big questions' as he studied hundreds of teachers from seventeen different disciplines:

- What makes a great teacher?
- Who are the teachers that students remember long after graduation?

Bain found sixty-three highly effective teachers[2] from seventeen disciplines. These teachers were distinctive in many ways, but one consistent aspect of their teaching was that they began with intriguing problems or questions to motivate their students or challenge their prior assumptions. Big questions are one way we can

---

[2] Bain and his colleagues used several criteria to determine whether a teacher could be considered 'highly effective', including exceptionally high student ratings, where available. But high ratings alone were not sufficient. Other evidence had to exist that demonstrated the teacher regularly fostered exceptional learning. The nature of that evidence varied with the discipline, but it might have included the syllabus, examinations, methods of assessing student learning, nominations by colleagues, observations of the teaching, learning objectives, examples of students' work, performance on departmental examinations, students' subsequent performance in other classes, and interviews with students. In the end, Bain and colleagues wanted evidence that the teacher was successful in reaching most, if not all, the students, and in helping an unusually high number of them achieve advanced levels of learning in their field or discipline. (Bain, 1994, p. 183)

invite learners, at any level, in any subject, into a topic that fascinates us.

It's not easy coming up with big questions. But the more you know about your subject, the more likely you will know the driving issues and questions that can motivate and guide people as they explore your field or discipline. Here are some big questions and their associated disciplines as generated by teachers in workshops we've conducted:

- What is professionalism and how should it be assessed? (health professions)
- How do microbes change the world? (microbiology)
- Why are some people healthy and others not? (public health)
- How does your brain work; and what can go wrong? (psychology)
- How has touch screen technology changed the way children learn? (education)
- How does society influence individual behavior? (sociology)
- Why don't a penguin's feet freeze? (biology)
- What is justice? (political science)
- What is intelligence? (education/psychology)
- What is the purpose of the humanities in today's society? (humanities)
- How does historical thinking differ from other forms of thinking? (history)
- What does it mean to be an 'educated' person? (philosophy)

Individually, these examples will be most meaningful if we know something of the field or discipline from which they came. But collectively they demonstrate how big questions can invite curiosity and wonder, even when we don't know much about their respective field or discipline. That's what big questions should do—they pique curiosity and invite interest, which hooks intrinsic motivation and results in learner engagement. They are the 'hook' at the beginning of a class or series of sessions that provides a motivating point of engagement for people to find relevance and confidence.

Most teachers, at one time or another, have to help learners with material or ideas that mark a departure from old and comfortable ways of knowing about the world. Previously known as 'troublesome knowledge', such ideas are also called 'threshold concepts'.

Threshold Concepts

Threshold concepts are difficult but essential concepts that may be contrary to people's common way of thinking and, thus, troublesome for learners. Yet, these concepts must be understood for learners to understand a subject area (Rhem, 2013). Once learned, they fundamentally change the way learners view the subject. In this sense, threshold concepts are transformative.

There is a good fit between threshold concepts and the Transmission Perspective on teaching because both emphasize content and invite teachers to focus on concepts that are critical to learning their subject matter. In other words, threshold concepts allow learners entry to that which their teachers seem to understand intuitively.

Threshold concepts apply in most every subject or field—from elementary school through graduate school. They are the building blocks for deeper, more complete understanding of a subject. Temperature, for example, is a concept that is relatively easy to understand, whether in Fahrenheit or Celsius. But the concept of heat transfer is not quite so easy to understand. Yet, it is essential to physics and to cooking. Yes, cooking! Imagine that you have just poured two identical cups of hot coffee. You poured them from the same container, so they are the same temperature. But because you don't like your coffee too hot, you want it to cool, but be ready to drink as soon as possible. Should you wait and add the milk after it has cooled; or would it cool quicker by adding the milk first and then letting it cool? You decide to try an experiment: You add the milk to the first cup immediately, wait a few minutes and then add an equal quantity of milk to the second cup. At this point, which cup of coffee will be cooler, and why? The physics of heat transfer gives the answer and the explanation: the second cup cools faster because in the initial stages of cooling it is hotter than the first cup with the milk in it and it therefore loses heat more rapidly because of the steeper temperature gradient (Meyer & Land, 2003).

Heat transfer, then, is a 'threshold concept' in physics. But heat transfer, or more precisely, controlling the rate of heat transfer, is also a threshold concept in cooking, particularly if you consider the source of heat (gas, electric, or barbecuing) and the nature of the container or pan in which you are heating something.

Threshold concepts have become increasingly important as we understand more about where students stumble when entering new

subject matter domains. But once students 'get' a threshold concept, it's hard for them to 'un-get it' (Rhem, 2013). This is the transformative aspect of such concepts. By focusing on threshold concepts,
we can create a leaner curriculum and more successful learners,
now and in their further studies. Threshold concepts are another
instance of less can be more.

Concepts (threshold or otherwise) are miniature frameworks
for organizing and applying knowledge. When we transfer learning
from one setting to another, it is the concepts that transfer. They are
abstract summaries of what we know. That's why they travel so well.
But if we have them wrong, we have difficulty transferring our
learning or building upon it for further learning or application;
all the more reason to identify those concepts that are most critical
to learning and to the transfer of learning, such as, threshold concepts.

It takes time and effort to learn threshold concepts or ideas.
They don't come quickly. Like much deep approaches to learning,
they require deliberation, negotiation, and recursive visits to the concept. This can take a long time. Rhem (2013) explains it this way:

> *We know that the recursive nature of this learning can take a
> long time, and the reason for that is that we have these prior
> ways of seeing things and the brain likes that, likes closure,
> likes to be settled, and letting go of that requires a lot of mental
> energy. It's uncomfortable and we don't like doing that for too
> long . . . that's the major source of troublesomeness in shifting
> your schema which new concepts require* (2013, p. 3).

He goes on to explain one strategy that has worked well: getting students to review each other's understanding of those concepts. Note that he's not talking about peer assessment, but about
peer reviews. The point is to get learners to understand concepts on
their own terms through a process of negotiating their understanding with 'near peers'. The distinction will be clear as you read the
following:

> *Students doing a draft of their work and having two fellow par-
> ticipant students anonymously reviewing it and in turn review
> two others . . . students gain much more insight by giving the*

feedback than in receiving it. Receiving is helpful, but they de-velop a very different set of skills by giving the feedback, by actually reviewing others' work. That seems to have a more important learning function (2013, p. 3).

It's not clear why Rhem recommends keeping the reviewer's identity anonymous. However, there are good reasons for not doing so, as explained by a friend that uses peer review in her teaching:

I am a big supporter of peer review, but I include students' review comments as part of their overall assessment so they need to put their names with them. If these reviews aren't val-ued in the same way as students' own written work, I don't think students think I value it as highly . . . and I want them to know that I take that seriously. (Michelle Riedlinger)

This process highlights the need for learners to explain and then discuss their understanding of a concept. This also points to the deliberation, negotiation, and recursive nature of learning thresh-old concepts. They are, after all, troublesome ideas. For such ideas or concepts understanding doesn't come quickly. But when it does come, it provides a foundation for further learning.

Isn't All Teaching Supposed to be Learner-Centered?

One of our favorite authors raises an on-going tension and ques-tion that we have tried to address throughout this chapter: Isn't all teaching supposed to be learner-centered? And if so, is the Trans-mission Perspective a legitimate approach to teaching if it is con-tent-centered? Here's what Parker Palmer has said about that ten-sion:

As the debate swings between the teacher-centered model, with its concern for rigor, and the student-centered model, with its concern for active learning, some of us are torn between the poles. We find insights and excesses in both approaches, and neither seems adequate to the task. Whiplashed, with no way to hold the tension, we fail to find a synthesis that might embrace the best of both. (Palmer, 1998, p. 116)

We feel quite strongly about this issue. That's why the Transmission Perspective is the lead chapter in this section of the book. Let's look at some of the reasoning behind our decision to emphasize this perspective on teaching.

First, when conducting the initial research that informed the first edition of this book we found a large number of teachers that self-identified with commitments, beliefs, intentions and actions that characterize this view of teaching. We can't be certain about the quality of teaching for everyone who described their teaching in this way. But we are certain that many of them had reputations as highly effective teachers. Indeed, we were directed to them because colleagues, students, or supervisors recommended that we interview them and/or observe their teaching. In other words, they came highly recommended as models of effective teaching.

Second, the dominance of a learner-centered view of teaching very quickly approaches an orthodoxy that excludes variations on 'good teaching' that don't fit within that particular view. Consider, for example, societies with long honored views of teaching that conceptualize learning and learners quite different from our own prevailing views. According to the work of several authors (e.g., Watkins & Biggs, 1997; Marton & Booth, 1997; Pratt, Kelly, & Wong, 1999; Wong, 1995), Chinese faculty and students, for example, commonly understand 'learning' and the role of teachers and learners quite differently than in Western societies. In this version of effective teaching, teachers are responsible for guiding students through their content, down a well-defined sequence of steps, toward mastery and then application of the knowledge, fully confident that they, the teachers, are in control of the knowledge and the stages of learning. In turn, students are to be willing and compliant recipients of the teacher's authority. Together, teacher and students enter into an equally well-defined set of reciprocal roles and relationships that give further meaning to learning and alternative forms of effective teaching. To understand this point of view, one must accept that there is a plurality, rather than a single orthodoxy, of the good in teaching (Pratt, 2002). The implications are important and the point is also clear: Learner-centered teaching can mean quite different things, depending on cultural context.

Third, the way in which learner-centered teaching is understood and promoted assumes that there is universal agreement as to what 'learner-centered' means. There is, within the educational discourse today, an implied assumption that our personal conception of learner-centered is (or ought to be) everyone's conception of learner-centered. Yet, context can greatly influence the nature of learner-centered teaching. Consider teaching in the workplace versus teaching in classrooms (see Chapter 5). The nature of the work and the extent to which teaching must be balanced against the demands of work will determine the nature of what 'learner-centered' means when teaching in a workplace. We (the authors of this chapter) work in medical education where teaching is often done alongside caring for patients. In these settings, as in classrooms, teaching is always 'situated' in ways that influence what can be done and what learner-centered can mean. Similarly, the role of learner and teacher vary across cultures such that 'learner-centered' might mean one thing in an Asian setting and quite another in an American setting (Pratt, 1991; 1992; Pratt et al., 1999). We are reluctant, therefore, to assume that 'learner-centered' has a universal meaning across disciplines, contexts, and cultures.

Finally, current notions of 'learner-centered' may also exclude many of our most memorable teachers, those whose passion for a subject ignited our interest and may have even redirected our lives. The Transmission Perspective represents that kind of passion and commitment. But the current mantra of 'learner-centered' teaching would exclude those teachers and their ways of teaching from consideration as potentially effective orientations to teaching. We would argue, instead, for a 'learning-centered' view of teaching. Consequently, as with all perspectives on teaching, Transmission Perspective teaching should be guided by one overarching principle: *What was learned is more important than what was taught.* Effective Transmission Perspective teachers demonstrate their commitment to that principle by attending to the three keys to engagement:

- Foster active, rather than passive, engagement.
- Avoid cognitive overload.
- Use advance organizers.

CONCLUSION

Transmission Perspective teachers are often viewed as 'yesterday's teachers', out-of-touch (if not out-of-date) with newer teaching philosophies. Yet, if we use our content to actively engage learners, we can be tomorrow's teachers. At the same time we can also address Palmer's feeling of being 'whiplashed', with no way to hold the tension between teacher-centered and learner-centered approaches. This chapter tries to calm that tension by presenting a synthesis that might do as he asks by embracing the best of both.

Others have recently taken on this synthesis as well by exploring imaginative ways of delivering content. An alternative way of thinking about teaching has taken hold in many classrooms, particularly in higher and further education. It's called 'flipping the classroom'. One of the early innovators and a good example of this is the Khan Academy (see www.KhanAcademy.org).

Created in 2006 by Salman Khan, the Khan Academy is a non-profit online educational organization that supplies a free online collection of thousands of video micro lectures on various subjects such as mathematics, history, healthcare, medicine, finance, physics, chemistry, biology, astronomy, economics, American civics, art history, and computer science. The Khan Academy's approach is based on the idea of using technology to aid learning and free the teacher to spend more time interacting with students instead of lecturing. In traditional classroom teaching scenarios, the teacher introduces a topic, lectures on the pertinent details and then assigns homework for students. In a flipped scenario students study the topic by themselves, typically using video lectures, and then during class time students and teachers interact with the 'homework'.

At a time when we are feeling the pressure to be something other than a Transmission Perspective teacher, technology-enabled flipped classrooms and online learning/teaching have created a growing need for good Transmission Perspective teaching. Salman Khan was a groundbreaker in disruptive innovation. But look closely; he's also a great teacher. His mastery of content is evident in his videos and he effectively controls the distribution of that content into manageable portions for those who use them for their learning. Innovative use of technology has created a brand new frontier for effective teachers that is dominant in the Transmission Perspective. We just need to pay attention to those keys to engagement and apply them in emerging forms of innovative education.

As we mentioned in the opening of this chapter, not only is the Transmission Perspective very common, it can also represent a default way to teach when you don't know any other way. If you're not sure how to teach or haven't reflected on what is important to you (particularly your beliefs about learning), and you are anxious about what's in your control as a teacher, then you may tend to 'fall back' on the content as your guide to a stand-and-deliver model of teaching. It can be particularly hard to engage learners in a large group, for example, so the tendency is to stay where we are comfortable – in our performance of content rather than opening it to allow learners into the questions and issues that make our discipline or content a world of excitement and exploration.

Being committed to content and the 'performance' of the teacher can be a strength when teachers learn how to transform such beliefs into skillful actions. It's no accident that we teach content that we enjoy; it comes comparatively easy to us, and, for some of us, it is our passion!

While we are passionate about our content, our students may not be. For those learners, our primary responsibility is to engage them in meaningful ways with our content. We do this most naturally through our enthusiasm and expertise, but we have other strategies to employ as well. Their engagement may not be as easy as ours, but it is every bit as important if we want them to learn and care about our content.

In closing, we want to give you our top five recommendations for books that can help you make your way of teaching a powerful means to advance student learning. Here are our top five books, available as of 2014, with a brief comment on each:

1. Bain, K. (2004). *What the best college teachers do*. Cambridge, MA: Harvard Press.

As mentioned earlier, this is one of the best research-based books on teaching in higher and further education. It isn't a quick read, but it is worth reading—more than once—to get a sense of what makes the difference between good teaching and highly effective teaching.

2. Brown, Roediger, & McDaniel (2014). *Make it Stick: The science of successful learning*, Cambridge: Harvard University Press.

This is a *tour de force* of cognitive psychology research on how *test-enhanced learning* can be used to best advantage by students and instructors. Senior Author (Henry Roediger) is the mover and shaker in this line of research and has dozens of studies confirming the power of quizzes and self-tests to help adults (and children) learn and retain what they learn.

3. Ambrose, Bridges, DiPietro, Lovett, & Norman (2010). *How Learning Works: 7 Principles For Smart Teaching*, Jossey-Bass Publishers.

Five scholars from Carnegie Mellon University have decades of experience in faculty development and their experience shines through in this readable summary of research and experience organized around seven principles. Each chapter begins with two case studies (very short) that set up a teaching situation, to which a principle is the solution. It is very credible and easily read with little or no jargon.

4. Palmer, P.J. (1998). *The courage to teach: Exploring the inner landscape of a teacher's life*, San Francisco: Jossey-Bass.

This is an enviably well written and thoughtful book. If you are given to teaching, you will be given to this book and to Palmer's characterization of what it means to have the courage to teach. We can't recommend this book too highly. Quite simply, it's been a game changer in higher education.

5. Benassi, Overson, Hakala (2014). *Applying Science of Learning in Education: Infusing Psychological Science into the Curriculum*. American Psych Assoc. Available on-line at: http://teachpsych.org/ebooks/asle2014/index.php

The main attraction to this text is two-fold: first, the authors are researchers and have produced some (if not all) of the findings presented on the topics within each chapter; and second, it's freely downloadable at the hot link given above. If you want to be selective and read only a chapter or two from many topics related to learning, this is for you.

REFERENCES

Ambrose, S. A., Bridges, M. W., DiPietro, M., Lovett, M. C., & Norman, M. K. (2010). *How learning works: Research-based principles for smart teaching*. San Francisco: Jossey-Bass.

Ausubel, D. P. (1968). *Educational psychology: A cognitive view.* New York: Holt, Rinehart & Winston.

Azer, S. A. (2009). What makes a great lecture? Use of lectures in hybrid PBL curriculum, *The Kaohsiung Journal of Medical Sci_ ences*, 25(3), 109-115.

Bain, K. (2004). *What the best college teachers do.* Cambridge, MA: Harvard Press.

Belluck, P. (2011). To really learn, quit studying and take a test. *New York Times*, January 20.

Benassi, V. A., Overson, C. E.,Habala, C. M. Eds.(2014). *Applying Science of Learning in Education: Infusing Psychological Science into the Curriculum.* American Psych Assoc. Available on-line at: http://teachpsych.org/ebooks/asle2014/index.php

Bordage, G. (2009). *Conceptual frameworks to illuminate and magnify*, Medical Education, 43(4), 312-319 (April).

Bowman, S. (2000). *Preventing death by lecture.* Bowperson Publishing.

Brown, S., & Race, P. (2002). *Lecturing — A practical guide. London: RoutledgeFalmer.*

Brown, P. C., Roediger, H.L., & McDaniel M.A. (2014). *Make it Stick: The science of successful learning.* Cambridge: Harvard University Press.

Burkill, S., Rodway, S., & Stone, M. (2008). Lecturing in higher education in further education settings. *Journal of Further and Higher Education*, 32(4), 321-341.

Christensen, C. M. & Horn, M. B. (2013). Going all the way: online learning as an agent of drastic change. *New York Times: Education Life*, November 3, p. 25.

Deci, E. L., Vallerand, R. J., Pellitier, L. G., & Ryan, R. M. (1991). Motivation and Education: The self-determination perspective. *Educational Psychologist*, 26(3&4), 325-346.

Dunlosky, J., Rawson, K.A., Marsh, E. J., Nathan, M.J., & Willingham, D.T. (2013). Improving students' learning with effective learning techniques: promising directions from cognitive and educational psychology. *Psychological Science in the Public Interest*, 14(1), 4-58.

Ernest, H., & Colthorpe, K. (2007). The efficacy of interactive lecturing for students with diverse science backgrounds. *Advances in Physiology Education*, 31 (1), 41-44.

Hopkins, R (2014). *Bridging the gap: Understanding the experience of basic scientists transitioning to an integrated curriculum*. A thesis submitted in partial fulfillment of the requirements for the degree of Doctor of Philosophy, the University of British Columbia, Vancouver, Canada.

Jarvis-Selinger S., Pratt D. D., & Collins J. B. (2010). Journeys to ward becoming a teacher: charting the course of professional development. *Teacher Education Quarterly*, 37(2), 69-96.

Jones, S. E. (2007). Reflections on the lecture: outmoded medium or instrument of inspiration? *Journal of Further and Higher Education*, 31(4), 397-406.

Kember, D. (1997). A reconceptualisation of the research into university academics' conceptions of teaching. *Learning and Instruction, 7*(3), 255- 275.

Kember, D., & Kwan, K. P. (2000). Lecturers' approaches to teaching and their relationship to conceptions of good teaching. *Instructional Science, 28*, 469-490.

Karpicke, J. D., & Roediger HL (2008). The critical importance of retrieval for learning. *Science*, 319, 966-968.

Klionsky, D. J. (2004). Talking biology: Teaching outside the textbook and the lecture. *Cell Biology Education*, 3, 204-211.

Klionsky, D. J. (2008). The quiz factor. *Cell Biology Education*, 7, 265-266.

Larsen, D. P., Butler, A. C., & Roediger, H. L. (2008). Test-enhanced learning in medical education. *Medical Education*, 42, 959-966.

Larsen, D. P., Butler, A. C., & Roediger, H. L. (2013). Comparative effects of test-enhanced learning and self-explanation on long-term retention. *Medical Education*, 47, 674-682.

Marton, F., & Booth, S. (1997). *Learning and awareness*, New Jersey: Laurence Earlbaum and Associates.

Meyer, J. H. F., & Land, R. (2003). Threshold concepts and troublesome knowledge—Linkages to ways of thinking and practising. In *Improving Student Learning—Ten Years On*. C. Rust (Ed), OCSLD, Oxford.

Nasmith, L., & Steinert Y. (2001). The evaluation of a workshop to promote interactive lecturing. *Teaching and Learning in Medicine: An International Journal,* 13 (1), 43-48.

Palmer, P. J. (1998). *The courage to teach: Exploring the inner landscape of a teacher's life*, San Francisco: Jossey-Bass.

Pratt, D. D. (1991). Conceptions of self within China and the United States. *International Journal of Intercultural Relations*, 15(3), 285-310.

Pratt, D. D. (1992). Chinese conceptions of learning and teaching: A Westerner's attempt at understanding. *International Journal of Lifelong Education*, 11(4), 301-319.

Pratt, D. D. (2002). Good teaching: one size fits all? In Jovita Ross-Gordon (Ed.) *An Up-date on Teaching Theory*, 5-16, San Francisco: Jossey-Bass.

Pratt, D. D. (2005). Personal philosophies of teaching: A false promise? *ACADEME, American Association of University Professors*, 91(1), 32-36, January-February.

Pratt, D. D., Kelly, M., Wong, W. S. (1999). Chinese conceptions of 'effective teaching' in Hong Kong: Towards culturally sensitive evaluation of teaching. *International Journal of Lifelong Education*, 18(4), 241-258.

Race, P. (2005). Making learning happen in large groups. In *Making learning happen: A guide for post-compulsory education*. London: Sage Publications.

Rhem, J. (2013). Thresholds are troublesome. *National Teaching and Learning Forum*, No. 66, reprinted in R.Reis (Ed.), *Tomorrow's Professor eNewsletter*, No. 1287, 4 November.

Roediger, H. (2014). Sunday review: How tests make us smarter. *New York Times*, July 20.

Samuelowicz, K., & Bain, J. (2001). Revisiting academics' beliefs about teaching and learning. *Higher Education*, 41, 299-325.

Trigwell, K., & Prosser, M. (2004). Development and use of the approaches to teaching inventory. *Educational Psychology Review*, 16(4), 409-424.

Watkins, D. A., & Biggs, J. B. (eds.) (1997) *The Chinese learner: Cultural, psychological, and contextual influences.* Hong Kong Comparative Education Research Centre: University of Hong Kong.

Wong, M. (1995). *Apprenticeship teaching among Chinese masters.* Unpublished masters thesis, The University of British Columbia.

Wood, W. B., (2009). Innovations in teaching undergraduate biology and why we need them. *Annual Review of Cell Development Biology*, 25, 93-112.

CHAPTER 5
The Apprenticeship Perspective

Robin M. Hopkins

What is learning? What does it mean to learn something? and how
do you know when you have learned it? I encourage you to pause—
yes, lift your eyes from the page, and reflect even briefly about
what learning means to you. There are multiple ways that these questions could be answered. Depending on your schooling and teaching background you will have different ideas about the role of teachers, the position of students, and what it means to "know" something.
Among the multiple, even competing, perspectives on learning, two
are most relevant here: *cognitive* and *social* learning perspectives.
In this chapter I will first explore these two outlooks on learning.
My goal is to lay down a conceptual foundation for the second part
of the chapter where the transmission and Apprenticeship Perspectives will be compared and contrasted.

PERSPECTIVES ON LEARNING

Each of us develops an idea of teaching that emerges from our areas of our expertise and/or practice. My background is in teaching
anatomy in health professional programs. Given my experience as
an anatomy educator I am inclined to draw examples from higher
education, particularly the context of medical schools. My experience as a graduate student is also inherently woven into the fabric of
examples supporting this chapter. Although my experience draws
from the context of higher education, the apprenticeship teaching
perspective is not limited in this way. The term *apprenticeship* has a
long tradition in the education of adults, often referring to learning
in applied situations, "on the job" or in practice. For example, apprenticeship conjures up images of learning in the trades,

mentorships, coaching, and workplace learning, to name a few. As
you work your way through this chapter, take time to think of how
each section and concept relate to you and your specific context of
teaching and learning. With this understanding of my background
as an educator I will start by exploring the most common way that
people think about learning—as a process of acquiring knowledge.

A Cognitive Learning Perspective[1]

The *acquisition* metaphor (Sfard, 1998) is commonly used to
describe a cognitive view of learning. The metaphor implies that
information and knowledge is external to the learner and can be
acquired and made our own through a process of learning (Mason,
2007). Once acquired, we can store this information, organize it in
our minds, and apply it to other situations. To "know" something
within this metaphor implies that you own that knowledge, much
like a possession or commodity. The acquisition metaphor, therefore, focuses predominantly on the minds of individuals. Teachers
are perceived as the providers of knowledge and students the recipients. Different words may be used to describe the acquisition process, such as internalization, appropriation, accumulation, and transmission (Sfard, 1998), but the fundamental idea remains the same:
learning is a process of acquiring knowledge.

An important concept within this perspective is *transfer*—applying what is acquired in one setting to a new setting. Research
related to the notion of transfer has shown that learning something
in a context similar to where the knowledge will be applied, enhances the learner's ability to retrieve and use that information in
the future (Mann, Dornan, & Teunissen, 2010). This is also referred
to as the *context-specificity* of knowledge. In other words, for transfer to be possible, there must be a strong and transparent relationship between the knowledge to be learned, and the context of its
application. This can be somewhat of a problem for many who hold
exclusively to a cognitive view of learning, a matter I will return to
later in the chapter.

---

[1] I acknowledge that there is more than one cognitive perspective on learning.
However, for purposes of this chapter, I am highlighting the most common
aspects of those views of learning, that is, the emphasis on individual acquisition of knowledge, skills, and attitudes or values.

Although we most often think of learning as acquisition, it is but one perspective on learning. Another view of learning starts not with the individual, but with the social context. From this viewpoint, learning is perceived as a process of enculturation, i.e., gradually becoming a legitimate member of a community and being able to competently participate within it (Lave & Wenger, 1991; Wenger, 1998, 2006).

The Social or Situated Learning Perspective

Situated learning has been interpreted in multiple ways, but it may be helpful to start with what situated learning is not. Firstly, although often used synonymously, situated learning is not just learning "in situ" as its title may imply (Lave & Wenger, 1991). In a biological context "in situ" means to study or observe something in the exact place that it was found. For our purposes situated learning includes more than just what goes on in a single classroom or a particular work site. The social context of professional practice goes well beyond these isolated physical spaces as we engage more broadly and interact within a community of a school or company. Secondly, situated learning is not just "learning by doing." That is, just because I am able to perform a task that is demonstrated to me doesn't mean I know how to properly engage and work with my peers. The concept of situated learning developed by Lave and Wenger (1991) proposes a shift from thinking about learning as an isolated, individual activity of learning "in situ" or learning by doing, towards a general theoretical perspective where learning is an inseparable part of all of our interactions in the world. According to this view, learning is a state of being or, more accurately, becoming. A metaphor often used to summarize this social orientation to learning is the *participation* metaphor (Sfard, 1998). Learning-as-participation is integrally tied to the context of real life practice, be it the practice of a trade, a profession, a sport, or a hobby. In sum, Lave and Wenger have developed a social theory of learning (Lave & Wenger, 1991), one that talks about learning as becoming a competent member of a *community of practice*.

Communities of Practice

As defined by Wenger (2006) communities of practice "are groups of people who share a concern or a passion for something they do and learn how to do it better as they interact regularly". Communities of practice are a collection of people working together within an occupation or towards a common goal (Wenger, 2006). In earlier work (1998), Wenger outlined three characteristics of practice that are a source of coherence for a community: mutual engagement; joint enterprise; and shared repertoire. These three dimensions are how the practice of teaching or the practice of a trade or profession, for example, comes to be defined as a *community* of practice.

Mutual Engagement

Mutual engagement is the interaction between members of a community of practice (Wenger, 1998). In order to be a member you need to interact with others in that community in pursuit of common goals. This does not mean that your offices need to be next door to each other; it means you need to communicate with each other on an ongoing basis. Conversation, then, is an integral part of your belonging. In the workplace, we might call this "shop talk". As a member of your community, you are entitled to your voice; you tell war stories, swap tales from the field, compare notes on your practice, share successes and commiserate over failures. Only "bona fide" members of that community can talk shop; those who cannot or are not invited, are on the outside of that community. Mutual engagement also does not require members to have similar perspectives or backgrounds, or to reach a particular agreement as a result of interaction. For example, anatomy educators have different academic degrees, research areas and perspectives on teaching. Yet by talking at department meetings, developing curricula together and teaching alongside each other in the lab they become members of, and continually define, a community of practice. Communities of practice are built through mutual engagement; but a sense of *joint enterprise* is what keeps the community together (Wenger, 1998, 2000).

The school, department, or organization where you work may have an official mission statement. Although this statement is the declared purpose of the collective group, the *joint enterprise* is how the community interprets that statement and engages together in working towards it (Wenger, 1998). In other words, a joint enterprise is what community members have come to understand as their shared sense of what they are trying to accomplish and why that is worth pursuing. Despite there being an explicit purpose statement, the actual joint enterprise of the community is defined by members of the community as they engage in practice. This sense of intention for the community creates relationships of mutual responsibility as members hold each other accountable to it. Over time, as the community engages with each other and as they work towards a sense of joint enterprise they develop a set of communal resources, a *shared repertoire*.

The history of a community's engagement with each other is reflected in their *shared repertoire*—the resources they use and share (Wenger, 1998). The repertoire includes tangible objects like documents, curricula, course materials, websites and lab equipment, but also implicit artifacts such as routines, certain ways of doing things, organizing concepts, and ways of teaching. The majority of the anatomy education literature reflects the development of the community's shared repertoire. The innovation of three-dimensional virtual models, computer-based microscopic anatomy, and the ongoing debate of the use of cadaveric dissection demonstrates how the tools and resources anatomy educators use to teach are changing. Language, an integral part of a community's shared repertoire, is one of the most tangible characteristics of a community of practice (Mann, et al., 2010). In higher education the university has been described as "a host of subcultures that speak in strange tongues" (Clark, 1985, p. 157). You have probably noticed the "strange tongues" of different communities of practice in everyday life, overhearing a pair of colleagues talking about work on the bus or in a coffee shop. Most of the time you can figure out what they do, but the terminology they use can be so specific to their profession that it often makes no sense to someone who is not part of the community. If you have come to education from another discipline or field you may have experienced the jargon that typifies educational writing. Education is notorious for its jargon, which can be a "strange tongue" to those who are not yet members of that educational community.

Learning within these communities is like being immersed in a foreign country; it requires you to learn another language, the fundamental tool for communication. Because our membership is enacted through communication, we must learn the words and expressions that help us navigate through these communities and among fellow members. For example, my father, a financial planner, advises me about my investments. When explaining what I should do about my finances he often forgets that I am not a financial planner. Recently he said, "There are some things you can do to make your investments more tax efficient. Your TFSA has some room, transfer a combination of cash and CLF stock to your TFSA, but you don't want to over-contribute to your TFSA as penalties may apply. You are transferring actual CLF shares to keep the brokerage fees to a minimum". My response - a blank stare. You may have felt similarly when a doctor is trying to explain a diagnosis, an IT person is talking you through a computer problem, or a mechanic is explaining the work that needs to be done on your car. The difficulty in such cases is that you do not share the repertoire of these practices, so you lack the language to be able to communicate fully and comprehensibly. As a result, you cannot relate to what they are saying. In addition to the other tools and resources developed by a community, a communal language is an essential part of a shared repertoire.

The concept of communities of practice will help us better understand the Apprenticeship Perspective in that it provides a language to talk about teaching as fostering the growth of students' *competence* within a field of practice. Competence within a social system is not just having a certain amount of knowledge or the ability to perform specific skills, but is something that is established within a community through engagement in practice.

LEARNING: THE TENSION BETWEEN COMPETENCE AND EXPERIENCE

In general, when you think about being competent it often refers to being capable or qualified to do something. A competent driver, for example, would have adequate knowledge and skill to be able to safely drive a car. In medical education there is a trend toward "competency-based education" where competencies are specified as a combination of knowledge, skills, and attitudes needed to carry out the tasks of a physician (Frank et al., 2010). Students attain competence once they demonstrate that they have acquired the appropriate knowledge, skills, and attitudes to become physicians. The emphasis in many such fields is on individuals acquiring those competencies. The Apprenticeship Perspective, however, adds another dimension of competence—*social* competence—as defined by Wenger's three dimensions of practice. Competent members of the community are those who can: 1) engage with other members as trusted colleagues, 2) understand the enterprise and be mutually accountable to each other, and 3) have access to the shared repertoire and can properly use it (Wenger, 1998, 2000). Rather than acquiring a body of information, "knowing" from a social perspective is defined as displaying competence and being recognized as a competent member of the community.

In their book, *The Question of Competence* (2012), Hodges and Lingard extend the conversation about competence to the context of teams. Through mutual engagement with other members of a community, a sense of competence emerges and individuals gain acceptance (or not) as legitimate members of that community. However, competent individuals can come together to form an incompetent (or less competent) team; and individuals who perform competently in one team may not in another. Thus, there emerges not only a sense of individual competence, but also a sense of "team competence". In this sense, competence is constantly evolving, distributed across individuals and tasks, and is learned through participation (Lingard, 2012).

Competence in a social system, or team, is reciprocal and dependent upon those with whom one is interacting. For a community to be competent, individuals must have an accurate understanding of the joint enterprise and knowledge of what others are capable of doing in relation to that enterprise. They must be able to recognize when a team member makes a mistake and be willing to offer relevant information or assistance before it is requested. However, in the absence of a sense of mutual accountability, it's unlikely that community members will negotiate and clarify their interdependent roles in critical situations (Lingard, 2012). Learning in this sense is not only a process of individual acquisition but also of mutual participation. Learning and competence, therefore, are best developed and assessed in contexts of participation.

In sum, learning can be viewed as a mental process of acquiring new information; but it can also be conceptualized as a change in the individual in relation to a community along the three dimensions of social competence (Wenger, 1998). Learning for the individual changes her ability to engage in practice, her understanding of why she is engaging in it, and the resources she has at her disposal to do so. Similarly, for the community, learning includes changes in how members engage in reciprocally beneficial ways, the shaping of their joint enterprise, and the ongoing development of a shared repertoire. Thus, learning is understood as a change in "knowing" as defined by the dimensions of social competence. Competence from this perspective still involves the acquisition of knowledge and skills, but in the context of, and at the service of, being able to participate in the community and embody the identity of a practitioner. Competence alone, however, is not how an individual or a community learns; it is the interaction between competence and personal *experience* that brings about learning for both the individual and the community.

Learning involves the interplay between life experience and social competence (Wenger, 1998). These two components are not necessarily or usually aligned, and it is in their realignment that learning occurs (Wenger, 2000). For example, my first class as a PhD student was "Philosophical Inquiry into Educational Research". Up to that point in my educational journey I had never touched the subject of philosophy and I was quick to find out that the rest of the students in the class had. The class discussion ensued in the "strange tongue" (Clark, 1985) of philosophy and I had no idea what anyone was saying because they kept referring to a long list of philosophers that I was not familiar with. My personal *experience* in this area was lagging behind the *competence* defined by the class. I felt an urgent need to learn all I could about philosophical concepts and scholars. My motivation was not only in service of me passing the course, but in allowing me to go to class and engage with others (without feeling like an idiot). Learning in this case occurred through the alignment of my experience (and repertoire) with the competencies demonstrated by class members. In other words, learning transpired when the competence of the class was advancing my competence.

We can see the same thing with employees who enter the workplace on their first day on the job. They have already demonstrated to those with some authority in the hiring process that they have what it takes to take up this new position. Their resume or CV has outlined their competence and their interview has shown them capable enough to be selected for the job. But on that first day of work, their experience now begins to catch up. As an individual, they are competent and are recognized as such. But in the context of their new job, they need time to align their individual competence in relation to other members of their community of practice.

The reverse can also take place where learning is a result of an individual pulling or advancing the competence of a community. For example, late in my master's degree I had an opportunity to visit another university where a scholar was giving a presentation on writing for publication in medical education. As my program was quite new, we had yet to be exposed to this genre of writing. I was hanging on every word of the presenter not only because he is a leader in the field, but also because the information was so useful for my future career as an academic. My experience opened my eyes to a new way of writing that I had not been exposed to. When I returned to my university I was filled with an overwhelming motivation to share this with my peers because I knew that they would find it helpful for their writing as well. I organized a talk during one of our academic half days to impart my experience with my fellow graduate students in hopes that it might improve the scholarship being produced from our program as a whole. In this case learning occurred with the alignment of my program's competence in writing with my experience of what good publishable academic writing looks like in medical education. In other words, my experience was pulling my community's competence along. Again, new employees also illustrate this concept. Their introduction into a new workplace changes the workplace itself through the knowledge and experience that they bring. Their addition to the community helps redefine the collective skill set of the group of employees within that workplace. In sum, learning can be defined as the realignment of experience and competence, and it is this interaction that is central to individual and collective change.

The examples above illustrate the need for a deliberate, but appropriate, tension between experience and competence. If tension between the two is lost, learning suffers. One way tension is lost is if experience and competence are too close or congruent, resulting in no challenges. For instance if you are comfortable teaching the same curriculum, continue to use the same materials and strategies, and do not consider how each unique group of students changes the context of your teaching, your practice likely becomes stale and stagnant. Tension is also lost if experience and competence are too far apart. For example, trying to have a conversation about finances with my dad is just too overwhelming for me to try to understand it all. When someone else's insider language becomes indecipherable jargon, you will probably begin to tune out. Learning from a social perspective entails the interaction of experience and competence; whenever the two are in constructive tension, with either pulling the other, learning takes place (Wenger, 2000). When learning occurs, it combines both personal changes with changes in the community as they continually work to realign with each other. Talking about learning in terms of the tension between competence and experience is just one way to think about learning within the social perspective. Another way to conceptualize learning from a situated or social viewpoint is through the process of legitimate peripheral participation.

LEARNING AS LEGITIMATE PERIPHERAL PARTICIPATION

A new or "peripheral" member of a community has limited experience and, therefore, limited competence. Participating alongside more seasoned practitioners, newcomers gradually learn to engage and communicate within the community of practice. Over time, with their experience and competence pulling each other they gradually become a more central member of the community. Lave and Wenger call this process *legitimate peripheral participation* (LPP) (Lave & Wenger, 1991). My aim in this section is to highlight some points about LPP that will be useful in our conversation about the apprenticeship teaching perspective.

The first is that newcomers are participating in real or actual practice of the profession or trade. Although engagement will be to a limited extent with less responsibility, the tasks performed are still considered valuable and essential to practice (Hanks, 1991; Johnson & Pratt, 1998). Newcomers are amidst and participate alongside experts or more experienced and competent members of the community. However, for their participation to be legitimate, the practices newcomers engage in must be *authentic*.

Secondly, describing newcomers as on the "periphery" does not necessarily mean that there is an ultimate "center" of participation to be acquired. Lave and Wenger (1991) note that it is "important not to reduce the end point of centripetal participation in a community of practice to a uniform or univocal 'center', or to a linear notion of skill acquisition" (p. 36). Rather, peripheral participation leads to *full* participation. Full participants can still to some degree be considered peripheral members. This has to do with the changing nature of practice itself. Experienced practitioners who have, for example, been teaching for years have developed and adopted from their own mentors a certain way of thinking about and participating in their field. Newcomers on the other hand bring to the community a fresh perspective and the potential to contribute ideas and suggestions for the constructive development and change of the practice. Lave and Wenger (1991) note that "insofar as this continual interaction of new perspectives is sanctioned, everyone's participation is legitimately peripheral in some respect" (p. 117). In other words, because practice is always changing and evolving, everyone, including experts and full members, can be considered a newcomer to some extent. The community and all its members learn, not just new members. As stated by Hanks (1991) "learning, as it were, is distributed among co-participants, not a one-person act" (p. 15).

Thirdly, it is important to grasp the complexity of LPP with respect to relations of power within a community. As newcomers gradually gain experience and are mutually engaged with old-timers, are accountable to the enterprise of the community, and use the language and tools of practice, they transition into a more empowering position. On the other hand, if newcomers do not have access to legitimate real practice and, for whatever reason do not have the opportunity to engage with more experienced members, they maintain a very disempowered position. As framed in the previous section, a lack of tension between experience and competence prevents the newcomer from becoming a full member of the community.

Lastly, it is important to understand that LPP is not a specific teaching technique or an educational prescription to be applied in the classroom. It is a way of thinking about learning that will be helpful for us to understand the Apprenticeship Teaching Perspective.

COMPARING COGNITIVE AND
SOCIAL LEARNING PERSPECTIVES

If we accept learning as a changing social experience, then one way to describe learning is the realignment of an individual's personal experience with the competence defined by the community. Part of this realignment is achieved through legitimate peripheral participation where a newcomer gradually becomes a member of a community of practice. This notion of learning is in contrast to the perspective discussed earlier in this chapter, where learning is perceived as the acquisition of knowledge and skills. As summarized in Table 5.1, learning from a cognitive perspective is thought of as the acquisition of something, where learning from a social viewpoint involves becoming a participating member of a community. The cognitive perspective positions teachers as providers of information and students as receivers of information. The social learning perspective positions the teacher as an experienced practitioner working in contexts of authentic practice alongside learners as legitimate participants. Unlike the cognitive perspective, where knowledge is considered an individual possession, knowledge in a social learning perspective is enacted through participation in the work of a community. In that participation, one's competence is dependent upon others as well as self. Consequently, competence, or "knowing", can only be demonstrated while working within that community.

Lave and Wenger show their leaning toward the social perspective in saying that "learning is a way of being in the social world, not a way of coming to know about it" (p. 24). What is important to note, however, is that *both* "being in the social world" and "coming to know about it" are important and useful in our conversations about teaching and learning.

Debate on the benefits and limits of each perspective has gone on for years. Despite efforts to identify the best ways to utilize both, the dichotomy still remains as the two are continually compared and contrasted (Cobb & Bowers, 1999; Greeno, 1997; Sfard, 1998). My intent here is not to discern some way to bridge the two perspectives but rather to emphasize that there are different ways to think about learning. All are valuable for informing our discussions about teaching, just in different ways (Greeno, 1997). For example, medical students spend two years learning the terminology of anatomy in the university setting. In subsequent years they enter teaching hospitals where they begin to use that language in the context of a community of medical practice. Medical students' acquisition of anatomical terms is an integral part of becoming a member of the medical community. As noted by Sfard (1998) it is helpful for us to think about these conceptualizations of learning as "offering different perspectives rather than competing opinions" (p. 11).

I will now turn to using the different perspectives on learning as a lens to compare and contrast the transmission and apprentice-

Table 5.1 Comparison of Cognitive and Social Learning Perspectives. Modified from Sfard (1998).

	Cognitive perspective	Social perspective
Learning	Acquisition of something	Becoming a participant
Teacher	Provider of knowledge	Full member, expert practitioner
Student	Recipient of knowledge	Newcomer, peripheral participant
Knowledge	Property, possession, commodity	Defined by the community of practice
Knowing	Having, possessing	Competence within and belonging to a community

ship teaching perspectives with a particular focus on exploring the latter. A cautionary note when considering the various ways of thinking about learning is to keep in mind that these frameworks are just different perspectives rather than competing ideologies. In other words, it is important to remember that cognitive and social learning perspectives are complementary rather than contradictory. Each way of understanding learning is important and provides a unique lens for understanding effective teaching.

In addition to trying to avoid the dichotomization of cognitive and social learning, another cautionary note regarding the adoption of different learning perspectives is best articulated by Cobb and Bowers (1999) in that "the two perspectives cannot be reduced to that of choosing between the individual and the social collective as the . . . unit of analysis" (p. 4). In other words, the contrast between cognitive and social perspectives should not be confused with the common distinction between the individual versus the social or collective. The difference between the cognitive and social perspectives is that they have fundamentally different answers to the question of "What is learning?" But the more relevant issue here is their complementary, but different, emphases on how learning takes place and what kind of learning we want to facilitate.

Taking caution not to privilege either perspective on learning or to reduce them to a comparison of the individual versus the collective, I will now turn to using these different ways of thinking about learning to contrast the transmission and apprenticeship teaching perspectives.

THE APPRENTICESHIP TEACHING PERSPECTIVE

In this section my goal is to explore the indicators of commitment (beliefs, intentions, and actions), as well as assessment strategies, within the apprenticeship teaching perspective and contrast those with the transmission perspective. The challenges and advantages of the Apprenticeship Perspective will then be considered. I will conclude by highlighting a few principles that characterize effective teaching within the Apprenticeship Perspective. We all have a different idea of what apprenticeship means, so before jumping into the apprenticeship teaching perspective itself it is important to address what we mean by "apprenticeship" in this perspective on teaching.

Examples of Apprenticeship versus
an Apprenticeship Teaching Perspective

What comes to mind when you think about "apprenticeship"? The first image that pops into my head is of Mr. Miyagi from the movie the *Karate Kid*, a wizened martial arts master passing the ancient teachings of his discipline to his young protégé Daniel San. Another image that comes to mind is that of a medieval blacksmith, adorned with dirt and sweat, pounding the red hot metal of a horseshoe as his apprentice observes attentively at his side. I am sure you are able to think of more insightful examples that span beyond 80's movies or feudal Europe, but the point I am trying to make is that the Apprenticeship Teaching *Perspective* is a way of thinking about teaching that is more encompassing than traditional notions of apprenticeship, i.e., those typically associated with a master passing down the traditions of a craft or trade to an individual trainee. These more typical illustrations of apprenticeship are only the beginning, connecting what we might have known about the term apprenticeship with what we are assimilating from this chapter. From here we can also consider the many different forms of apprenticeship learning in other fields, though not exactly named as such, for example, health professions, law, academia, various trades, sports and the arts. These make for some good *examples* in which to explore the apprenticeship teaching perspective. In addition, although we can explore the pedagogical beliefs, intentions and actions (assessment and strategies) of the apprenticeship teaching perspective through examples of apprenticeship, it doesn't mean that every instance of apprenticeship necessarily or inevitably fosters this teaching perspective. The distinction between examples of apprenticeship and an apprenticeship teaching perspective will become clear as we move to discussing the beliefs, intentions and actions that characterize this perspective.

Beliefs, Intentions, and Actions
as Indicators of Commitment

As we compare the beliefs, intentions and actions of the transmission and apprenticeship teaching perspectives you will notice how each reflects a different understanding of learning. In many respects these teaching perspectives parallel the cognitive/social-learning orientations. For example, transmission teachers tend to believe that learning is a cognitive process occurring in the minds of students. They believe that a systematic organized approach to learning will make it easier for students to receive information, organize it in their minds, and recall it at a later time. Apprenticeship teachers, however, believe that learning is both the process (verb) and the product (noun) of participating in a community. Thus, rather than focusing on efficiently delivering of content, as in the Transmission Perspective, this perspective conceives of teaching as a process of mentoring, guiding, coaching, and enculturating learners into the ways of the community. Learning necessarily starts on the periphery and requires legitimate participation within contexts of real practice.

In general, the overriding difference between these teaching perspectives is that transmission is focused on *content;* whereas the Apprenticeship Perspective focuses on *context*—physical, temporal, social, and cultural contexts—where people are learning how to engage and work in relation to others. Transmission teachers are concerned with how information is arranged and taught in a way that students can better receive and accurately give back that information. Apprenticeship teachers on the other hand worry not so much about *what* is being taught in terms of learning objectives or a well-defined body of knowledge, but that learners are actively engaged with experts in the setting of genuine practice. For example, a student teacher during her practicum is not only learning the mechanics of how to manage an effective class, she is re-learning the content in ways that now have to bend to the learners, accommodating their different motivations and predispositions. They are a vital part of the social context she has to 'learn'. As she engages with more experienced teachers in the school, and receives feedback from staff observing her classes, she is slowly learning her identity as a teacher and what her role is in the context of both the school and the profession. In this sense, context IS the teacher. (Pratt, Harris, & Collins, 2009; Pratt, Sadownik, & Jarvis Selinger, 2012). She will learn things during her practicum that she could not have learned in university or college classrooms while training to be a teacher. Whereas the Transmission Perspective foregrounds 'content', the Apprenticeship Perspective foregrounds 'context'.

Foregrounding either context or content changes what is meant by "curriculum" within each of these teaching perspectives. Curriculum for a transmission educator is clearly articulated and specifically designed and defined in advance either by the teacher or by some external mandate. Alternatively, from an Apprenticeship Perspective, curriculum is created from the context of the community. It arises from opportunities within the natural rhythms of practice rather than being prescribed and planned ahead of time. These different conceptions of curriculum parallel Lave and Wenger's (1991) distinction between teaching and learning curriculums where a *teaching* curriculum is something that is constructed for the instruction of newcomers, and a *learning* curriculum consists of moments of learning situated within the natural ebb and flow of practice. Foregrounding either context or content not only has implications for the meaning of curriculum, but also for the nature of knowledge.

Knowledge within the Transmission Perspective is in the form of content and concepts that can be clearly identified and conveyed from educator to student. But knowledge gained within the context of practice as within the Apprenticeship Perspective may not be, or is difficult to explicitly verbalize. This "craft knowledge" is embodied in the routines of expert practitioners. It is what comes naturally to them after years of being in the field. Rather than the acquisition of content for testing or future application, this type of knowing is learned through participation alongside expert practitioners. With a curriculum that arises out of practice, and the need to learn within sites of practice, the intention of apprenticeship teachers is to help build learners' competence within the community and to assist them in developing their identity as a full member. They do this by being aware of, and teaching and assessing students within, their *zone of proximal development*.

Originally developed by Vygotsky (1978), the zone of proximal development (ZPD) is an area where learning and development is maximized. More specifically, it is defined as the zone between what a learner can do independently without any help, and what cannot be done safely, even when assisted by a more competent member of the community (Lave & Wenger, 1991). Between those extremes lies the most productive zone of learning—the zone of proximal development.

The application of Vygotsky's ZPD in the field of education fostered the development of *scaffolding*; a process where an expert practitioner or a more experienced peer provides a lot of initial help to a student, and then tapers off the assistance as the student becomes more competent. As the name implies this strategy is much like the scaffolding of a building. At the beginning of construction, scaffolding predominantly provides structure to the building, similar to how a practitioner will provide more help and support to newer members of the community. For example in the first weeks of clinical immersion a dental student may only observe the practicing dentist as he articulates his thoughts and actions while he carries out procedures.

As a building continues to be built it gradually gains its own structural integrity and less support is needed by the scaffolding. In the same way, as a student gains experience and becomes a more competent member of the community the assistance of the expert practitioner will gradually "fade" (Johnson & Pratt, 1998), providing less support and allowing the student to have greater responsibly. To maximize learning the strategy of scaffolding must occur within the newcomer's ZPD. This means that in order for teaching to be meaningful the expert practitioner must be aware of the student's level of competence.

In sum, the underlying difference in understandings about learning, and thus the foregrounding of either content or context, has implications for what effective teaching means and looks like within the transmission and apprenticeship teaching perspectives as summarized in Table 5.2.

Table 5.2 Comparison of Transmission and Apprenticeship *Teaching* Perspectives

	TRANSMISSION	APPRENTICESHIP
General Orientation	Content	Context
Beliefs	Learning is a cognitive process of gaining, organizing, and retrieving knowledge Learning is facilitated by clear and organized presentation of information	Learning is a process of socialization into a community of practice Learning requires authentic participation in the context of practice
Intentions	Build a base of essential knowledge and/or skill in learners	Develop learner's competence and identity as a member of a community of practice
Actions Assessment	Frequent testing Testing understanding of foundational knowledge	Assessment aligned with authentic practice Awareness of, and assessment within learner's zone of proximal development
Strategies	Structured and systematic approach to the presentation of information	Scaffolding Engaging with learners in the context of authentic practice

Benefits and Challenges of the Apprenticeship Perspective

Broadly speaking, the benefits and challenges within the Apprenticeship Aerspective stem from the affordances and difficulties associated with teaching within the context of authentic practice as well as the nature of expert practitioners' knowledge. The overlying advantage of having students immersed in genuine practice is that they are motivated to learn. This motivation arises because they are working alongside those who they want to become—master practitioners who are full members of the community. Although as newcomers they hold less responsibility and perform simplified tasks, these tasks are still regarded as valuable to the practice, which makes learning relevant. As their competence increases, learners continue to be motivated by knowing that their contributions to practice have gained more value to the community. In sum, the prioritization of context within the Apprenticeship Perspective does much for motivating learning. Students are encouraged by the relevance of authentic practice and being able to legitimately contribute to and play a valued role within the community they are working to join. But although beneficial for motivating students, the context of genuine practice poses multiple challenges for educators and learners, including the following.

The ill-defined nature of the context of real practice

The context of practice is uncertain and ever transforming. Every physician's office, construction site, and classroom is unique. As the flow of work changes from day to day so does every teaching opportunity for educators. Therefore, there is no straightforward or standard response for teachers to follow. As previously discussed, the "curriculum" is created by practice itself, "unfold[ing] as opportunities develop for learners to become engaged in practice" (Johnson & Pratt, 1998, p. 92). Educators may feel more or less equipped to manage such uncertainty or to capitalize on such teaching moments as they arise. The situated nature of real practice also poses a challenge in assessing learners in that the level of task difficulty is not well defined (Pratt, et al., 2012), nor can it necessarily be implied by the age, grade, or years spent within a professional program.

No practice to participate in

Our conversation to this point has assumed that there is a definable practice, craft, or profession which learners aspire to be a part of. But what about contexts where students are not all going to become nurses, lawyers, mechanics, or engineers? Take elementary and secondary schooling for example, or even general introductory courses within higher education where there may be multiple communities and professions in which students are hoping to become members. As noted by Sfard (1998) "real life situations that would be likely to become for mathematics or science students what a craftsman's workshop is for the apprentice are extremely difficult to find" (p. 10). So there is ambiguity for educators that are not immersed in the context of practice that learners wish to gain access, making the task of fostering "authentic" learning experiences difficult.

Lack of access

If students are denied access to a community and are unable to engage in the activities of practice, movement towards becoming a full member will be limited. One can be kept from participating by the structure of the curriculum or by individual educators. For example, the curriculum of most professional programs includes classroom-based teaching prior to immersion in the context of practice. During the initial part of the program, which can span from months to years, students are largely denied access to participating with full members of the community. The learning that they are doing is still legitimate but as noted by Lave and Wenger (1991) "there is a difference between talking *about* a practice from outside and talking *within* it" (italics in original) (pp. 107-108). Students learn the language of a community but not necessarily how to properly use that language in the context of real practice. Apart from how a program or curriculum is organized, educators themselves can also deny access to practice. Full members or expert practitioners have control over how much or little they wish to involve newcomers in the tasks at hand. This has as much to do with the level of motivation and incentive an educator has to teach and share the profession as it does with the relationship with the students and the knowledge of their levels of competence.

The embedded nature of expert knowledge

Drawing from the work of Schon (1983) and Weinstein and Hamman (1994), Johnson and Pratt (1998) bring attention to the tacit "knowing in practice" of master practitioners. They explain how this tacit, or "craft" knowledge, is embodied in the master's actions making it difficult to articulate to others (Johnson & Pratt,

1998). I would add that this tacit knowledge of expert practitioners consists not only of the embodied knowledge of habitual manual tasks but also the social and cultural knowledge of the community including how to properly act, talk, and engage with other members. This "socio-cultural" knowledge or awareness is rarely spelled out for newcomers but is of utmost importance to developing competence in a community. An expert practitioner with his embodied knowledge runs the risk of assuming that what is apparent to him in the context of practice is also apparent for his students (Pratt, et al., 2012). This can be extremely dangerous in professions involving patient care or workplaces, such as, construction sites where safety consciousness is embedded though unstated in one's actions. This challenge points to the need for teachers to make explicit what has become natural to them over years of practicing their profession. This means an educator needs to put her expertise into words, no matter how obvious she believes the situation or reasoning to be. The same can be said for learners in needing to talk through their application of knowledge and skills. Without knowing the reasoning behind student's actions, teachers can struggle to give adequate feedback within the learner's zone of proximal development (ZPD).

Tension between teaching and practice

Although the image of a newcomer working alongside a master practitioner may give the impression of a seamless unified activity, educators are required to both teach learners and complete the day-to-day work needing to be done. The pressures of time and productivity in the context of real work make it difficult to weave the teaching of newcomers into the rhythm of practice. Depending on the nature of assessment in the program, students face a similar conflict in whether they should be learning to become a competent member of the community or learning to display knowledge on a test. Although teaching and practice are largely intertwined according to the Apprenticeship Perspective, finding balance between the two remains an ongoing and changeable challenge for the teacher (Ellaway, et al., 2014; Goldman, 2009; Gordon, 2013)

This list of challenges is by no means exhaustive. If you take some time to reflect, I am sure you could generate more challenges specific to your experience and context of practice. As you may have concluded, my intention is not to propose solutions to these difficulties. Every teacher's situation presents its own unique set of conditions, and therefore how one may most appropriately address the challenges within the Apprenticeship Perspective will be different.

CHARACTERISTICS OF EFFECTIVE APPRENTICESHIP TEACHERS

When considering what makes good teaching, we might look first to our dominant perspectives according to the Teaching Perspectives Inventory (Chapter 11). TPI Profiles present graphic portraits of what we value as educators and help us think about what we can do to improve our teaching. Although some characteristics of good apprenticeship teaching are particular to each individual, this chapter constructs a general framework of effective teaching that differentiates the Apprenticeship Perspective from other perspectives on teaching. I will conclude with a listing of principles and characteristics that are central to the Apprenticeship Perspective. While the convenience of a list is used to enumerate these principles and characteristics, it is important to acknowledge that they are not exclusive to this perspective, but are central to it. That is, if someone is working in a situation that requires an appreciation of the context and community in teaching, these principles and characteristics provide a guide to improving or even evaluating their practice. Consequently, it is best to consider them as a whole rather than as separate, as they overlap and inform each other. Finally, while some of these characteristics are more distinct to the Apprenticeship Perspective they are not confined solely to this perspective and may also speak to the other four perspectives presented in this book.

Principles and Characteristics

Effective teaching happens within the context of authentic practice.

As previously mentioned the core tenet of apprenticeship is that teachers "involve you within" an actual, physical and social context of practice rather than "tell you about" it (Johnson & Pratt, 1998; Pratt, et al., 2009). Although uncertainty within the fluctuating context of authentic practice can be challenging, the opportunity to engage with practitioners in real practice is paramount in motivating student learning.

Effective teachers understand learning as participation within a member of a community

Teachers within the Apprenticeship Perspective tend to think about learning in a social rather than cognitive way. This implies that instead of focusing on organizing and delivering content for students to consume they are concerned with engaging with learners in the context of practice so that they may become a member of the community. Pratt et al. (2012) note that this "orientation to the social and cultural aspects of learning and teaching is . . . one which clearly differentiates it from other perspectives" (p. 110).

Effective apprenticeship teachers are role models

As one of Pratt's (2012) eight qualities of effective teachers, educators within the Apprenticeship Perspective are role models in that they "teach as much by what they DO, as by what they say". This is emphasized within the Apprenticeship Perspective in that students immersed within the context of practice work alongside expert practitioners, observing and learning not only from how they perform tasks and carry out procedures, but also from how they deal with unexpected, critical, or difficult situations. If someone is watching, you are teaching, and they are learning how to be a member of the community.

Effective apprenticeship teachers teach and assess within learners' zone of proximal development (ZPD)

Over time as practitioners engage with newer members of the community they gain a sense of what they are able to do on their own and what they can accomplish with assistance from a more competent member of the community. Effective apprenticeship teachers instruct within this range of ability in order to maximize learning. Along with role-modeling, teaching within learner's ZPD is also one of Pratt's eight qualities of effective teachers (2012).

Effective apprenticeship teachers build relationships with learners

Fundamentally connected to the ability to identify each learner's ZPD is that educators establish relationships with students. This is facilitated by apprenticeship teachers working alongside newcomers in the context of practice. However, if educators do not have enough time to spend with learners or are pressured by the productivity of work, they will most likely not build the amount of rapport needed to gauge a student's learning and provide meaningful feedback.

Effective apprenticeship teachers make the implicit explicit

As "craft" knowledge is tacit and difficult to put into words master practitioners must make an effort to articulate to learners what has become intuitive and habitual to them over years of practice. This includes not only the manual skills of the profession, but also the unspoken "knowing" of the social and cultural environment including how to properly engage and communicate with other members of the community. Apprenticeship teachers not only make an effort to articulate their own reasoning, but also encourage learners to do the same so they are able to better assess student learning and, again, provide more meaningful feedback.

Effective apprenticeship teachers are co-participants within an evolving practice

Relationships of power are complex within a community of practice. Expert practitioners in the field are the most competent and experienced members of the community; yet newcomers bring useful naïve ideas and recommendations that can bring positive development and change to the practice. Effective apprenticeship teachers recognize that despite their empowered position as a full member of the community, they are still co-participants with newcomers and are humbly open to the fresh perspectives they may offer in order that it may better the community as a whole. In other words, effective apprenticeship teachers foster the mindset of life-long learners despite the power differential implied within the culture of a community of practice.

To close I will remind you what Dan Pratt has emphasized here and elsewhere (2012). There is one characteristic of effective teachers than spans across all five teaching perspectives: "They truly believe that what is learned is more important than what is taught" (Pratt, et al., 2012, p. 208)

REFERENCES

Clark, B. R. (1985). Listening to the professoriate. *Change: The Magazine of Higher Learning, 17*(5), 36-43.

Cobb, P., & Bowers, J. (1999). Cognitive and situated learning perspectives in theory and practice. *Educational Researcher, 28*(2), 4-15.

Ellaway, R., Pusic, M., Yavner, S.,Alet, A. L. (in press). Context matters: Emergent variability in an effectiveness trial of on-line teaching modules. *Medical Education.*

Frank, J. R., Snell, L. S., Cate, O. T., Holmboe, E. S., Carraccio, C., Swing, S. R., et al. (2010). Competency-based medical education: theory to practice. *Medical Teacher, 32*(8), 638-645.

Goldman, E. (2009). Learning in a chaotic environment. Journal of Workplace Learning, vol. 21(7), pp. 555-574.

Gordon, M. (2013). When shifting context: the role of context dynamics in educating and understanding handover. *Medical Education*, vol. 47, pp. 434-442.

Greeno, J. G. (1997). On claims that answer the wrong questions. *Educational Researcher, 26*(1), 5-17.

Hanks, W. F. (1991). Foreword. In J. Lave & E. Wenger (Eds.), *Situated learning: Legitimate peripheral participation.* Cambridge: Cambridge University Press.

Hodges, B. D., & Lingard, L. (2012). *The Question of Competence: Reconsidering medical education in the twenty-first century.* Ithaca, New York: Cornell University Press.

Johnson, J., & Pratt, D. D. (1998). The Apprenticeship Perspective: Modeling Ways of Being. In D. D. Pratt (Ed.), *Five perspectives on teaching in adult and higher education.* Malabar, FL: Krieger Publishing Company, Inc.

Lave, J., & Wenger, E. (1991). *Situated Learning: Legitimate Peripheral Participation.* Cambridge: Cambridge University Press.

Lingard, L. (2012). Rethinking Competence in the Context of Teamwork, In Hodges & Lingard (Eds.). *The Question of Competence: Reconsidering medical education in the twenty-first century.* Ithaca, New York: Cornell University Press, chapter 2, pp.

Mann, K., Dornan, T., & Teunissen, P. (2010). Perspectives on Learning. In T. Dornan & K. Mann (Eds.), *Medical Education: Theory and Practice*: Churchill Livingstone.

Mason, L. (2007). Introduction: Bridging the Cognitive and Socio-cultural Approaches in Research on Conceptual Change: Is it Feasible? *Educational Psychologist, 42*(1), 1-7.

Pratt, D. D. (2012). Teaching Perspectives: Why can't everyone be like me? . Presentation to Harvard Macy Institute, Harvard Medical School, January: Cambridge, Massachusetts.

Pratt, D. D., Harris, P., & Collins, J. B. (2009). The power of one: looking beyond the teacher in clinical instruction. *Medical Teacher, 31*(2), 133-137.

Pratt, D. D., Sadownik, L., & Jarvis Selinger, S. (2012). Pedagogical BIASes and Clinical Teaching in Medicine. In L. M. English (Ed.), *Adult Education and Health*. Toronto: University of Toronto Press.

Schön, D. A. (1983). *The reflective practitioner: How professionals think in action*. New York: Basic Books.

Sfard, A. (1998). On Two Metaphors for Learning and the Dangers of Choosing Just One. *Educational Researcher, 27*(2), 4-13.

Vygotski, L. S. (1978). *Mind in society: The development of higher psychological processes*. USA: Harvard University Press.

Weinstein, C. E., & Hamman, D. (1994). Acquiring expertise in specific content areas: Implications for teaching novices. *Journal of Staff, Program and Organizational Development, 12*(1), 57-60.

Wenger, E. (1998). *Communities of Practice: Learning, Meaning and Identity*. Cambridge University of Cambridge Press.

Wenger, E. (2000). Communities of Practice and Social Learning Systems. *Organization, 7*(2), 225-246.

Wenger, E. (2006). Communities of practice: A brief introduction. Retrieved January 16, 2012, from http://ewenger.com/theory/index.htm

CHAPTER 6
The Developmental Perspective

Ric Arseneau

INTRODUCTION

Before getting into medical school I took a course in comparative vertebrate anatomy. I found the course difficult to understand and overloaded with facts. In addition to my disinterest in the course, I was suffering from "grade anxiety"—from the fear of not getting into medical school. I tried to understand the material but was not rewarded for comprehension. Extra reading outside of class notes was actually detrimental to my grade. The teacher seemed to give a mixed message. Although he said he wanted us to understand and be able to compare and apply what we knew, he actually rewarded us for the reproduction of his own ideas. In fact, word for word reproduction from class notes was the most valued. As the final exam approached I realized I needed an A+ to get an overall A average. Because of time constraints and the competing demands of other exams, I decided to rehearse and memorize the lecture notes for the semester without any attention to understanding. I knew what would be rewarded: the reproduction of well-rehearsed answers. This strategy resulted in a grade of 90% — my best mark to date for the course.

From the example above can you infer the teacher's espoused theories? What evidence do you have of the teacher's theory-in-practice? Do you suppose he is aware of any discordance? The discordance between espoused theory and theory-in-practice is a common problem in higher education. For example, the concept of excellence, and the goals for teaching and learning usually include variations on the following themes (Ramsden, 1992):

- To teach students to analyze ideas or issues critically.
- To develop students' intellectual/thinking skills.
- To teach students to comprehend principles or generalizations.

Yet, my experience in the example above is likely more in keeping with the usual experience of learners. Several studies (Ramsden, 1992; Dahlgren, 1984) seriously question the effectiveness of higher education and conclude that:

- Many students are accomplished at complex routine skills including problem-solving algorithms.
- Many students have amassed large volumes of detailed knowledge.
- Many students are able to reproduce large quantities of factual information on demand.
- Many are able to pass examinations.

But many are unable to show that they understand what they have learned, when asked simple yet searching questions that test their grasp of content. They continue to profess misconceptions of important concepts; their application of their knowledge to new problems is often weak; their skills in working jointly to solve problems are frequently inadequate.

Ramsden (1988) cites one particularly striking example in which 80-90% of U.S. college students were unable to explain concepts from ninth grade algebra despite being able to manipulate the symbols and pass behavioral objectives. They were unable to demonstrate that they understood. This example illustrates the central theme of the Developmental Perspective: learning has occurred only when learners are able to demonstrate understanding. Therefore, teaching from this perspective has to do with facilitating the learner's intellectual development (i.e., development of the intellect). The goal, then, is to close the gap between teachers' espoused theory and theory-in-practice by challenging learners to think critically, to solve problems, and to understand for themselves.

This chapter, as well as the others in this book, reflects a particular orientation toward the theory and practice of teaching. Not only does it provide a set of beliefs and intentions to guide specific instructional techniques, it also describes an educational philosophy consistent with my practical and theoretical understanding of cognition and learning. The Developmental Perspective parallels a

theoretical perspective of learning and knowing termed con-
structivism (e.g., Candy, 1991; Jonassen and Land, 2012). The
constructivist perspective is consistent with a lot of current philosophical and neurophysiological views of brain function (e.g.,
Anderson, 1992).

It is worth emphasizing that the Developmental Perspective represents a set of beliefs as opposed to a set of teaching behaviors. In
other words, teaching is not merely the application of specific rules
in specific situations. Teaching is the visible expression of an underlying set of beliefs a teacher brings to the learning environment—
beliefs that help the teacher to better navigate the murky waters of
practice. Therefore, the degree to which your practice reflects a particular teaching perspective in this book is a matter of the degree to
which your personal theories resonate with the set of assumptions
belonging to a particular perspective. Recall that most of us operate
from more than one perspective. I hope to persuade you that operating from the Developmental Perspective is important in bringing
about understanding. Even if your practice is primarily informed by
one of the other perspectives in this book, I believe that having the
Developmental Perspective operate in the background will improve
your teaching.

The remainder of this chapter is divided into three main sections: key ideas, developmental teaching principles, and bridging
knowledge. I will begin by presenting two key ideas underlying the
Developmental Perspective. The main concepts underlying the Developmental Perspective will be presented as a set of seven "developmental teaching principles." This will be followed by a discussion
of the "special knowledge" required to teach from this perspective.

KEY IDEAS

Before embarking on the main discussion of the chapter, it is important to consider two key ideas underlying the Developmental Perspective: (1) How we come to understand something, and (2) The
relationship between teaching and learning.

How We Come to Understand

*Have you ever wondered how a child comes to learn and un-
derstand the concept of "dog"? The child may notice, or the
parents may point to a dog and say "dog." What the child sees*

and attends to will depend on that particular child. Does the child notice the size, the color, short ears, long ears, pointed ears, straight tail, curly tail, etc.? What is it that the child un derstands when the parents say "dog"? On another occasion, the child may see a cat and say "dog." The parents will correct the child and say, "No . . . Cat." The child must now take her concept of dog and change its internal representation so that it more closely matches that of her parents. With time and inter action with her parents, the child will develop a very good un derstanding of what a dog is (i.e., an accurate and appropri ate internal representation of the concept "dog").

Obviously, the concept of dog was not transferred from the parents to the child. The child had to construct an internal representation of the concept. She used the concept to interpret (i.e., construe) and make sense of new situations (e.g., mistaking a cat for a dog). By interacting with her parents, she constructed increasingly more sophisticated and more accurate internal representations of the concept (e.g., not all small furry animals are dogs). She developed better conceptions (i.e., parents' preferred conception).

Conceptual understanding then, has to do with the dual acts of constructing and construing. Internal models are constructed and used to construe (i.e., interpret) new situations. Testing one's constructions with those of others allows us to reach a common understanding.However, given the personal manner in which internal representations are constructed, all constructions are necessarily idiosyncratic; we all have a different understanding of the same concept. Concepts may overlap sufficiently with those of others so that we can understand and communicate with each other.

The concept of "dog" is relatively unproblematic; we can all agree on what a dog is. However, higher levels of abstraction are needed to understand concepts such as justice, health, and education. Each one of us understands these concepts differently based on our history with the concept. For instance, what does the word "mother" bring to mind? How might it differ in the following situations? What if you were adopted? What if you were an orphan? What if you were abused? The possibilities are endless, as are the subtle and not-so-subtle difference that each one of us carries for the concept of mother. Although, personal constructions are idiosyncratic, there may be sufficient overlap among individual constructions within a group for agreement and understanding to occur (i.e., social constructions). These constructions are related, if not analogous, to the shared repertoires explored in the Apprenticeship Perspective (Chapter 5). For instance, the concept of "healthy looking" is a social construction. There is no such thing as healthy looking; the concept simply represents a more or less agreed-upon definition by a specific group. Considering a lean muscular woman as fit and healthy looking is a social construction of western society in the 21st century. The same outward look may have a totally different meaning to a different social group or at a different time. Would this lean and muscular woman evoke the idea of health looking in the 1800s? Not very likely. Therefore, despite their idiosyncratic nature, personal constructions may overlap sufficiently for a common meaning to occur. However, common meanings may differ for different groups or at different times.

In summary, understanding comes from the personal construction of internal representations of concepts. Constructions are used to construe new situations. The iterative acts of constructing and construing allow us to refine our understanding of a concept. Further, dialogue between individuals allows the development and sharing of common meaning for some concepts (i.e., social constructions). However, social constructions are necessarily constructions and do not represent an external reality, but simply an internal representation of reality. For a given group, some constructions may be more acceptable or correct.

The Relationship between Teaching and Learning

The relationship between teaching and learning was called into question by a cartoon in which a boy told his friend that he had taught his dog how to whistle. With his ear up to the dog's face, the friend said, "I don't hear him whistling." The boy replied, "I said I taught him. I didn't say he learned it" (Whitman, 1990).

The less than direct relationship between teaching and learning is obvious but often forgotten. It is beyond the scope of this chapter to provide a detailed discussion of this relationship. My goal is to challenge a taken for granted assumption held by many individuals: that teaching necessarily results in learning. Given that this is a book on teaching, it is important that you not lose sight of the indirect relationship between teaching and learning. You will need to ask yourself what other forces have a positive (or negative) impact on learning. My view of the relationship between teaching and learning will become obvious as the ideas in this chapter are developed.

DEVELOPMENTAL TEACHING PRINCIPLES

Consider the following anecdote:

> *I once had the opportunity to supervise a junior colleague during his first clinical teaching assignment. After observing one of his clinical teaching sessions, I asked him to comment on what he thought the students learned. He was caught somewhat off guard and replied, "I think I did some good teaching, but I've actually never thought, have the students done good learning?"*

Teaching from the Developmental Perspective is Machiavellian: "the ends justify the means." Therefore teaching from this perspective, as with every perspective, has more to do with what is learned, than with what was taught. The focus, then, is on the development of learners' thinking, reasoning, and judgment rather than on specific teaching performances. There is no one right way to teach, only better ways depending on the content, the context, the learners, and the teacher. Therefore, this chapter will focus on the beliefs and intentions that inform teaching from a Developmental Perspective in the hopes that individual teachers will creatively interpret these into teaching actions that work for them. In reading this chapter, it might be helpful for you to consider your own teaching. Note any similarities and differences, paying particular attention to your underlying beliefs and intentions as a teacher. If you have never taught, read this chapter from the perspective of when you were a learner.

I believe the best way to understand this perspective is experientially. The following seven principles and discussions will highlight the Developmental Perspective. They will be presented sequentially for you to discover. Each principle will build on the preceding ones. The last principle will be a guiding principle. These seven Developmental Teaching principles are based largely on the works of Ramsden (1988), Marton, Hounsell, & Entwistle (1984), on student learning, and on the work of Schmidt (1993) on the principles of cognitive learning.

Principle 1: Prior knowledge is key to learning

Read the following paragraph as though you were preparing for a test.

Simple Malfunctions and Their Remedies: Air in the Fuel System.

The fuel injection system consists of the fuel tank, fuel feed pump, fuel filter, fuel injection pump, injection line, and fuel injection valve. If air enters any part of the system, with the exception of the fuel tank, fuel will not be injected into the cylinders. Check the fuel injection "sound" in the following manner: (1) Pull out the knob for engine warm-up and place the control lever in the "half speed" position; (2) Open the delivery cock of the fuel tank; (3) Loosen the fuel strainer air-bleed bolt; (4) Move the priming lever of the fuel feed pump up and down. All the air has been bled out of the fuel line when only fuel flows out. After bleeding, retighten the bolt; (5) To "bleed air" from the fuel line, loosen the air-venting bolt on the fuel injection pump and move the priming lever up and down until all the air bubbles out.

How well would you do on the test? Why? Unless you are a marine diesel mechanic, you probably don't understand the information. Given enough time to rehearse, you could commit the short passage to memory. But how long would you remember? What if you were asked to provide an explanation, or worse, asked to carry out the steps?

Prior knowledge is the most important determinant of new learning. If you couldn't make sense of the above information, it was because you had no prior knowledge in this area. You couldn't understand because you couldn't connect it to something you already knew. Prior knowledge is the foundation on which new knowledge is constructed; new knowledge is built from (or onto) existing conceptions (prior knowledge).

Learners always have some relevant prior knowledge. It is your role as a teacher to access the right starting point for your learners. Make it real. Start with something they know. Stay within their "zone of proximal development" (Vygotsky, 1978): not too easy, not too difficult. And as with the Apprenticeship and Transmission Perspectives, limit your use of jargon and be aware that your students may not yet be fluent in the 'communal language' of your field.

There is a direct relationship between the amount of learners' prior knowledge and the amount learners can learn. The less they know about something, the less they can take in. Paradoxically, as teachers we often try to present the most to those with little prior understanding. This is also evident in the Transmission Perspective when discussing cognitive load (see: Chapter 4, Figure 4.1, on page 81).

Implications for teaching

- Start with the learner.
- Teaching requires an understanding of the range of learners' prior conceptions (and misconceptions).
- It is the teacher's responsibility to adjust the content to the learners' prior understanding of it.
- Pay close attention to your language (i.e., limit the jargon)
- For learners in an unfamiliar content area: "less can be more."

Principle 2: Prior knowledge must be activated

Read the following paragraph as though you were preparing for a test.

The whole procedure is basically quite simple. First, the units are distributed in different categories. One single category may of course be sufficient if you do not have too much to work with. If one has to leave for another place, because of a lack of resources, this is the next step; if not preparation is now completed. It is of vital importance not to over-commit oneself. This means in this context that it is preferable to do a few things at once, than to let things pile up. In a short time perspective this may not seem important, but complications may easily emerge. Mistakes may be expensive. In the beginning the procedure may appear as complex. But soon it is only a detail among others in our everyday life. It is difficult to foresee an end to this activity in the near future, but we know very little about such things. When the procedure is completed you allocate the material in different groups anew. Thereafter, they can be brought back to their respective places. Soon they will be used again and the whole cycle has to be repeated anew. But, on the other hand, this is only part of our lives.

How well would you do on the test? Would you have done better than in the example from principle 1? What if I said you already know quite a bit about this? Then I told you it was about 'washing clothes'? Now reread the paragraph, keeping in mind washing clothes. This example shows that prior knowledge is a necessary but not sufficient condition to learning; it must be activated (Schmidt, 1993).

As a teacher, it isn't enough to only have an idea of where your learners are and to start from there. First of all, your estimation may be wrong; you may be outside their zone of proximal development (i.e., too advanced or not advanced enough). Second, even if you are right, what your learners already know may not be at the front of their mind ready for use; prior knowledge needs to be activated to be most useful.

It has been suggested that the best starting point is common sense and everyday experiences—remember, learners always have some relevant prior knowledge—and to progress to abstraction, then back again to the application of theory in practice (Ramsden, 1992). Consider the following example:

Medical students are often so caught up in "thinking medicine" that they block out their common everyday experiences. Here's a typical exchange:

Teacher: *How long does it take for someone to excrete a free water load?*

Students: *(Puzzled look. No response.)*

Teacher: *Oh, come on (jokingly), you all know this . . . If you go to the movies and buy a super jumbo 10 gallon drink, what are the chances that you'll sit through the movie without having to go to the washroom?*

Student 1: *Not long, maybe an hour or so?*

Teacher: *How full does your bladder have to be before you feel you have to go?*

Student 2*: I see, it must start being excreted almost immediately; it just takes time for the bladder to fill before you get the sensation to go.*

Teacher: *If a patient is receiving too much free water IV (intravenous), what should happen?*

Student 1: *The patient should start excreting it almost immediately.*

Teacher: *Exactly . . . you'd expect the same "Movie Theatre Phenomenon, " unless there is something wrong . . .*

In the case above, the medical students had useful prior knowledge but couldn't use it. A simple question from an everyday experience activated that prior knowledge and allowed them to understand. The case also illustrates the easy flow from common sense and everyday experience to abstraction, then back again to the application of theory in practice.

An alternative strategy for activating prior knowledge is "planting." Its use and application are similar to that in literature and movies. The hero of the story should not get herself out of a tight situation with a hand grenade she just happened to be carrying in her purse. The author better have introduced the hand grenade earlier in the story for it to be believable. Similarly, you can "plant" important concepts by reactivating them from the learners' memories at the beginning of the lesson. A review and reactivation of important concepts will help with the believability, understandability, and flow of your lesson.

Finally, the reactivation of prior knowledge has a diagnostic component. It allows you to diagnose the level of your learners and to determine whether or not your lesson plan is within their zone of proximal development. For example, a teacher who begins a class by reviewing the previous class often tells the learners what they learned last time. Instead, the learners could tell the teacher what they actually learned. Based on this information the teacher can determine if the day's lesson plan is appropriate.

Implications for teaching

It is insufficient to make assumptions about your learners' prior knowledge; let them tell you (and activate it).

A good way to activate prior knowledge is to cite common sense and everyday experience. From there, move to abstraction, then back again to the application of theory in practice.

Principle 3: Learners must be actively involved in constructing personal meaning (i.e., understanding) —the links are more important than the elements

Case 1

A humanities teacher is leading a small group discussion based on an assigned reading. Although the students have obviously read the paper, based on their ability to recite parts of the text, few of them seem to have grasped the main "point" of the author.

Case 2

A physics teacher is correcting an exam. The students had no problem "plugging" numbers into formulas, yet few were able to satisfactorily answer questions in a second part of the exam that required them to explain concepts underlying the formulae.

Case 3

A disgruntled student comes in to challenge a recent low mark on an essay. The essay assignment presented a statement and asked the students to agree or disagree, and defend their opinions. The student complains and says "all the facts" are included. The teacher points out that the student has simply arranged a series of facts, but hasn't really interpreted the information or made an argument. Further, the impression given by the essay is that the student just started writing and stopped after fulfilling the required number of words; the essay wasn't organized or structured. Finally, the student had not used data as evidence. In fact, there was no indication that the difference between evidence, opinion, or example was understood.

What do the learners in these three cases have in common? How are they similar to the learner studying comparative vertebrate anatomy in the anecdote in the introduction to the chapter? How are they different when compared to the child who comes to understand the concept of dog? From a Developmental Perspective, learning occurs only if learners give meaning to knowledge and link it to what they already know (i.e., prior knowledge). The learners in the above cases focused on reproducing the content rather than understanding it. I would argue that little(if any) useful learning occurred.

The processes of teaching and learning have many features in common with the example of how a child comes to understand the concept of dog. The parent does not tell the child what a dog is; the child must come to understand the concept internally. The parent has in mind the desired conception and becomes involved in a dynamic dialogue with the child. The child has the opportunity to test his or her conception with that of the parent and the parent has the opportunity to correct misconceptions. Eventually the child and parent negotiate the meaning of dog, and the child's understanding comes to overlap the parent's conception.

Teachers and learners often assume that knowledge is transferred intact from teachers (and textbooks) to learners; they fail to appreciate the personal and idiosyncratic nature of learning and knowledge. According to White and Gunstone (1992),

> . . . understanding develops as new elements are acquired and linked with the existing pattern of associations between elements of knowledge. Addition of new elements will often stimulate reorganization of the pattern *as the person reflects on the new knowledge and sees how it puts older knowledge in a different light"* [emphasis added]. (p. 13).

Given that learners and teachers (in fact all individuals) necessarily have different patterns of associations (i.e., internal representations or maps), it is impossible for teachers to transfer a piece of knowledge to learners. Meaning and understanding have to do with the connections of a new element of knowledge to existing knowledge, rather than the new element itself. Without some way of linking the new knowledge into their current and personal maps, learners usually forget. Learners must be actively involved in constructing personal meaning from the raw materials provided by teachers if teachers are to help learners achieve understanding.

Here we find more strong connections between the Developmental and Apprenticeship Perspectives. What better model for encouraging active involvement by students than apprenticeship? When students are provided access to real-world context they are able to link new knowledge into their own personal maps organically and, one could argue, relatively effortlessly. The main overlapping idea between the Developmental and Apprenticeship Perspectives is the belief (as put forth time and again by Pratt et al., 2009; 2012) that context is indeed a great teacher. More will be presented on the importance of context below (Principle 5).

Teaching should therefore focus on helping learners construct personal meaning. Approaches to learning aimed toward this end have been termed "deep" (i.e., an emphasis on meaning) and "holistic" (i.e., an emphasis on organizing principles to understand "wholes") in contrast to those methods of learning with a focus on reproduction (i.e., "surface" approach) (Eizenberg, 1988; Marton & Saljo, 1984). According to this perspective, true learning and understanding can only occur when learners search for personal meaning by organizing information into an integrated and structured whole (i.e., use of a deep/holistic approach). The learners in the three cases above used a surface approach as evidenced by their lack of understanding and emphasis on reproduction.

Therefore, teaching from the Developmental Perspective emphasizes a qualitative change in learners rather than a quantitative one; learning has to do with knowing differently rather than knowing more. Teaching has to do with promoting a structural or morphological change in learners' thinking rather than adding to the number of facts in their knowledge base.

Given that each learner will have a different set of prior knowledge elements, each learner will necessarily have a different understanding of a concept—that is, they will construct a different sense of the information. Despite the idiosyncratic nature of each individual's understanding, it is possible for their prior knowledge

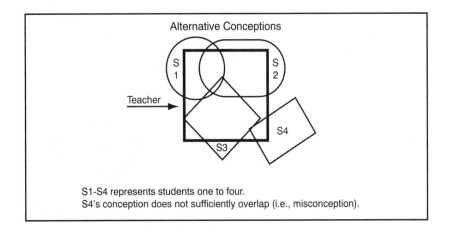

Figure 6.1 Comparison of teacher's conception of an idea
with that of four students

to overlap sufficiently to come to a common understanding. This is represented in Figure 6.1.

Notice the conceptions of students SI, S2, and S3 have much in common with the teacher's conception. However, S4 has a conception of the idea that is significantly different than the teacher's.

You should now have a better understanding of one of the teaching implications from principle 1: Teaching requires an understanding of the range of learners' prior conceptions and misconceptions. Further, you should appreciate that teaching from this perspective assumes a desired endpoint (i.e., preferred conception or range of conceptions). Therefore, the teachers' role is to lead the learners from their existing conceptions to the preferred conception. For instance, learners may have a naive conception of selling price as reflecting the cost of materials and production. An economics teacher may want to move the learners to a more sophisticated understanding that includes supply and demand.

Good Developmental teachers will not only have a good idea of learners' starting points and the desired endpoint, but will also know effective ways to help learners cross the bridge to new understanding. This "bridging knowledge" (Pratt, personal communication) has also been termed "pedagogic content knowledge" (Wilson, Shulman, & Richert, 1987) and will be discussed in the next section. It is different from simple content expertise and has to do with effective ways of representing the content for learners' understanding. Bridging knowledge is what separates an expert teacher from a content expert (one can imagine many Developmental teachers with good bridging knowledge working in apprenticeship positions).

Implications for teaching

- The Developmental teacher is a guide, a coach, and a co-inquirer more than a source of knowledge and information. This is analogous to the 'co-participant within an evolving practice' from the Apprenticeship perspective.
- Teaching expertise has to do with ability to help learners cross from old conceptions to new ways of understanding (i.e., bridging knowledge).
- Teachers should encourage the development of a "deep" (i.e., an emphasis on meaning) and "holistic" (i.e., an emphasis on organizing principles to understand "wholes") approach to learning and discourage a "surface" approach (i.e., an emphasis on reproduction).
- Teachers should not accept verbatim reproduction as evidence of learning but should become adept at probing for understanding.
- Learners' wrong answers should be seen as evidence of misconceptions that need to be addressed.

Principle 4: Making more, and stronger, links requires time

An undergraduate anatomy student spends considerable time making a set of anatomy flash cards for all the major muscles including their origin, insertion, innervation, and major action. An envious (but less industrious) student convinces the first student to lend him the cards to study for the exam. Both students adopted a deep, holistic approach to learning, but one student does significantly better on the exam. What is a plausible explanation?

The first student constructed the cards according to her prior knowledge. She therefore had an advantage. But, there is another factor as well. The second student may think that the first student wasted a lot of time making up the cards, but efficiency may not be effective in the long run. This is the paradox that underlies principle 4.

Learners need time to dwell and cognitively manipulate new ideas in order to increase the number and the strength of the links to new knowledge as it is incorporated into their personal construct system. Cementing new knowledge into the framework through meaning takes time; it cannot be short-circuited in pursuit of efficiency. Unfortunately, the period for making sense of it all and building personal conceptions is often neglected (Brookfield, 2006).

Learners who focus on the links between knowledge elements rather than the knowledge elements themselves are said to be elaborating their knowledge base (Coles, 1991). An elaborated knowledge base is associated with better examination scores, and also with the ability to apply knowledge to new situations and problem solving. The greater the number of links to a piece of knowledge, the greater the number of ways to access that piece of knowledge (i.e., retrieval pathways or cues). Elaboration takes time. Learners need time to link ideas both within and between subjects, and for learners in the professions, to link theory and practice. Unfortunately, in the hectic pace to cover content, teachers often leave little time for learners to reflect on what they are learning. The endpoint of learning, then, is the development of an elaborated knowledge base through the use of a deep holistic approach to learning.

Implications for teaching

- Teachers need to build in time and opportunities for learners to elaborate their knowledge base (i.e., increase the number and strength of links).
- Teaching more (e.g., covering the syllabus) may result in learning less.
- Teachers make knowledge more accessible, more transferable, and more usable when they help students make links within and between subjects, as well as between theory and practice.

Principle 5: Context provides important cues for storing and retrieving information

Case 1

Almost everyone has had the following experience. You are walking down the street and you meet someone who greets you with a familiar tone. You smile, return the greeting, and con-

tinue walking. But you just can't seem to "place" the person. Try as you might, you don't remember where you know her from. The next day at work, you come across the same person and immediately recognize her as a coworker from another department.

Case2

Undergraduate medical education is traditionally separated into two stages: preclinical education taught by basic scientists and clinical education taught by practicing clinicians. Many students go through growing pains as they make the transition from preclinical to clinical medicine. Although they have spent 2 years learning anatomy, physiology, and pathology, they can't seem to access the information to understand or solve clinical problems. To many students, preclinical and clinical education embody two separate and unrelated bodies of knowledge. Their understanding of glucose metabolism from the preclinical years is not very helpful for understanding diabetic emergencies when they start seeing patients. Many students, therefore, see their task as "relearning" once they enter the clinical years.

How are the two cases above similar? Can you provide an explanation? In the first case, you knew the person in a work context but were unable to access that information in a different context. Similarly, medical students are unable to retrieve information learned and stored in the context of basic scientists once they are seeing patients (i.e., clinical context). Since basic scientists and clinicians think differently, their knowledge base is linked differently and therefore accessed by different cues (i.e., retrieval pathways or cues; see principle 4); their knowledge base has a different structure or morphology (see principle 3). Some medical students recognize their task as re-contextualizing the information: changing the links, the associations and the cues of their knowledge base. For other students, it becomes a matter of learning twice.

The term *context* is used in different ways in the literature. In this discussion, context means the perspective from which the content is understood. Other 'contexts' will be discussed later. Just as with the Apprenticeship Perspective, from a Developmental Perspective content cannot be separated from context. The information must be understood in relation to some perspective. Therefore, learning cannot be context free. Knowledge, and its organization into the student's personal construct system, is highly dependent on the context in which it was learned. Recall the anecdote from principle 1 in which the learners had prior knowledge of the "Movie Theatre Phenomenon" (i.e., large volumes of water don't take long to excrete) but couldn't explain a clinically related situation. Their prior knowledge was activated in order to have them understand and personally connect with a new concept. One could argue that they already understood the concept, albeit in another context.

The same anecdote could therefore be used to explain principle 5. Prior knowledge does not transfer across contexts very well, just as new knowledge does not. The idea is to have learners "reach across contexts" to make links and understand new concepts in light of what they already understand (i.e., re-contextualize information). Further, the more contexts from which information is learned, the more accessible and usable it is. We believe that learners can be encouraged to do such "reaching" and thus link what they are learning with what they already know. This is how we understand a deep approach to learning (see principles 4 and 5). That is, when studying new material, learners should be encouraged and assisted in relating the content to other situations. Practitioners of the Apprenticeship Perspective should also take note of this idea. Context itself may be a great teacher, but multiple contexts tend to multiply the learning opportunities.

Implications for teaching

*   Learners should be taught in the context from which they will eventually use their knowledge.
*   Teaching from several contexts makes knowledge more usable, if learners understand the links between contextual representations of knowledge.

Principle 6: Intrinsic motivation is associated with deep approaches to learning while extrinsic motivation, and anxiety are associated with surface approaches to learning

This principle involves you in a simple exercise while reading the following vignettes. Decide whether the learner is adopting a deep or surface approach to learning and comment on what you think is driving the learner to adopt that particular approach (i.e., what is the motivating force?).

Vignette 1

The first vignette is from the movie River's Edge. *The scene depicts a classroom the day after one of its students has been found murdered at the river's edge. An animated and emotional teacher, who can best be described as a throwback to the 60s, is indulging himself in a long diatribe on the meaning of this senseless killing. One of the students in the class interrupts by lifting his hand.*

"Yes?" asks the teacher.

"Will this be on the test?" responds the student.

Deep approach/Surface approach (choose one)

Drivingforce(s):_____

Vignette 2

Two students are taking a postgraduate course in anthropology. The first student, from another department, took the course because it fit his time slot and still allowed him to play varsity soccer. Besides that, his faculty advisor strongly suggested that he take this course. The second student, from the department of education, was relieved to get into the course from the waiting list because she plans on conducting some qualitative research as part of her thesis; this course would be very helpful in understanding qualitative research methodology.

As part of the course requirements, the students have to write an essay on an assigned topic. When reading the source materials, the first student concentrates mainly on finding suitable quotes. He starts his essay by defining the concept. He makes sure to include many quotes, which he groups and arranges into subheadings. He churns out his essay in time to go drink-

ing with his buddies. The second student is concerned that the essay topic is not relevant to her needs and negotiates with the teacher to write on a topic more closely related to her thesis. She spends several days reading source materials and finds many contradictory opinions. In fact she notes that the same data is used to support opposing points of view. She interprets the information in light of her thesis proposal and adopts a particular point of view. She organizes her essay as an argument, using evidence from the literature to back her position. Further, she highlights some of the inconsistencies and possible misinterpretations from opposing camps.

Student 1

Deep approach/Surface approach (choose one)

Drivingforce(s):_____

Student 2

Deep approach/Surface approach (choose one)

Drivingforce(s):_____

Vignette 3

It's the night before the biology exam. A student sits in front of a pile of lecture notes and textbooks. How could she have left all of this to the last minute? As she reads, she is consumed by a feeling of dread and keeps thinking, "there's so much to cover and so little time left." She has difficulty concentrating and her mind keeps drifting to thoughts of failure.

Deep approach/Surface approach (choose one)

Drivingforce(s):_____

Vignette 4

A final year medical student is studying for his internal medicine exam. He finds that the demands of patient care are both exciting and arduous. For the first time, he sees the relevance of much of what he is learning. Unfortunately, the end of rotation multiple choice (MCQ) exam has been hanging heavily over his head throughout the rotation. On the one hand, he wants to read topics relating to his patients to understand their illnesses and to answer questions that come up regarding their management. Unfortunately, his past experience with MCQ exams tells him that understanding is not rewarded. He knows that memorized facts are quickly forgotten but he really needs an "A" on this exam if he wants to get into the residency of his choice.

Deep approach/Surface approach (choose one)

*Drivingforce(s):*_____

Vignette 5

A student attends an engineering lecture. The teacher is obviously interested in her work and concerned that her students understand many aspects of engineering. Her enthusiasm is infectious and the student listens intently, forgetting to take notes. The teacher specifically illustrates the relevance of concepts to the real world of engineering by relating vivid and humorous anecdotes. At one point during the lecture, the student has an "Aha!" experience, as a concept he has been struggling with in another course suddenly becomes clear.

Deep approach/Surface approach (choose one)

*Drivingforce(s):*_____

Vignette 6

Sam is taking part in a small group calculus tutorial. The tutorial leader poses a question to each student in order by seating arrangement. Sam's turn is next. The tutorial leader is impatient with students who cannot provide immediate answers and ridicules them before moving on to the next student. Sam can't "think." The only thoughts that enter his mind are how stupid he will look if he can't answer his question.

Deep approach/Surface approach (choose one)

*Drivingforce(s):*_____

Now consider each vignette in terms of the driving force (i.e., learner motivation). Is the source of motivation from within the learner (i.e., intrinsic motivation) or is it perceived as an external pressure (i.e., extrinsic motivation)? Also speculate on the level of anxiety experienced by the learner. Go back and label each vignette as I. M. (intrinsic motivation) or E. M. (extrinsic motivation). Also identify those vignettes in which the learner is experiencing a high level of anxiety (H. A.). Can you detect a relationship between motivation (intrinsic vs. extrinsic) and approach to learning (deep vs. surface)? Can you detect a relationship between high anxiety and learning?

It is important to note that the approach to learning adopted by a particular learner does not represent a stable characteristic of that learner. Both the institutional context (i.e., departmental demands, exams, marking, teaching) and the personal context (i.e., intrinsic motivation, interest, prior experience, future goals) play an important role in determining the approach taken by a learner. Different learning materials themselves or even teaching styles or sessions may promote the adoption of different approaches to learning. Finally, high levels of learner anxiety are usually associated with a surface approach to learning.

Thus far, we have used the terms deep and surface approaches to learning without defining them to any great extent. By now, you should have a good grasp of these concepts based on the examples used. Below is a list of important characteristics of deep and surface approaches as they apply to a reading task, i.e., learning from reading (Ramsden, 1988, p. 19).

Deep Approach—the readers' intention is to understand, therefore they will:

- focus on what is signified (e.g., the author's argument);
- relate and distinguish new ideas and previous knowledge;
- relate concepts to everyday practice;
- relate and distinguish evidence and argument;
- organize and structure content;

- have an internal emphasis: driven by personal and immediate reasons for learning this content.

Surface Approach—the readers' intention is to complete the task requirements, therefore they will:

- focus on the signs (e.g., the text itself);
- focus on discrete elements;
- memorize information and procedures for assessments;
- unreflectively associate concepts and facts;
- fail to distinguish principles from evidence, new information from old;
- treat tasks as an external imposition;
- have an external emphasis: driven by the demands of assessments, knowledge cut off from everyday reality.

What then is your role as a teacher in encouraging learners to adopt a deep approach to learning? There is evidence in the literature that attempts to drive learners toward a deep approach to learning has the paradoxical effect of having them take a surface approach (Marton & Saljo, 1984). For example, learners that use a deep approach when reading an assigned text have been found to interact with the text by asking themselves questions while reading (e.g., Can I summarize this section in one or two sentences? What is the relationship between sections? What are the main points?). When similar questions were used in an attempt to foster a deep approach to a reading task, the learners used a surface approach. It seems that the predictability of the "demand structure" was at fault; the questions themselves became the end-point of learning rather than a means toward deep learning.

How then can you encourage your learners toward deeper approaches to learning without such a paradoxical effect? Focusing on motivation and the learning environment is key. You should nurture your learners' intrinsic motivation. You should also, as much as possible, reduce extrinsic motivation and learner anxiety.

The presence of intrinsic motivation has been associated with a deep approach to learning and spending more time on task (Ramsden, 1992). There is a synergistic and reciprocal relationship between intrinsic motivation and a deep approach. That is, the use of a deep approach while learning a concept and the resulting understanding in itself results in increased intrinsic motivation. As noted in the Transmission Perspective (Chapter 4), intrinsic motivation may be stimulated by focusing on what is relevant to learners: specific interests, immediate real world concerns, prior experiences, future goals, etc. Highlighting positive growth and gains rather than deficiencies can have a similar effect. Even more importantly, providing learners freedom of choice in content and learning style is associated with a deep approach to learning (cf., vignette 2, student 2 writing an essay on a topic relevant to her interests and needs).

When it comes time to consider our students' motivations we find significant overlap with concepts from the Nurturing Perspective (Chapter 7). Modes of motivation and the needs of learners are always at front of mind for the Nurturing teacher, who first and foremost aims to identify with the students and bring empathy to the teaching practice. So it must go for the Development teacher. Intrinsic motivation among students will flourish when their teacher is willing and able to put him or herself in the students' shoes.

What about the engineering student attending the lecture (vignette 5)? How did you label his motivation (i.e., intrinsic or extrinsic)? What did you describe as the driving force? His motivation isn't truly intrinsic, in that it isn't from within. Yet, it isn't really perceived as an external pressure. His source of motivation can be thought of as vicarious (Hodgson, 1984). The student is experiencing interest, enthusiasm, and relevance vicariously through the teacher. There is evidence that vicarious motivation may be just as effective as intrinsic motivation in promoting a deep approach to learning. Vicarious motivation may be a bridge to intrinsic interest and motivation.

The learners in vignettes 1, 3, and 4 are preoccupied with the notion of evaluation (as was the comparative vertebrate anatomy student in the introduction to the chapter). The medical student in vignette 4 realizes that memorized facts are quickly forgotten (i.e., surface approach) but is faced with the conflict of wanting to do well on the test. Unfortunately, there is evidence that those learners who rely heavily on memorization for studying in medical school are overrepresented in the top quartile of the class and are thus being rewarded for adopting a surface approach (Regan-Smith, cited in Small et al., 1993). It would seem that the espoused theory and theory-in-practice of the medical school are at odds.

Even when learners would prefer to use a deep approach, experience tells them that teachers often undervalue answers that are not close to verbatim reproduction of what they have been taught. It is argued (Ramsden, 1988) that "the most significant single influence on student learning is their perception of assessment" [italics added] (p. 24). Therefore, learners' *perception* of evaluation is the most important source of extrinsic motivation leading them to adopt a surface approach to learning. It is important to note that it is learners' perception of evaluation and not the evaluation itself. For instance, the medical student in vignette 4 has not taken the internal medicine exam yet. For all he knows, it may very well require and reward a deep understanding of concepts. Unfortunately, this student's past experience with multiple choice type exams has left him with a perception of what is required (i.e., rote memorization). Therefore, teachers need not only change exam requirements, but also, they must alter the learners' perception of what is required of them.

A factor that may further aggravate the problem of perceived evaluation requirements is that of curriculum overload. Principle 4 informs us that a deep approach to learning takes time; the concept of "efficient" learning is not compatible with the Developmental Perspective. What happens when learners are given too much to learn in a given amount of time? By predicting and attending to the perceived demands of evaluation, learners can save effort and energy. Therefore, curriculum overload compounds the problem by providing another source of extrinsic motivation leading learners to adopt a surface approach to learning. Unfortunately the strategy is "penny wise and pound foolish"; learners are successful on exams but understand and retain little.

Now, consider Sam in vignette 6, anxiously waiting his turn to be questioned. How did you describe his approach to learning? You may argue that he was so anxious that no learning occurred at all; he was preoccupied with preserving his self-esteem. Interactive teaching and learning occurs in an ego-intensive environment where learners and teachers hate to say "I don't know" (Whitman, 1990). In an effort to preserve self-esteem, learners may try to hide areas of deficiency in understanding. It has been my experience that learners' prior experience with inquisition style questioning under the guise of the Socratic method leaves them uneasy with not knowing. Learners often mistake questioning as a method of teaching with questioning as a means of evaluation.

Other sources of anxiety may come from past failure and lack of self confidence. Anxiety may also be related to evaluation (cf., vignette 3, student studying for biology exam). It becomes easy to see how anxiety may inhibit learners from taking a deep approach to learning.

This brings us to an important question: Can you teach from the Developmental Perspective without also operating from the Nurturing Perspective? (See Chapter 7.) Conversely, can you teach from the Nurturing Perspective without also operating from the Developmental Perspective? I argue that both perspectives are closely linked and that one needs to operate from both to be successful in either. That is, one perspective becomes foreground while the other becomes background. The Nurturing Perspective is concerned with facilitating personal agency. There is a high regard for the learner's self-concept and a concern in developing the relationship between learner and teacher. One could argue that the goal is to help change learners' conception of themselves. This is accomplished in part by fostering a climate of trust and respect. Therefore, both perspectives focus on changing conceptions (i.e., understanding) in an atmosphere of trust and respect. To teach from the Nurturing Perspective requires helping learners change their self-concept and self-efficacy. Similarly, to teach from the Developmental Perspective requires an ability to have learners want to take risks in an ego-intensive environment.

As seen in vignette 6, learners may not engage in deep approaches to learning if the environment is not supportive of their self-concept. Therefore, successful teaching from the Developmental Perspective requires reducing learner anxiety by operating from the Nurturing Perspective in the background. Learners are more likely to engage in a deep approach to learning in a climate of mutual trust and respect. Learners know when teachers are genuinely interested in them; they can recognize a fake in 2 seconds flat. Further, by enhancing learners' self-esteem through encouragement and support, intrinsic motivation may be nurtured and therefore facilitate a deep approach to learning.

Finally, let's consider the student (vignette 2) who demonstrated no real interest in anthropology, and took the course because of the time slot and persuasion from his advisor. Extrinsic motivation is manifested by the way he approached the essay assignment. He can be distinguished, however, from the other extrinsically motivated learners in the other vignettes. The source of extrinsic motivation in the other learners can be ascribed to the "institutional context" (i.e., departmental demands, exams, marking, teaching). His extrinsic motivation is a result of "personal" context (Gibbs, Morgan, & Taylor, 1984). Learners undertake schooling or take courses for various reasons. Some may simply attend to be part of collegiate culture (i.e., sports and fun). Others may be focused towards gaining qualifications and employment or self-improvement. Finally, some may be stimulated by academic interest (i.e., intellectual interest). Given that teachers are driven by academic interests, they may be at odds with learners' personal contexts. It is unlikely that most, or even many, learners will be academically oriented; and teachers are unlikely to have a significant influence on learners' personal context. Therefore, teachers need to understand that there are some sources of extrinsic motivation over which they have little control. Be careful of labeling a learner as lazy; reasons for taking different courses may vary. This person may in fact be academically oriented and intrinsically motivated in other areas.

Implications for teaching

- Teachers should focus on nurturing intrinsic motivation, and diminishing extrinsic motivation and anxiety by:
  - attending to what is relevant to learners;
  - giving learners some control in learning;
  - showing enthusiasm for their content area (i.e., vicarious motivation).
- Teachers need to change learners' perceptions of evaluation demands as well as the evaluations themselves by:
  - demonstrating how understanding and evaluation requirements overlap;
  - avoiding curriculum overload (i.e., teaching too much content);
  - creating a safe place where learners can risk not knowing (c.f., Nurturing Perspective).
- Attempting to manipulate approaches to learning should be undertaken with caution, as the predictability of the demand structure may have the paradoxical effect of encouraging a surface approach.

Principle 7: The Guiding Principle

Unlike the first six Developmental teaching principles, principle 7 does not directly concern cognitive development and therefore does not build on the others; instead principle 7 "over-sees" and guides the other principles by providing an ideal (cf., General Model of Teaching in Chapter 1). It is therefore not possible to provide you with a cognitive exercise to illustrate principle 7. Instead, a quote will introduce the ideal that guides the first six principles.

> *Thomas C. King . . . believes that the overriding purpose of education is to make the learner independent of any need for a teacher (1983). Dr. King contends that anything you do to build dependency is bad, and anything you do as a teacher to build independence is good. Thus, he concludes that the teacher as an information giver is performing an immoral act!* (Whitman, 1990, p. 85).

Although thought provoking, this quote is impractical and overly simplistic. Learner dependence-independence in learning does not exist as a dichotomy but rather as a continuum. Teaching from the Developmental Perspective, then, focuses not only on the development of the intellect, but also on movement along the continuum toward greater independence.

Teachers often burden themselves with the impossible task of teaching everything (or as much as they can) about their area of expertise. This is not only unrealistic but can be counterproductive in the long run (cf., principle 4 and Transmission Perspective, Chapter 4). Instead, teachers should see themselves as occupying a brief but important role in the student's development, not unlike a pair of training wheels on a child's first bicycle. Anything we do that fosters learner dependence in learning counters our espoused theory of helping learners become independent self-directed learners. If we are working toward this end, we should feel increasingly unnecessary as our learners take charge of their own learning. Unfortunately, teachers may mistake the feeling of being needed with that of being helpful.

•   Principle 1: Prior knowledge is key to learning.

- Principle 2: Prior knowledge must be activated.
- Principle 3: Learners must be actively involved in constructing personal meaning (i.e., understanding)—the links are more important than the elements.
- Principle 4: Making more, and stronger, links requires time.
- Principle 5: Context provides important cues for storing and retrieving information.
- Principle 6: Intrinsic motivation is associated with deep approaches to learning, and extrinsic motivation, and anxiety are associated with surface approaches to learning.
- Principle 7: Teaching should be geared toward making the teacher increasingly unnecessary: that means, the development of learner autonomy as well as the intellect.

How then can we help learners become more effective and independent learners? Addressing this important and controversial question requires more space than can be provided in this section (see Candy, 1991, for an in-depth treatment). I will only provide you with food for thought and some general guidelines for practice.

It is often assumed that providing learners with opportunities to exert control over learning will ultimately result in greater learner autonomy. Learner control is an important and necessary condition, but not a sufficient condition for promoting independence. Providing learners with opportunities to exert control over learning is only the first step in fostering personal autonomy in learning. Other means are needed to complement and reinforce learners' independent efforts. One often neglected, but effective, way to foster learner independence is to make learning an object of reflection (Candy, 1991). Learners are usually so caught up in trying to learn the content of courses that they seldom consider the process of learning itself. Teachers need to help make learners aware of the strategies and approaches used in learning (e.g., surface vs. deep). Further, they need to help learners recognize the relationship between the strategies used and learning outcomes.

As mentioned earlier, context is all important in learning—the same applies to learning about learning. Therefore, the techniques for helping learners acquire such awareness should not be taught as a self-contained set of learning skills. Instead, they should be built into all subject matter being taught. Perhaps the most important factor in promoting learner autonomy is helping learners believe they can. This aspect of developing learner autonomy is more likely the domain of the Nurturing Perspective, with its focus on building confidence and competence (i.e., self-efficacy). Either way, teachers need to encourage learners to believe in their own abilities.

An important corollary is helping learners identify the sources of their successes and failures. Success should be attributed to hard work rather than luck or favoritism. Conversely, failure should be understood as resulting from lack of effort rather than lack of ability. It is now possible to appreciate that shifting control to learners is not sufficient for promoting autonomy in learning. Teachers holding to this misconception can unwittingly have an adverse effect on autonomy. For instance, learners thrown into the "deep-end" and required to fend for themselves may only end up learning that they are incapable of taking control of their own learning. The ideal of fostering learner autonomy in learning is not a call for "bootstrapism."

From a practical point of view, teachers have three main ways of influencing personal autonomy in learning (Candy, 1991): (1) helping learners develop a sense of personal control (cf., Nurturing Perspective); (2) providing access to learning resources; and (3) helping learners develop the competence to take control of their learning and to demonstrate their competence socially (c.f., Apprenticeship Perspective). Some of the competencies that might be built into all subject matter being taught include:

- locating and retrieving information
- setting goals
- time management skills
- question-asking behavior
- critical thinking
- self-monitoring and self-evaluation

Principle 7 says that effective teaching should be geared toward making the teacher increasingly unnecessary. Pay particular attention to the word *increasingly*. Above, I discussed the concept of the student's "zone of proximal development" in terms of the complexity of content in learning (principles 1 & 2). Similarly, each learner has a zone of proximal development in exerting independence in learning. The outer limit of this zone should be out far enough to challenge the learner but not so far as to cause frustration and self-doubt. Likewise it should not be too close as to bore the learner. Further, each learner will necessarily occupy a different place on the dependence-independence continuum.

It is important to recognize that the dependence-independence continuum is represented as linear and unidimensional for the sake of conceptual clarity. It is actually better understood as multiple continuums each representing a different capacity or skill (e.g., goal setting; locating and retrieving information). Each learner will necessarily differ in amount and kind of autonomy in learning. As mentioned, throwing all learners into the deep-end may be detrimental in the long run in that it undermines the goal of helping learners develop a sense of personal control. Teachers should start by providing adequate support and direction in learning with the intention of slowly phasing these out as learners take greater control and responsibility for their learning (Pratt, 1988).

The teaching skills of providing adequate support and phasing out are similar to the skills of scaffolding and fading discussed in the Apprenticeship Perspective of teaching. They also provide a rare incongruity with the precepts of the Nurturing Perspective. As Dave Smulders points out in Chapter 7, Nurturing teachers "do not seek to minimize their presence," nor do they "proceed from the position of invisibility." As learning progresses, Nurturing teachers attempt to "place themselves more definitively in relationship with learners." Although Developmental teachers are not seeking invisibility *per se*, they do tend to prize learner autonomy slightly more than the maintenance of a long-term teacher-learner relationship. Perhaps the difference here is merely one of degrees, but it is worth noting.

Different learners will necessarily start at different points on the continuum, move at different rates, and need different kinds of help on their journey toward greater independence in learning. Further, autonomy in learning is a situational attribute rather than a personal one. That is, learners may display varying amounts of self-direction depending on the specific content area and situation (Pratt, 1988).

Implications for teaching

- Teachers should start by providing learners with opportunities to exert control over their own learning.
- Teachers need to go further in promoting learner autonomy by:
  - making learning an object of reflection.
  - encouraging learners to believe in their own abilities.
  - helping learners identify sources of successes and failures.
  - helping learners develop the competencies needed to learn independently (e.g., goal setting).
  - helping learners identify learning resources.
- Teachers should provide the necessary support and direction to move learners along the dependence-independence continuum by:
  - becoming aware of the types and range of independence in your learners.
  - providing learning tasks that accommodate this range and allow for different rates of progression and different endpoints.

Now that you are familiar with the seven Developmental Teaching Principles, I will consider the special knowledge needed to be a good Developmental teacher.

BRIDGING KNOWLEDGE:
TEACHERS' SPECIAL KNOWLEDGE

Consider the following example:

A student is attending a seminar as part of her course work. The seminar leader is enthusiastic. He tries to engage her. He asks questions. She just doesn't seem to understand. The harder he tries, the more confused and frustrated she becomes. He obviously knows his stuff; he just can't get her to understand. She leaves feeling that she understands less than when she came in.

What characterizes gifted and inspired teachers? Do they have a better understanding of their subject area? Do they use more effective teaching behaviors? If not, what specialized knowledge and skills distinguish them?

To view and assess the quality of teaching in terms of methods and techniques is simplistic and narrow; unfortunately this has been the focus of much research and evaluation in adult teaching (e.g., Chapter 12 on Evaluating Teaching). Moreover, this instrumental view provides insight into the assumptions that underlie the teaching and learning relationship. These assumptions include the beliefs that effective teaching or specific methods are necessarily related to (and responsible for) learning, and that a focus on improving teaching behaviors (i.e., skills) will therefore result in better learning. If learning does not improve, blame is usually placed on the learner. This limited view of teaching denies the complexity of learning and its emphasis over teaching. It also reduces teaching to a decontextualized set of effective teaching behaviors.

The idea of generic and transferable teaching skills is of limited usefulness; the separation of content and process is artificial. You can't just teach; you have to teach something. Unfortunately, much research has been preoccupied with what teachers need to do rather than what they need to know. From this perspective, the teacher's role is that of installing or implementing the curriculum. A more useful idea is that of teachers occupying an important place between the curriculum-as-plan and the curriculum-as-lived experience (Aoki, 1991). The teacher's role, then, becomes one of interpreting the curriculum plan into meaningful experiences from the student's viewpoint. It is this ability to serve as bridge or translator, we argue, that separates gifted and inspired teachers from merely adequate teachers.

Consider the similarities between a teacher as interpreter and a language translator as interpreter. The ability to translate from English to Japanese requires more than a knowledge of translation. It requires a special ability to translate that specific language. You cannot separate the skills of translation from the language itself. You cannot simply translate; you must translate something. Otherwise, the special translation skills would be transferable to another language. Further, translation has to do with understanding and getting a message across. The focus is on meaning rather than the elements of speech or text. For instance, "Boys' night out" has nothing to do with male children playing outside in the evening.

Therefore, to teach from the Developmental Perspective is to act as a bridge from the curriculum-as-plan to the curriculum-as-lived by the learners. It requires more than subject matter expertise (i.e., content expertise); special skills in translation are required.

However, translation skills are content-specific; they cannot be use-fully separated from the subject area. Finally, the primary focus of translation is to get the message across—i.e., focus on learners' un-derstanding.

Bridging knowledge occupies an important place among the other types of knowledge used by teachers: knowledge of content area, knowledge of other content, knowledge of curriculum, knowl-edge of learners, knowledge of teaching and learning process. Un-fortunately, bridging knowledge has been neglected. More empha-sis has been placed on content expertise (i.e., subject matter expertise) and process expertise (i.e., expertise in the general prin-ciples of teaching). Content expertise is necessary but not sufficient for becoming a good teacher. The seminar teacher in the example above "knew his stuff" but was unable to communicate it to others. On the other hand, a process expert, unfamiliar with the content area, is just as unlikely to promote learner understanding. Bridging knowledge is the knowledge needed to transform the content for the purposes of teaching: "We use the general term 'transformation' to designate the set of activities engaged by the teacher to move from her own comprehension of a matter, and the representations most useful for that understanding, to the variations of representation, narrative, examples, or association likely to initiate understanding on the part of the student" (Wilson, Shulman, & Richert, 1987, p. 113). It is no longer useful to think of effective teaching as a two-sided coin comprised of content expertise and process expertise. A space must be created for bridging expertise.

Teaching from the Developmental Perspective has to do with helping learners cross the bridge to understanding: the bridge from "not knowing" to "knowing." More importantly, teachers help learn-ers cross the bridge to knowing differently: the bridge from "lay conceptions/unsophisticated conceptions/misconceptions" to "bet-ter/more useful/more appropriate conceptions." Teaching from the Developmental Perspective assumes a knowledge of learners' start-ing points (prior conceptions or misconceptions), a knowledge of where you want to take them (better or preferred conception(s), and a knowledge of effective routes for the transition (i.e., bridging knowledge, Figure 6.2).

The seminar teacher in the example above is lacking in bridg-ing knowledge and is not unlike many experts who have difficulty teaching. Content experts or other people with subject matter ex-

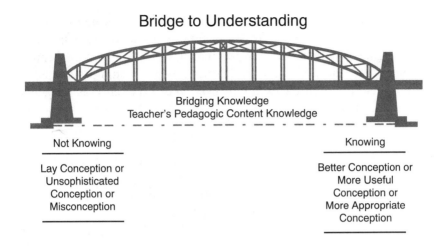

Figure 6.2 Bridging Knowledge: moving students from "not knowing to knowing"

pertise sometimes have difficulty with the unthinking of an idea or concept which has become commonplace or reflexive for them (Marton, Hounsell, & Entwistle, 1984). These teachers can't remember not knowing and therefore make assumptions about what learners know and don't know. These assumptions are usually not conscious in that they are usually taken for granted. A similar phenomenon can occur when lecturers don't interact with their learners. As their content expertise increases over the years, they become increasingly less able to communicate their understanding to learners; they no longer speak the same language.

Our discussion about bridging knowledge so far has been somewhat vague and theoretical. Unfortunately, there is no way around this. Bridging knowledge is very specific—not only to a content area, but also to specific learners. The knowledge needed to make nuclear physics understandable to first-year university students is necessarily different from that needed to make anthropology understandable. Further, the knowledge needed to transform the content of respiratory diseases into learning will be different for medical students, nursing students, and respiratory therapy students. Even the same learners will require different representations of knowledge at different levels of training. First-year medical students will have different needs than medical interns and residents.

Although I cannot be more explicit in my discussion of bridging knowledge, we can make some general comments to help guide you in the development of bridging knowledge for your specific subject area and your specific learners. When reading each of the points below, search for examples from your experience as a teacher in a specific content area.

- Become familiar with:
  - The usual range of learners' conceptions and misconceptions;
  - The teaching strategies, methods, and activities that make your content more understandable;
  - The progression and changes in learners' conceptions over time;
  - The "sticky points" and conceptual stumbling blocks that slow learners' understanding and require special attention and extra time;
  - The appropriate pace for introducing new and more complex concepts. Watch for cues from learners that your pace is too slow or too quick. Learn to choose, adapt, and use curricular materials that facilitate understanding in your content area.
- Develop, collect, and use analogies, anecdotes, metaphors, and examples that are striking and provide insight.
- Develop the capacity to introduce variations on a theme: alternative representations of your subject matter. That is, develop a representational repertoire for the subject matter you teach (Wilson, Shulman, & Richert, 1987).
- Learn to juxtapose elements in order to provide your learners with an "Aha!" or "Eureka!" experience.
- Speak the same language as your learners; don't make assumptions about what they know and don't know.
- Sequence your teaching to promote understanding. A good starting point is common sense and everyday experiences moving to abstraction, then back again to the application of theory in practice.
- Maintain a balance between the "forest" and the "trees" in your presentations. Bring the focus back to the big picture before introducing the next element.

- Don't burden yourself with providing a complete understanding of concepts all at once. Sometimes "white lies" are OK. Simplified or incomplete representations may be appropriate depending on learners' level of understanding and sophistication. Think of these as "transitional" representations. Increasing levels of complexity can be added in layers, as learners master each level. For instance, having first-year medical students think of the heart as two pumps in series is a good first approximation of a difficult and complex concept. A common mistake made by many content experts who teach is to deny the importance of transitional representations. They confuse transitional representations with misrepresentations and misinformation. They err on the side of comprehensive coverage of concepts and usually confuse learners.

Those of you with considerable teaching experience can probably think of examples for each of the points above. Those of you with less experience may need to rely on your experience as learners for insight. Our goal has been to provide you with a framework for interpreting and understanding the special knowledge that enables you to transform your content for the purposes of teaching.

Experience will play an important role in the development of your bridging knowledge. Experience is necessary but not sufficient in developing bridging knowledge expertise. Ten years of experience without reflection is just 1 year's experience repeated nine times. Teaching should be a reflective, thinking activity (Calderhead, 1987). Unfortunately, many teachers are "surprisingly unreflective about their work" (Ashton, 1984, p. 31). Reflection will enable you to learn from your experience as a teacher. Recall that teaching from the Developmental Perspective has to do with helping learners cross the bridge to understanding. Reflection on your experience will help you in refining the routes and creating alternative routes (i.e., expand your representational repertoire). Make reflection a routine part of your work as a teacher. Questions to ask yourself after a teaching session might include the following:

- What worked? Why?
- What didn't work? Why?

- Was the sequencing of material appropriate and helpful?
- Was the pace appropriate?
- What would you do the same next time?
- What would you do differently next time?

SUMMARY

I won't bore you by repeating and summarizing the main points in this chapter. If you're interested in doing so, just go back and read all the bulleted lists. Instead, I want to present you with an argument: all learning (not just that associated with teaching) follows the key points outlined in this chapter. Reflect on your experience as a reader of this chapter (i.e., learning from reading). If I have done a good job of presenting the material in this chapter, several examples of the Developmental Teaching Principles will come to mind. For instance, I often introduced new concepts with examples from everyday experiences (e.g., activation of prior knowledge). I required active engagement with the text to promote the construction of personal meaning. I also spent a lot of time (cf., more links = more time) approaching concepts from several angles rather than simply stating things once.

I don't take credit for the concepts presented in this chapter, as they are not my original thoughts, but the work of many researchers and practitioners. I do, however, take credit for its representation. I can now cite a specific example of bridging knowledge (i.e., pedagogic content knowledge). I could have simply listed the seven Developmental Teaching Principles and provided brief explanations. I chose instead to represent the ideas using examples, anecdotes, analogies, and metaphors that I thought would be helpful in promoting understanding. That was my use of 'Bridging Knowledge'. I assumed (perhaps wrongly) that you would not have an extensive understanding of these concepts, so I sequenced the material in a way that developed and demanded an increasingly sophisticated understanding. Only you can determine how successful I have been in transforming the words and ideas of others for your learning.

Finally, I hope to have provided you with opportunities for the "having of wonderful ideas" (Duckworth, 1987). I tried to let you figure it out as often as I could. My main goal was to have you understand, which is the main focus of the Developmental Perspective. I hope to have convinced you of the strengths of this perspective by having you experience it. Hopefully, you will try to apply some of my ideas to your own context.

REFERENCES

Anderson, O. R. (1992). Some interrelationships between constructivist models of learning and current neurobiological theory, with implications for science education. *Journal of Research in Science Education*, 29 (10), 1037-1058.

Aoki, T. (1991). *Inspiring curriculum and pedagogy: Talks to teachers*. Calgary, AB: University of Alberta.

Ashton, P. (1984). Teacher efficacy: a motivational paradigm for effective teacher education. *Journal of Teacher Education*, 35(5), 28-32.

Bateman, W. L. (1990). *Open to question: The art of teaching and learning by inquiry*. San Francisco: Jossey-Bass.

Brookfield, S. (2006). *The skillful teacher*. San Francisco: Jossey-Bass.

Calderhead, J. (1987). *Exploring teachers' thinking*. London: Cassell Education.

Candy, P. C. (1991). *Self-direction for lifelong learning* (1st ed.). San Francisco: Jossey-Bass.

Coles, C. (1991). Is problem-based learning the only way? In D. Boud & G. Feletti (Eds.), *The challenge of problem based learning* (pp. 295-307). London: Kogan Page, Ltd.

Dahlgren, L. (1984). Outcomes of learning. In F. Marton, D. Hounsell, & N. Entwistle (Eds.), *The experience of learning* (pp. 19-35). Edinburgh: Scottish Academic Press.

Duckworth, E. (1987). *'The having of wonderful ideas' and other essays on teaching and learning*. New York: Teachers College Press.

Eizenberg, N. (1988). Approaches to learning anatomy: developing a programme for preclinical medical students. In P. Ramsden (Ed.), *Improving learning: New perspectives* (pp. 178-198). London: Kogan Page, Ltd.

Entwistle, N., & Marton, F. (1984). Changing conceptions of learning and research. In F. Marton, D. Hounsell, & N. Entwistle (Eds.), *The experience of learning* (pp. 211-228). Edinburgh: Scottish Academic Press.

Gibbs, G., Morgan, A., & Taylor, E. (1984). The world of the learner. In F. Marton, D. Hounsell, & N. Entwistle (Eds.), *The experience of learning* (pp. 165-188). Edinburgh: Scottish Academic Press.

Hodgson, V. (1984). Learning from lectures. In F. Marton, D. Hounsell, & N. Entwistle (Eds.), *The experience of learning* (pp. 90-102). Edinburgh: Scottish Academic Press.

Jonassen, D. H. & Land, S. (Eds.) (2012). *Theoretical Foundations of Learning Environments* (2nd Ed). New York: Routledge.

Kegan, R. (1994). *In over our heads: The mental demands of modern life*, Cambridge: Harvard University Press.

Marton, F., Hounsell, D., & Entwistle, N. (1984). *The experience of learning*. Edinburgh: Scottish Academic Press.

Marton, F., & Saljo, R. (1984). Approaches to learning. In F. Marton, D. Hounsell, 8c N. Entwistle (Eds.), *The experience of learning* (pp. 36-55). Edinburgh: Scottish Academic Press.

Napell, S. M. (1976). Six common non-facilitating teaching behaviors. *Contemporary Education*, 47(2), 79-82.

Pratt, D. D. (1988). Andragogy as a relational construct. *Adult Education Quarterly*, 38(3), 160-181.

Pratt, D. D., Harris, P., Collins, J.B. (2009). The Power of One: Looking beyond the instructor in clinical teaching. *The Medical Teacher*. Vol. 31, No. 2, February, pp. 133 – 137.

Pratt, D. D., Sadownik, L., Jarvis-Selinger, S. (2012). Pedagogical BIASes and Clinical Teaching in Medicine. In L. M. English (Ed.), *Health and Adult Learning*. University of Toronto Press, pp. 273-296.

Ramsden, P. (1988). Studying learning: Improving teaching. In P. Ramsden (Ed.), *Improving learning: New perspectives* (pp. 13-31). London: Kogan Page, Ltd.

Ramsden, P. (1992). *Learning to teach in higher education*. New York: Routiledge.

Rando, W. C, & Menges, R. J. (1991). How practice is shaped by personal theories. In R. J. Menges & M. D. Svinicki (Eds.), *College teaching: From practice to theory* (pp. 7-14). San Francisco: Jossey-Bass.

Reynolds, A. (1992). What is competent beginning teaching? A review of the literature. *Review of Educational Research*, 62(1), 1-35.

Schmidt, H. G. (1993). Foundations of problem-based learning: Some explanatory notes. *Medical Education*, 27, 422-432. *Scientific American*, 267(3), September, 1992

Small, P. A., Jr., Stevens, C. B., & Duerson, M. (1993). Issues in medical education: Basic problems and potential solutions. *Academic Medicine*, 68(10 October Supplement), S89-S98.

Vygotsky, L. S. (1978). *Mind in society: The development of higher psychological processes.* Cambridge, MA: Harvard University Press.

White, R., & Gunstone, R. (1992). *Probing understanding.* London: The Falmer Press.

Whitman, N. (1990). *Creative medical teaching.* Salt Lake City: University of Utah School of Medicine.

Wilson, S. M., Shulman, L. S., & Richert, A. E. (1987). '150 different ways' of knowing: Representation of knowledge in teaching. In J. Calderhead (Ed.), *Exploring teachers' thinking* (pp. 104-124). London: Cassell Education.

CHAPTER 7
The Nurturing Perspective

Dave Smulders

THE VARIABILITY OF LEARNERS AND LEARNING

Try to imagine yourself in this position. You are the instructor in this story. You're sitting at a table in a classroom of self-paced learners, looking down at a written assignment. It's a short essay. The author of the essay, a student, is sitting next to you, waiting while you read the paper. You have to give it a mark out of 25, as set out in the course syllabus, and you have to provide some feedback. By the time you finish it, you figure it is worth a respectable 18 or 19/25, or 78 per cent, or B+ or a "meeting expectations". Although you don't bother to check, you know that it fits the grading rubric you use for this course. If you were to pass this paper around to a group of colleagues, you are reasonably certain that they would come up with the same overall assessment. Now before you pen the designated mark on the paper, you look up and think about what you're going to say to this learner.

But before you do that, let's consider a few of the people who may be sitting across from you.

First there is Noor, a recent immigrant, whose schooling as a child was sporadic, given an upbringing in a country consumed by wars. She is motivated to learn, but she has considerable gaps in her knowledge and the mechanics of her writing are a disaster. She has been slaving away over this paper and making incremental progress from draft to draft. She is trying to reach this current standard on her first rather than her fifth draft. She will be relieved that she can write to an instructor's estimation of a B+, but she wants to know how to do that more efficiently.

171

Another student is a young single mom, Cynthia. She comes to the classroom when she can, usually late in the afternoon between getting off work and picking up her toddler from daycare. One of her challenges is that she quickly becomes defeatist and dismissive when confronted with obstacles. One time, in response to your attempt to explain a few key rules about punctuation, she burst into tears, slammed her book shut and fled from the classroom. This has happened before.

Eric is very timid. He seems nervous at all times but none more so than when he's in a test environment or any situation where he's being evaluated. He has relayed to you that counseling hasn't helped with this, and he feels that it is simply a part of his personality, reaching as far into his past as he can remember, wreaking havoc with his ability to succeed in an academic environment. Nonetheless, he is an extremely hard worker and that he has come this far is a testament to his determination and good will. He sighs audibly at every jot of the pen on the paper. You sense him sinking in his chair as you keep reading through the paper, and you can hear him begin to beat himself up with self-reprimanding comments about his work. "Maybe I should have . . . " "Why can't I remember to . . . "

Finally, there is Hasti. She is a relentless hard worker, always early for class and late to leave. She seems to have dedicated her life to this class though somehow she's got other classes on the go as well where she is undoubtedly just as fierce in her commitment. Her long-term goal is ambitious—entry to medical school. It is a long way off, yet for her every class represents a potential grade that will bring up her overall Grade Point Average (GPA). Every discussion becomes a focus on grades. At the beginning of every class, she announces that her goal is to get above 95% in order not to drag down her average. She is sure there's nothing left an instructor can detect so she'd like to submit this draft for the grade now. In her view, she's achieved perfection and feels that it's time for her to score 100%. Every time you write a comment, question or correction on the paper, she jumps up to lean over and see what you are doing and insists, "I was told to change it to that."

Now we ask the question that guides any instructor's actions: what do you do next? What do these feedback sessions look like for you? Are they uniform? That is, could you capture a single boilerplate style explanation and deliver that unchanged for each student or would you need to vary your explanations? How would your conversation change with each student? Should you try these questions with a friend or colleague and see what they say - are their answers the same as yours?

Even if I were to state right here in this text precisely what I insist you should learn from these examples, what I think each particular student's description illustrates, with accompanying tips, tricks, principles, and little lessons on teaching and learning, you would still perceive the lessons of this chapter differently than other readers (Postman and Weingartner, 1969) because of what you bring to this moment.

Above all, what does teaching consist of in these examples? And of course what are the variables that influence learning with these students?

Before you continue with your analysis of how you would work with each student in this scenario, it might help further to consider a few of the variables that have emerged from the descriptions.

- How important is the grade in each of these cases? More broadly put, how important are standards?
- What subject matter does each learner need to focus on in order to proceed? Indeed, what would be the learner's next move based on your feedback?
- How much does the learner's background influence your thinking about your forthcoming discussion?
- How much does the learner's emotional state at the time of your reading the assignment influence your thinking about your forthcoming discussion?
- What role does confidence play in the writing of these assignments and in the possible reception to your feedback?
- In which learners is there a physical manifestation of their attitude or thinking about the assessment you are conducting?
- In which cases do you feel you'll emerge from the class thinking you've had a good day? Which cases have warning flags plastered all over them with exclamatory notes of caution stuck here and there at the corners?

- How important or relevant is your subject matter expertise? Which cases require something else of you?
- For which learners, if any, do you want to have a more open conversation about their work? Which ones need to be told what to do? What does it mean to "do the right thing"?
- Do you have a box of tissues in your office for days like this? Are they for you or your students?
- Apart from wondering why you've chosen to become an educator in the first place, are there any other questions you would want to pose for yourself here?

While you're dwelling on that, let's flip the scenario around. Put yourself in the position of the learner. You have just completed your assignment and you've just handed it over to the instructor to review, right there as you sit and wait. What are you expecting from your instructor? What feedback are you looking for? What are you hoping from this exchange? What would be the best thing the instructor could say to you to help with your learning?

This little scenario quickly becomes complicated because of the limitations a single example poses, although we can see how these different learner profiles can conjure up a myriad of issues for any teacher. Even though I'm attempting to depict of mix of the institutional (a college-level class) and the unconventional (a self-paced, one-to-one experience), I cannot hope to capture an archetypal teaching moment except that it involves a teacher and a learner in some way. The students in the scenario are not meant to represent the totality of possibilities that we could face with your learners on any given day in any given subject area. Also, in these examples we are looking at a very specific task in a fairly well defined context: delivering some feedback to a single piece of assigned student writing in a postsecondary learning environment. However, what you consider to be of particular importance for your and your learners' well being is certainly applicable across a wide range of teaching situations. The first principle we have arrived at with the Nurturing Perspective is that the learners will inform your next move. As a Nurturing teacher, that is what you have been preparing yourself for.

But I'm framing this scenario and its collection of unique learners based on my own connection to teaching, my experience. I have a colleague who works along with me in the environment described above. By watching her, I discovered a model of nurturing in her approach with students. As she takes her seat beside the student to begin introduce herself and begin her work, she soon arrives at the question for the student: "What's your story?" For my colleague, and now for me, this helps mark the beginning of the teacher-learner relationship. As teachers, we come in at different moments along each learner's own unique learning journey, which goes back and extends far beyond our own small part in it. By asking "What's your story?" we are attempting to catch up to that point in the journey where we are enlisted to help make a difference. Our job is fundamentally to help and being able to do that involves knowing where our learners are and where they think they're going.

Similarly, when it comes to teaching, and understanding what teaching means to each of us, we need to ask ourselves what our stories are. Apps recommends a similar exercise to those trying to develop a teaching philosophy (1991, p. 7). We can begin our inquiry into our own role as teachers by writing stories about our practice and then reflecting on those stories and the details they conjure up; in effect, by this exercise, teachers can explore that all-important starting point for their learning, the moment where we can take charge of our learning and, in turn, our teaching.

The parallel between teachers and learners in this type of inquiry is not coincidental. Teachers who invest much of their energy in learners as their primary focus do so because their notion of "being a teacher" seems to run on a parallel track with their efforts as a learner in that experience. Freire's classic synthesis on teaching and learning makes a kind of reciprocal puzzle: "Whoever teaches learns in the act of teaching, and whoever learns teaches in the act of learning" (Freire, 1998).

READINESS TO LEARN

Learning as Journey—A Metaphor

When you set out on your way to Ithaca
you should hope that your journey is a long one:
a journey full of adventure, full of knowing.
Have no fear of the Laestrygones, the Cyclopes,
the frothing Poseidon. No such impediments
will confound the progress of your journey

if your thoughts take wing, if your spirit and your
flesh are touched by singular sentiments.
You will not encounter Laestrygones,
nor any Cyclopes, nor a furious Poseidon,
as long as you don't carry them within you,
as long as your soul refuses to set them in your path...

(from *Ithaka,* by Konstantine Kavafy, translated by Stratis Haviaras, lines 1-12)

As teachers, we often seek to find out what the souls of learners may or may not be setting in their paths. Knowing about this can become a kind of journey, and it places us willingly at the crossroads of teaching and learning. A primary focus when teaching from the Nurturing Perspective is assessing and enabling an individual's readiness to learn. Nothing can move forward until this is in place, and this perhaps distinguishes this perspective from the Developmental Perspective, which, as Arseneau has pointed out in the previous chapter, shares many features in one's approach and actions. The conditions of good learning for individuals are so bound up with each other that it's difficult to separate them out. The lines of the poem above offer a few ideas: we want to participate in that adventure of learning, we help to remove impediments, we seek to incite learners to singular sentiments so their thoughts can take wing.

Here is where teaching can begin. However, a teacher working from the Nurturing Perspective would not be done if all that happened was an increase in confidence on the part of the learner (Pratt, 1998). From the Developmental Perspective, teachers place emphasize the quality of reasoning, in order to support learners in their efforts to understand and work with new subject matter, in new or changing environments. Similarly, from the Nurturing Perspective, teachers regard a positive self-concept as a starting point for learners. This is where the Nurturing Perspective intersects with the other perspectives. From the idea of a positive self-concept, a teacher may see the other elements of teaching as they appear on the horizon. That is, by establishing a readiness to learn from the point of self-concept, a Nurturing teacher may then recognize how the other elements in Pratt's General Model of Teaching (Chapter 1) fit in: the organization of one's subject matter (Transmission); the need to determine relevant contexts for practice (Apprenticeship); the value in proceeding from individual to societal perspectives to transform society (Social Reform). For teachers from other perspectives, the notion of self-concept might seem distant from their concerns, but for Nurturing teachers it remains at the forefront of their attention.

Emotion and Learning

If we look back to those students from the beginning of this chapter, we can detect a variety of emotions in evidence, many of which are directly influential on the context described above and many certainly which have an effect on both teaching and learning, but primarily on the latter. We might even be tempted to reduce each description to an emotional state: the hopeful student, the angry student, the doggedly determined student, the terrified student, and so on. It's easy to see how learning can be regarded as an emotional-laden process, with multiple effects for everyone involved, both positive and negative.

Research on the connection between emotions and learning has long been part of the concerns of adult educators (Dirkx, 2008), although it seems to have gained more attention in the past decade, particularly through the lens of educational psychology (Schutz et al. 2006). This latter research links effective teaching to the notion of "emotional regulation"—that is how both teachers and learners can influence emotions with a longer-term intention of supporting learning. In trying to determine what constitutes an appropriate response for teachers, the authors explain how one way of emotional regulation is through "goal congruence" or assessing how the learning is proceeding. Are they making progress? Are there setbacks? What is next for a learner in the attainment of one's goals? If a teacher can help facilitate an honest appraisal by the learner, there is greater opportunity to regulate emotions for the better, such as reducing anxiety, anger, and fear. This is only possible if the teacher and the student share an understanding of the goals in question.

How teachers regard the influence of emotions in their teaching is indicative of their dominant perspectives. Reacting to the scenario with the students above, one teacher may see the need for painstaking distinction for each student, while another may argue that time demands a more general approach to the task. Some teachers may feel that they should themselves address personal issues related to learning, while others may call on the aid of other designated experts like counselors and advisors. These divergent approaches will likely never be resolved because they draw lines in the sand of our fundamental views of education, teaching, and learning. While it is important to recognize the potential impacts of emotions on learning, we will nonetheless feel obligated to deal with these differently in our practice. Nurturing teachers, however, tend to see this as a fundamental part of their practice. It is not something added on or addressed in specific, unique cases, apart from the regular work of teaching; it *is* the regular work of teaching.

Negative associations with school and learning often involve teacher-delivered feedback and the placement and effect of that activity on the learner's sense of well-being. If we look back to the example students at the beginning of this chapter, the teaching-learning context we've outlined is founded on an act of feedback: the varying emotional states of the learners are directly related to what's going to happen next in the scenario. Part of the difficulty in anticipating what to do for each of those students is knowing how feedback fits into the general practice of teaching.

In our example scenario, we are looking at some kind of an assessment (a written assignment) and the verbal provision of feedback by the teacher along with a mark of some kind. So feedback appears to be both entwined with learning (how each student is progressing with this activity) and assessment of performance (as implied by a mark to be attributed to this particular effort), as well as personal and institutional expectations of progress. Again, feedback here is predicated on a connection to the learner's goals for this particular task. This does not mean that there may not still be difficult conversations to have with learners in regard to their assessed work. But there is likely to be less conflict as a result of misunderstanding and a greater likelihood of being able to focus on the details of the assessment itself. Ultimately, each of these learners should be able to determine what their next steps are and what they need to do in order to learn.

Above all else, Nurturing teachers want their students to be successful at learning. For both learners and teachers, the source of enjoyment of an event like a course, derives from that experience of learning. On the other hand, teaching becomes a burden when, despite all efforts, learning doesn't seem to happen. Because of the inherent hope for the success of learning, in times of difficulty, it can be easy to fall prey to anxiety about work and insecurity about one's ability to "get through" to learners, creating frustration, even resentment, at the job. But when things go well—"thoughts take wing"—there can be an excitement and energy about learning, and teaching becomes this great reward that we seek to replicate in subsequent situations.

Building Self-Efficacy

Confidence is tied to success in learning through what is known as self-efficacy. According to social cognitive theory, self-efficacy refers to "people's beliefs about their capabilities to produce designated levels of performance that exercise influence over events that affect their lives. Self-efficacy beliefs determine how people feel, think, motivate themselves and behave" (Bandura, 1994, p. 71). In other words, the ability to learn begins with belief in one's own ability to learn. A stronger sense of self-efficacy will yield greater results for learning, increasing not only confidence but also competence. By contrast, low self-efficacy will set up internal barriers for an individual. Similarly, success that comes too easily will only set up individuals for failure in the long run. Being challenged and overcoming difficulties and obstacles work together rather than in opposition to each other. As one succeeds, an individual demands greater challenges in order to sustain one's growing sense of self-efficacy.

In many contexts, learners still need to satisfy standards set externally, such as professional competencies, grades, and certification benchmarks. In this way, the Nurturing instructor's expectations remain high. Good teaching involves not only supporting learners but challenging them as well and helping them to see achievement as a process that they can work at (Dweck, 2009). In the examples provided in the beginning of this chapter, we can see that each of the learners in question deserves a different response in light of this issue of self-efficacy. Some learners, perhaps Eric and Cynthia, may seem more sensitive to critique; others, like Hasti, will require it. Delivering feedback in these instances is not a case of "telling it like it is" for each assignment, unless we agree that "what it is" is quite different from learner to learner.

MAKING MEANING FROM LEARNING

We could look at two contrasting examples as an illustration of what's involved in a positive and negative learning experience, and how important elements like emotion, needs, motivation, and context weave their way into the learning process.

Example 1: Learning Arabic

> *I once took an Arabic language course. At the time, I thought I was finally getting it right. I had been travelling and working abroad for a few years and made it my practice to learn the language where I was staying. While my attempts at Greek and Slovak had been fairly successful, I had learned those languages more or less "on the streets" taking no formal lessons. So when I arrived in Kuwait one sultry summer's day, I decided I'd try to avoid making all my previous mistakes and get down to some formal instruction, which happened to be offered by my employer at the time. Every Wednesday evening, I and about 6 or 7 other foreign workers would gather in a classroom somewhere in Kuwait City and try our hand at Arabic. It was a collective disaster, mostly, I have to say, because of the teacher. It seemed his lessons were designed to completely confuse us and our weekly vocabulary consisted of mumbles of words that we would hardly expect to use in our day-to-day life in the country.*

> *Every day our teacher would write a list of words on the board for us to practice. A typical list would look something like this:*

> *Cat*
> *Hot*
> *Car*
> *Rabbit*
> *Red*
> *Blue*
> *Yellow*
> *Sky*
> *Pneumonia*
> *Surprised*

> *After meticulously going through each word, practicing our pronunciation, discussing different usages, trying to imagine how we might apply our new-found vocabulary, the teacher, satisfied with our progress, would announce,*

"Let's have a conversation!"

So we would get into pairs. We'd quietly introduce ourselves while he explained the rules of the activity. We were trying to try talk to each other, using our new words and any others we might have come across (whether the other person knew our personal stock of vocabulary or not).

Conversations ensued. They sounded like this:

Hello.
Hello.
Me . . . Car is red.
Oh! Rabbit has pneumonia.
MmHmm. . . . Sky blue and hot.
Hot?
Yes, and blue.
Good night . . .

Presumably as the vocabulary increased, we would become more and more adept at striving for a conversation that made sense. Or maybe that wasn't important – only the words mattered. I didn't stick around long enough to find out. Most of us bailed after only a few befuddling classes. While living in Kuwait, I never had the opportunity to announce that a camel had pneumonia, but I was always ready.

Example 2: A moment in literacy learning

Contrast this with a story Paolo Freire relates about a literacy student learning to write:

I had told Odilion about the emotion I felt when a literacy student named Joaquim wrote his first word, "NINA," and exploded into nervous uncontrolled laughter. I, involved in the emotion of the moment, asked him, although I guessed the answer, "What's the matter, why do you laugh so much?"

"Nina, Nina," he said, not laughing anymore, as if he was certain he had reinvented a person. "Nina is my wife's name. It's my wife."

That moment, rich in humanity, I lived intensely in my practice
as an educator. I shared the happiness of someone who wrote,
for the first time, his wife's name. (1996, p. 138)

As Knowles (1980) suggests, when we encounter learners in
our classes, we find eventually that learners bring with themselves a
rich, detailed and intensely personal set of circumstances that affects their learning. Embedded in their role as learners are their other
social roles as well, family member, worker, community member,
nationality, etc. According to sociocultural learning theory, we recognize that learning is itself not an isolated, independent kind of
experience but rather something that is affected by the world of the
individual, his or her context and culture (Hansman, 2001). While
teachers who are dominantly from the Apprenticeship Perspective
might see the context that is most relevant for learning as their area
of focus, Nurturing teachers, by way of contrast, recognize and often accommodate those other innumerable factors that each learner
brings forward. The difference with the Nurturing Perspective in
this regard is the belief that this context is rooted in the individual's
experience, as the first point of departure for acquiring information
and applying new knowledge to existing situations or old knowledge to new situations.

MOTIVATION AND NEEDS OF LEARNERS

In my Arabic lessons, not even a "crazed pedagogic medic waving
an oversized syringe full of fluid marked 'motivation' to administer
a hefty dose of teacher encouragement" (Brookfield, 2006, p. 20)
would be of much help. My motivation is tied up into what I am
seeking to achieve and how I am progressing, along with how I feel
about this process; it is closely related to my sense of self-efficacy;
it is bound up with the variable characteristics of adult learners, and
it is often in a state of flux. This is what makes teaching such a
variable, changeable activity; we have to be ready to adjust those
identifications as we get to know our learners better and become
familiar with them. If we are truly attending to the needs of our
learners, then we are constantly building up and tearing down structures to make our teaching relevant.

Addressing and responding to learner needs are critical actions
for educators (Vella, 1996) and are of particular relevance to Nurturing teachers. There are two cautions to add to this idea. First we

should be strike some kind of balance between what our students want or need and what we as teachers believe we can provide; sometimes those two things don't overlap completely, and sometimes students don't always know what they need or have a full picture. Moreover, teachers simply cannot provide what's needed or wanted given the constraints imposed by the learning and teaching environment; this makes teaching rather more complicated than a straightforward commercial transaction. But determining needs and wants is still worth exploring; we can incorporate in our efforts to find out about students. We also need to remain realistic about what's possible and still feel we're working to our full capacities. Secondly, learning does not have to be predicated exclusively on needs. As a teacher, you have something to say. This might be out of the purview of students or perhaps even contrary to their original expectations. That doesn't negate the value of what you're trying to do. So needs should become a moment for negotiation and consensus. Settling on these should be an opportunity for dialogue between teachers and learners. A teacher's skill is revealed in the way this dialogue is conducted and how prepared she or he is to work in this way.

READINESS TO TEACH

> . . . *Hope that your journey is a long one.*
> *Many will be the summer mornings*
> *upon which, with boundless pleasure and joy,*
> *you will find yourself entering new ports of call.*
> *You will linger in Phoenician markets*
> *so that you may acquire the finest goods:*
> *mother of pearl, coral and amber, and ebony,*
> *and every manner of arousing perfume—*
> *great quantities of arousing perfumes.*
> *You will visit many an Egyptian city*
> *to learn, and learn more, from those who know.*

(*Kavafy, Ithaka*, lines 13-23)

Who are "those who know" and what can they teach us?

Feeling confident and competent in one's teaching role is not something exclusive to the Nurturing Perspective. Everyone who teaches strives to know that he or she is first of all capable of teaching and then secondly capable of figuring out how to get better at it. You are reading this text in part to find out where you fit in as a teacher and what you can do within your own profile to improve your teaching. This is part of your own development as a teacher. Your self-concept as a teacher, therefore, is very similar to your self-concept as a learner. Perhaps more so than with the other teaching perspectives, teachers from the Nurturing Perspective identify with their learners and seek to make that kind of empathy meaningful for their practice. By putting themselves in the learners' shoes, they are taking on a role that they see to be necessary as teachers. Just like our learners, if we don't feel that we're ready to teach, we're not likely to be very good at it, never mind learning how to get better and more accomplished over time. And so good teaching becomes very much a mirror to good learning.

Palmer (1998) writes about the "inner teacher" which connects us to our true identities. The inner teacher gives us the authority to take up the role of the teacher in an authentic way, with confidence and a sense of potential. We all have this in ourselves. If this is how we think about ourselves as teachers, it only follows that we would have the same ideas about individuals as learners. Beyond all the external impositions on learners (like grades, credits, job requirements, expectations of others, and so on), there is the person who wants to learn. If we can get through those other distractions, we have a chance to work successfully with our learners (Brookfield, 2006).

Defining the Authenticity of a Teacher

Most likely, you have wondered about how you've ended up as a teacher. You can trace your life history back from your present moment and consider what decisions and events, serendipitous and deliberate, led you to where you are now. This can almost feel like an inexorable process, as though it was bound to happen. But in moments of crisis, we might even ask that question of ourselves at a particularly bad time in our teaching experience: "Oh no, how did I get here? (. . . and will I make it?)."

Being a teacher certainly can feel like a risky venture. It's not uncommon to have doubts about your readiness to teach. Even the most experienced and celebrated educators confess to having moments of anxiety and uncertainty about their role, in books like *The*

Skillful Teacher (Brookfield, 2006) and *The Courage to Teach* (Palmer, 1998). When I first read these confessions, I thought to myself "Whew, if these guys are having doubts, then maybe there's hope for a working stiff like me." But then, as I continued to think on this, I wondered, "If they can't figure it out, what hope is there that I can?" This is part of being a reflective practitioner, and challenging those doubts is part of our learning.

One reason that we may struggle in our profession, particularly when we are closer to the beginning than the end of our careers, is that we are not certain how to resolve the idea of "teacher" with our own personality. How can we be ourselves and be the teacher at the same time? And then, how can learners believe in us as their teacher? And why is that even important? According to Cranton (2006), what we're looking for is a way of describing our *authenticity* as teachers. This is relevant for the Nurturing teacher in particular because authenticity as a teacher is closely tied to credibility in the eyes of one's learners. Paradoxically, we need to develop the confidence to express our insecurities freely as part of the process of building relationships with learners. Without that credibility, every effort made in the service of one's learners may be discounted or not taken seriously.

Brookfield (2006) provides a manageable definition of authenticity in the context of teaching in higher education, including some suggestions about how this quality translates into action:

> *Authenticity . . . is defined as the perception that the teacher is being open and honest in her attempts to help students learn. Authentic teachers do not go behind students' backs, keep agendas private, or double-cross learners by dropping a new evaluative criterion or assignment into a course half way through the semester. An authentic teacher is one that students trust to be honest and helpful. She is seen as a flesh and blood human being with passions, enthusiasms, frailties and emotions, not as someone who hides behind a collection of learned role behaviors appropriate to the title 'professor'.* (pp. 56)

We can come up with different ways of understanding what authenticity means. It might be an expression of one's self in our community of practice Cranton (2001); Parker (1998) calls that the "true self" while Rogers (1969) refers to the "realness" of the facilitator. In practical terms, authenticity means that you have a clear awareness about yourself as a teacher and you try to communicate that candidly with learners. So if you have particular strengths, you share that with them as a way of implying that they are invited to call upon you for your knowledge, expertise, and experience. You are also honest about your limitations or uncertainties, which brings you in solidarity with your learners and helps you to avoid feeling like an imposter or unqualified for the task of teaching. But mostly you want to be able to explain how you work as a teacher and why you think your way of teaching will be valuable in this relationship you've just struck up with a new group of learners.

Being authentic would seem to be a natural state, but it is also something we must work at, as it paves the way for effective teaching from the Nurturing Perspective. Understanding and being able to communicate your authenticity can help identify what makes you unique as a teacher. The work that you do to arrive at this understanding is a learning process and it is something that Nurturing teachers encourage for their learners. "Becoming authentic, is, in many ways, individuation. It is not only being genuine but understanding what genuine means in a deep way for ourselves, and this involves critically questioning the world outside ourselves" (Cranton, 2006,). This is more or less the same notion that Nurturing teachers apply in their thinking about encouraging learners to feel ready to learn through individuation, a Jungian concept that refers to our efforts to distinguish ourselves from the collective of humanity by knowing where we share similarities and where we are different. In order to make a compelling case to learners that their learning begins with a healthy sense of self-concept, it only makes sense to put one's own house in order first.

Establishing Relational Trust

Suddenly, this discussion is wholly taken up with ourselves, what we represent as teachers, how we're supposed to define ourselves. What happened to the learners?

The reason authenticity is considered here in the context of this chapter on the Nurturing Perspective is that it sets the foundation for the relationships that we seek to establish with our learners. Teaching is a social activity—we are dealing with people after all, not brains in jars. When considering how I should act as a teacher, it is impossible to avoid the idea of building relationships with learners. From the Nurturing Perspective, these relationships are important as they create a connection between teacher and learner, which becomes the locus of teaching. Without that connection, it's hard to see teaching as a complete act because of the way we pose that earlier question, "What can I do (as a teacher) to help my students learn?"

Because establishing relationships is an essential aspect of teaching from the Nurturing Perspective, it is something that we need to consider more carefully than just recognizing its value. Relationships in the teaching-learning environment also have implications of power and authority, and teaching is more authentic and effective when those issues are clarified and made transparent. Being candid with learners about our intentions as teachers, being honest about each other's role, setting expectations for course activities such as assignments and other graded work, cultivating mutual respect, and working to get the best and most out of students all contribute to the development of the student-teacher relationship. But it's not surprising that this can be a highly personal endeavour. What about the individuals involved—getting along, developing friendships or the opposite effect, not liking someone, sensing incompatibility—where do these fit in? For it is impossible to get to know someone and not develop personal feelings about them, for better or worse. Some might argue that this focus on relationships leads to dangerous territory, including such risks as losing confidence, overstepping boundaries, or burning out. These are valid concerns, so it is worth looking at relationships further.

Relationships can be tested, even broken, as a result of these awkward situations, and the experience can be extremely demanding for both the educators and the learners in question. There is no rule of thumb about where to draw that line, and we might even say that this is a continual risk that one must take as a teacher looking at the world from the Nurturing Perspective. Teachers and learners may not all agree on what is permissible within a close relationship or how that relationship affects learning and teaching, not to mention how it affects each other. The intensity of this type of work can lead to teacher burnout. Seeking to maintain appropriate boundaries requires constant effort and can feel like a resistance to the natural inclination of getting to know and like someone. On the learner's side, there can be unintended consequences of developing a closeness with one's learners. Sometimes, too, relationship can have the opposite effect than what is intended by the teacher—that is, learner independence. Particularly, those learners who have revealed their vulnerability or disclosed their past negative experiences may feel that they can't learn from other kinds of teachers.

Rogers (1969), however, maintains that learning not only benefits from but, more critically, depends on the development of the teacher-learner relationship, and trust and empathy are qualities the teacher has to cultivate in order to be competent. Nonetheless, in terms of enjoying student-teacher relationships, both parties have to recognize the conditions imposed upon that relationship by outside forces (Chapman & Sork, 2001). That doesn't eliminate the potential for sincere friendships or long-term mentoring, but one needs to recognize the challenges that these relationships pose and be prepared to work with them. On the other hand, research shows that good teacher-learner relationships are not only beneficial to those who take part in them, but they also have positive influences on academic performance (Palmer, 2003) and general classroom management (Meyers et al., 2006).

Authenticity in the individual and its role in the teacher-learner relationship return us to the idea of readiness. We want to reach an environment in which we can be honest and open about giving feedback or expressing emotions like joy or anger. There is a loyalty inherent in a strong relationship that avoids the expectation that we will be merely conveyers of information or the full vessel amid a sea of empties. Accepting that one must get to know people in order to teach fully should help ensure against the temptation to put on a show or be someone you're not.

There are a few points to consider about relationships in educational settings. First of all, there is a forced quality in the coming together of learners and a teacher. We may have been hired to be teachers, not to meet people, but that is a fact of the job. The educational event in question—whether a one-to-one tutoring situation, a conventional classroom at a school, a course in some other setting like a church or community centre, or a networked environment such as an online course—is an opportunity to achieve mutual goals —both from the learners and the teacher. Intentions are meant to be reciprocal. When this occurs, there will be uncertainty, governed by variations of motivation, interest, ability and willingness to take part in such an event. Relationship building in this context is really about setting the scene for learning.

Despite their close focus on learners, teachers working from the Nurturing Perspective do not seek to minimize their presence in this experience. Although it would be true to say that Nurturing teachers do seek to promote the learner's self-efficacy and independence, that doesn't mean they proceed from the position of invisibility or step aside in the experience of teaching and learning. If anything, Nurturing teachers try to place themselves more definitively in this relationship with learners. Forming this relationship and working within it as a place to start and support learning are central characterizations of the Nurturing Perspective. So such teachers are not disappearing from the teaching and learning experience, not at all— they declare themselves to be an integral part of this experience. It is part of who they are as teachers.

As a reflection of one's self, teaching from this perspective involves "Nurturing the soul" of others (Dirkx, 1997). This does not mean an altruistic, selfless act of kindness. A mistaken view looks at the Nurturing Perspective bathed in an uncritically positive light whereby the Nurturing instructor appears as a kind of educational saint, prioritizing the needs of each individual learner above all else, including oneself. However, focusing on the learner as the first act of teaching is not the moral imperative of one with superior skills in the kindness of humanity though we might retreat to that kind of comfort in times of stress. We do want to acknowledge, nevertheless, how the unique and individual worlds of each learner can inform an educational context. Rather than ignoring that unique context, as Nurturing instructor we believe that it is important to encourage learners to delve into that context deeply, to draw on their past experiences and their personal histories as part of their learning. Dirkx (1997) writes eloquently about the ineffable subject of "soul work" in education. This is an aspect of learning that any teacher experiences with groups of learners, though it is hard to pin down. However, his description of his classes is as accurate as any in defining how teachers can effectively give due attention to learners in a Nurturing way to support learning:

> *When we nurture soul in adult learning, we assume that the unconscious represents the primary source of creativity, vital-*

ity, and wisdom within our lives—is the source of life itself. We recognize how the deeper aspects of our individual and collective unconscious come to express themselves. We encourage engagement with the unconscious through imagination, creativity, and intuition. (p 86)

Employing Expertise

One of the potential myths of the Nurturing Perspective is the separation of the content from the teacher, in contrast to the characterization of the Transmission Perspective. A misguided interpretation goes like this: "If I cater to learners exclusively and work in an entirely responsive way, I'll manage to do my job. By doing so I can also avoid what I suspect may be real teaching, i.e., talking with conviction, demonstrating my expertise, exemplifying authoritative knowledge and practitioner wisdom." This way of thinking not only does a disservice to good instructors who know their stuff and are well regarded for their context expertise, but it also ignores the learners and their expectations for teachers. It implies that good will alone will suffice for Nurturing teachers when rarely would learners concede to such a premise.

Knowing one's subject area and being recognized for that serve multiple purposes apart from merely being the one chosen to do the job of teaching. First, content expertise serves to introduce a teacher's credibility. It is not unnatural for learners to appeal to someone who has knowledge and insight about a topic in their interest. And being attentive to learners doesn't reduce the important of one's own teaching and subject matter expertise. Within the teaching perspectives, it is tempting to tick off expertise as a responsibility for those who are dominant Transmission and Apprenticeship teachers, but its necessity does not reside there exclusively.

Recognizing the value of content also includes the understanding that content is continually changing, not just for learners but also for those who purport to be the very content experts we rely on for our education. So if content is changing for these people, why can't we just enlist the participation of students in this response to change? In this way, teaching can become more inclusive and participatory and expertise needn't be regarded as the provenance of the instructor alone. Just as learning can become a shared activity, so can other critical elements of the teaching and learning environment such as teaching itself and content. Content exists in multiple formats and media, like books, movies, reports, performances, through the lives of others, their testimonies, interpretations, theories, and stories, and with the support of the teacher much of this can be derived from students as part of their learning experience.

As a teacher, it's important to share that philosophical position with students so that they don't misunderstand your intentions. In many cases, learners themselves haven't given much thought into what constitutes good teaching apart from what they've gathered in their learning experiences. They may have very conventional expectations of the teacher as the primary authority in the room. So when the teacher begins a class or session by declaring that they're leaving everything up to the learner to figure out, there is a danger in communicating a counter-intuitive message (Brookfield, 2006). Bringing one's content expertise into the discussion and the role of that expertise is, like these other critical features, part of setting the scene for learning.

STRATEGIES FOR NURTURING TEACHING

There is a potential risk in separating out any of these teaching perspectives and looking for associated methods or techniques that one can apply readily to suit one's perspective. In discussions about the five teaching perspectives with both educators and students (some who are filling both roles at once), I often hear and see and have participated in some ruthlessly left-brained discussions in the attempt to link methods to perspectives. It seems simple at first: Transmission teachers like to lecture; Apprenticeship teachers demonstrate; Developmental teachers question. But when you carry on with this type of exploration, you quickly find that we employ methods that align with our purpose and our understanding of effective teaching.

Recognizing the variety in human nature is one reason why a regimented accumulation of teaching techniques does not guarantee effective teaching. To break the ice, bring out the juggling balls; to calm them down, get them writing; to wake them up, conjure up a role-play—it doesn't really work that way. How often have teachers found that the same approach will work one day to great effect while the next time it will be an unqualified disaster. This is because with any new group of learners, you will experience different group dynamics, motivations, reservations, and concerns. Research can tell us to vary our methods, break our lectures into smaller, more manageable chunks, match activities and assessments to learning objectives, but it can rarely give a consistent answer for how to deal with different individuals and groups of learners from one experience to the next. Writing about teaching in nonformal settings, Taylor (2008) argues that teaching is an ongoing process of reading learners for cues that can suggest how to proceed, whether to change up the approach or intensify it.

So establishing a list of ready-made instructional methods that you can take out of this book and into your teaching situation will not really be helpful or worse may set you off toward disaster. Even knowing that group discussion, let's say, is favoured by Nurturing educators as an effective method does not really shed any light on how you can incorporate it in your teaching. However, Nurturing educators certainly do employ strategies and adopt traditional methods for their teaching. Nurturing teachers also lecture. It's true; they don't adopt the Transmission Perspective for this purpose. In fact, I would be hesitant to think of teaching in this way at all. We don't leap from one perspective or another depending on our aims or feeling at the moment.

I prefer to think of this as setting up the conditions for learning or readiness to learn, as I have described earlier. Such conditions might help summarize what I would see as the primary features of this perspective:

- *Condition 1*: We need to feel that we have something to offer as teachers. Identifying what that is becomes part of a design for learning.
- *Condition 2*: We need to make connections with learners. Teaching happens within the teacher-learner relationship. It is not an act that is presented or performed for an audience.
- *Condition 3*: We need to create opportunities where learning can best occur. Providing feedback, therefore, is the primary teaching method available to nurturers. Feedback enables the development of self-efficacy, addresses motivational concerns, and creates opportunities for teachers to help learners make meaning of their experiences.
- *Condition 4*: We need to celebrate success and address failure. Both constitute achievements in learning but with different results and subsequent responses.

Rogers (1969) writes that his goal in teaching is to establish the "freedom to learn." In his book of the same name, he offers some edifying examples of teachers across the disciplines who have revised their practices in accordance with many of the ideas discussed here in this chapter. One of these teachers, Gay Swenson, a high school French teacher, refers to her primary method of teaching as "implementing such a belief system" requiring most of all "one's courage, one's students, and one's commitment to trust the human ability to discover one's self. It is then we begin to become more of what we really are—free excited learners and growers."

CONCLUSION

Teaching, no less than learning, is a journey. This is what makes it so puzzling and uncertain from moment to moment and why it can feel like a precarious risk one day and a great reward the next.

Let's look back to Kavafy's poem and finish with a sense of the constant, unfinished business of teaching and learning. If we read the concluding lines of *Ithaka*, we can ask ourselves what we hope to gain from our experience of teaching and where it is leading us.

> *Bear Ithaca always in your thoughts.*
> *Arriving there is the goal of your journey;*
> *but take care not to travel too hastily.*
> *Better to linger for years on your way;*
> *better to reach the island's shores in old age,*
> *enriched by all you've obtained along the way.*
> *Do not expect that Ithaca will reward you with wealth.*
>
> *Ithaca bestowed upon you the marvelous journey:*
> *if not for her you would never have set out.*
> *But she has nothing left to impart to you.*
>
> *If you find Ithaca wanting, it's not that she's deceived you.*
> *That you have gained so much wisdom and experience*
> *will have told you everything of what such Ithakas mean.*

(*Ithaka*, lines 24-36)

REFERENCES

Apps, J. (1991). *Mastering the teaching of adults.* Malabar, Florida: Krieger.

Bandura, A. (1994). Self-efficacy. In V. S. Ramachaudran (Ed.), *Encyclopedia of human behavior,* 4, 71-81.

Blumberg, P., & Alsardary, S. (2009). Interactive, learner-centered methods of teaching mathematics. *PRIMUS: Problems, resources, and issues in mathematics undergraduate studies,* 19(4), 401-416.

Brookfield, S. (2006). The skillful teacher. *On Technique, Trust and Responsiveness in the Classroom.* Second Edition. San Francisco, CA: Jossey-Bass.

Chapman, V., & Sork, T. (2001). Confessing regulation or telling secrets? Opening up the conversation on graduate supervision. *Adult Education Quarterly,* 51: 94-107.

Cranton, P. (2006). Integrating perspectives on authenticity. *New Directions For Adult & Continuing Education,* (111), 83-87. doi:10.1002/ace.230

Cranton, P., & Caruseta, E. (2004). Perspectives on authenticity in teaching. *Adult Education Quarterly,* 55(1), 5-22. doi:10.1177/0741713604268894

Dirkx, J. (1997). Nurturing soul in adult learning. *New Directions for Adult and Continuing Education,* 74, 76-88.

Dirkx, J. M. (2006). Authenticity and imagination. *New Directions For Adult & Continuing Education,* (111), 27-39. doi:10.1002/ace.225

Dweck, C. S. (2007). The perils and promises of praise. *Educational Leadership,* 65(2), 34-39.

Dirkx, J. (2008a). Care of the self: Mythopoetic dimensions of professional preparation and development. In Timothy Leonard & Peter Willis (Eds). *Pedagogies of the Imagination Mythopoetic curriculum in educational practice.* Springer: Dordrecht, NLD.

Dirkx, J. (2008b). The meaning and role of emotions in adult learning. *New Direction for Adult and Continuing Education.* 2008(12), 7-18.

Dweck, C. S. (2009). Can We Make Our Students Smarter? *Education Canada,* 49(4), 56-61.

Freire, P. (1996). *Letters to Cristina. Reflections on my life and work.* Routledge: New York.

Freire, P. (1998). *Pedaogy of freedom: Ethics, democracy and civic courage*. Rowman & Littlefield Publishers: Lanham, MD.

Hansman, C. (2001). Context-based learning. *New Directions for Adult & Continuing Education*, 89, 43-51.

Hattie, J., & Timperley, H. (2007). The power of feedback. *Review of Educational Research*, 77(1), 81-112.

Holt, J. (1976). *Instead of education. Ways to help people do things better*. E. P. Dutton and Co.: New York.

Kavafy, K. (2004). Ithaka. *The Canon*. Translated from the Greek by Stratis Haviaras, Hermes Publishing.

Knowles, M. (1980). *The modern practice of adult education: From pedagogy to andragogy*. Follett Pub. Co.: Chicago.

Meyers, S., Bender, J., Hill, E., & Thomas, S. (2006). How do faculty experience and respond to classroom conflict? *International Journal of Teaching and Learning in Higher Education*, 18(3), 180-187.

O'Neill, G. & McMahon , T. (2005). Student-centred learning: What does it mean for students and lecturers? *Emerging Issues in the Practice of University Learning and Teaching*. All Ireland Society for Higher Education (AISHE): Dublin.

Palmer, P. (1998). *The courage to teach: Exploring the inner landscape of a teacher's life*. Jossey-Bass: San Francisco.

Palmer, P. (2003). Teaching with heart and soul: Reflections on spirituality in teacher education. *Journal of Teacher Education*, 54: 376

Postman, N. & Weingartner, C. (1969). *Teaching as a subversive activity*. Dell Pub. Co.: New York.

Reich, A. (1983). Why I teach. *Chronicle of Higher Education*.

Rogers, C. (1966). *Freedom to Learn*. Charles E. Merrill Publishing: Columbus, Ohio.

Schutz, P. Hong, J., Cross, D. & Osbon, J. (2006). Reflections on Investigating Emotion in Educational Activity Settings. *Educational Psychology Review*, 18(4), 343-360.

Taylor, E. (2008). Teaching and emotions in a nonformal educational setting. *New Directions for Adult and Continuing Education*. 120, 79-87.

Vella, J. (1996). *Learning to listen, Learning to teach*. Jossey-Bass: San Francisco.

Wlodkowski, R. J. (1999). *Enhancing adult motivation to learn: a comprehensive guide for teaching all adults*. San Francisco: Jossey-Bass.

I want to offer my thanks to faculty and students at two institutions where I teach, the University of British Columbia and Vancouver Community College, from whom I have drawn many examples and ideas for this chapter.

CHAPTER 8
The Social Reform Perspective

John P. Egan

One way to think of learning is as the historical production, transformation and change of persons (Lave & Wenger, 1991, p. 51).

INTRODUCTION

I had been warned about him before the course started—and my colleagues' predictions were coming true. Ali was not doing well; in fact, he was failing miserably. He sat near the back of class every day, sometimes falling asleep shortly after arriving. He never answered or asked any questions. But he was always on time and always smiled and responded politely, if hesitantly, when I spoke to him.

He was new to Canada, like perhaps one-third of his classmates, though he had come as a refugee from Somalia. His participation in this (vocational) certificate program was funded by the federal government, with an aim to facilitate new Canadians' entrée into the workforce. Most of his peers were much more engaged and did much better, though all of them struggled with English at times. I wasn't sure if it was language or his attitude that was the barrier. But I was irked: there were, no doubt, other new Canadians who would happily have taken his funded place in the program.

After failing another quiz I asked him if we could chat in private. I explained my concerns about his performance and offered to help him improve his performance. He just smiled. And shrugged.

197

"Did you study for the quiz?"

"No, not really."

"Have you been reading the textbook?"

"Some. I try."

"Is it the language...do you find it hard to understand the text?"

"No, it's not that...I can't find my family. I left them in one of the refugee camps so I could get established first, but now I can't find them. No one knows where they are. I'm calling all night to see if I can find my wife and child. I don't sleep much, anyways. But I like coming to school. I feel connected to Canada. I am learning."

I felt like an idiot. "That makes perfect sense. Your family is more important. But I'm here to help if you want."

I realized that for Ali, success wasn't about grades or certificates or even getting a job: it was about trying to keep going, trying to find his family, and trying to rebuild a shattered life. And that my job, as his teacher, was to support him on that journey. He did not complete the certificate.

There is no neutrality in teaching and learning. As part of the human experience, learners—and, therefore, teachers—are socially, culturally, and historically situated. Learners bring into the learning context, be it a classroom, meeting room or online learning space, whatever is on their minds or in their hearts: life is not left at the threshold or log-in page. Lifelong learning is a component of their lives, rather than experienced in isolation. This principle also applies to teachers. All teachers experience days where the forces in our own, non-teaching lives pull more strongly on us than others. Some days we feel we are "on" (working at our best), others "off" (struggling to achieve anything, or perhaps to avoid losing ground). Are our situated selves, as learners and teachers, to be managed or mitigated? Or embraced?

Perhaps not aiming for neutrality, most teachers nonetheless generally strive to be fair and impartial, even when encountering learners whose personalities, values or ideas conflict with our own. Conflicts or dissonance with respect to the ways learners and their teachers view the world (ontology) and their place in it (positionality) arise. Life's experiences, ways of making meaning out of them, and their impact on what we do (or do not do) are all significant. There can, however, potentially be one substantive difference: the extent to which individual teachers are mindful and reflective of their beliefs and the impact on their practice. And, by extension, how teachers support learners to be similarly mindful and reflective. This idea of mindfulness is not the unique domain of any one of the five perspectives described in this book. Indeed, teaching from any perspective is likely to be more effective when it is mindfully reflective with respect to actions, intentions, and underlying beliefs.

What sets apart the Social Reform Perspective is a belief that teaching is a political act—an act whose overarching objective is to transform society to better align with particular principles and values. As a result, the mindfulness related to practice seeks to evaluate how well what teachers do aligns with the sort of society they want to create. However, one common misperception is that the Social Reform perspective is always characterized by a commitment to social justice or progressive, leftish politics (Hall et al., 2012). This is not true. The Social Reform perspective is found among those who teach in faith-based, socially conservative contexts, in business education, even in technology education. No singular ethos of societal transformation defines this perspective. It is defined by transforming society, writ large, as a driver of education.

My interaction with Ali (above)—in one of the first courses I ever taught—was transformative for me as an early career adult educator. At that phase of my career, my work as a teacher was distinct from what was my driving passion in life: social justice. I had unconsciously compartmentalized my vocational adult education classroom (and its students) as training, and mistakenly conflated training with competency-based, skills building. Certainly acquiring skills is a large component of adult vocational education (and was of the program in which I taught). But the constraints in that classroom were imposed by me. In hindsight I had no pedagogical training when I was first hired and felt wholly unprepared to teach. As a novice adult educator, focusing on skill acquisition with my students made me less anxious and gave me more of a sense of being in control. Good for me, perhaps, but not always in the best interests of my students, and certainly not in the best interests of Ali. Ali's story reminded me that my commitment to social justice was not only compatible with my emerging practice as an adult educator. Social justice could drive that practice.

In this chapter I examine education as Social Reform from theoretical, experiential and pedagogical lenses. I will briefly introduce the work of three prominent educational theorists in the context of the Social Reform perspective: Malcolm Knowles, Paulo Freire, and Pierre Bourdieu. I will set out some specific pedagogical strategies—in terms of content delivery and process facilitation—that characterize the teaching of some Social Reform educators. Throughout I will reflect upon my own experiences as an adult learner and adult educator, primarily (though not exclusively) in the realm of community adult education.

EDUCATION FOR WHAT?

In both social and economic terms, the evidence of the transformative potential of education is powerful. After nineteenth century educational reforms in the industrial United Kingdom (UK), United States of America (US), and Canada (where a need for a workforce with the rudiments of literacy and numeracy emerged) a much broader social (rather than merely economic) transformation took place. Compulsory public education, initially only at the primary years, but expanded to the secondary level, transformed these economies and social order of the day. Arthur, Davies and Hahn (2008) write: "In the 18th and 19th centuries concerns for citizenship education accompanied the growth of nation states and the expansion of public or state education in many parts of the world." (p. 4). From educating workers, public education rather quickly focused on creating engaged citizens who could participate in civil society. Regardless of the initial intention, education as an entitlement has shaped the modern democratic citizen as an empowered and engaged actor.

Universal public education has also driven similar social and economic change across Europe, Asia, Latin America and Australasia, including primary, secondary, and post-secondary education, as well as workplace learning. From the South African context, where a post-apartheid democracy in its infancy faced numerous social and economic challenges, Groener (2006) argues for a transformative approach to workplace learning in particular. This approach aims to address persistent inequities in access to paid work that provides a living wage. Transformative workplace learning "must be premised on the values, ethics and purposes of a transformative political economy of adult education" while integrating elements of "employment equity, equal opportunity, (and) eliminating discrimination," among others (Groener, 2006, p. 12).

Some might find this emphasis on Social Reform in workplace learning (training, in other words) surprising. Nonetheless, what began as an education movement to satisfy a privileged class of capitalist business owners relatively quickly became one to create citizens who could participate as equals in democratic societies— even as the tensions between these (and other) competing sets of interests have persisted. Today there are competing discourses on education and society in the 21st century: school "choice", public versus private, secular or faith-based, and outcomes-driven, all of which demarcate a much more contested space for public education.

If your dominant perspective is Social Reform, then your practice, your ideals and your commitment to transforming society through education are part of a 100+ year tradition. The movement has, in many parts of the world, disrupted colonialism, led to (near) universal suffrage, and granted millions a greater degree of personal agency—economic, interpersonal and social—previously unknown to humanity. The Social Reform Perspective has also helped disrupt normative practices related to family life, land ownership and individual rights.

For Social Reform educators, the practice of teaching is intensely political and personal. Their stories, and the stories of their students, sustain them in their commitment. They view teaching and learning as a uniquely powerful enterprise, through which they create a better society. Their pedagogy reflects this passion and their strategies include challenging, interrogating, strengthening and celebrating. Such work is part of a broader tradition in education, particularly adult education, as evident in the work of Knowles, Freire, and Bourdieu. Each of these authors will be discussed in turn next.

KNOWLES' PERSPECTIVE

The transformative potential of teaching adults is found in a wide range of work, most often framed in the context of social justice or grassroots activism. This includes Malcolm Knowles' (1970) canonical work on andragogy (the process of educating adult learners).

Every society has used adult education processes to continue the development of the kind of citizens visualized to be required for the maintenance and progress of that society; and the perception of the kind of adult required is different in each society . . . The challenging fact is that every adult educator is the agent of several different societies whose needs he is expected to serve simultaneously. And one of the measures of his artistry is the extent to which he is able to understand and serve these differing needs. (p. 32)

While Knowles' work is sometimes critiqued as too bourgeouis, too middle class and too American, the hope for adult education to transform society is there. Knowles's conceptualization of andragogy is positioned within a powerful discourse around citizenship and personal agency. Pratt (1993) writes that this reflected a predominant view of the adult learner during the 1970s and '80s in the context of the United States:

. . . operating as if he or she has risen above the web of social structures... [such a view] does not acknowledge the vast influence such structures have had on forming the person's identity and ways of interpreting the world, much of which is received and accepted without conscious consideration or reflection . . . implying complex social, cultural, political, and historical factors are largely reduced to matters of individual perception, experience, need, and ultimately, human agency. This is, in part, a product of a particular historical period in the U.S.; it is also a continuation of the pre-eminence of psychology in education, wherein complex social and educational issues are framed [and reduced] in psychological terms (p. 17).

Even so, Knowles cautions that "a society in which gaps between people (youth vs. adult, black vs. white, East vs. West, rich vs. poor) are becoming better defined and less tolerable requires a citizenry that is liberated from traditional prejudices and is able to establish open, empathic and collaborative relationships with people of all sorts" (pp. 32-33). Thus for those of us who have lived in "democracies" and have nonetheless experienced marginalization, stigmatization or social exclusion, much of what Knowles describes as adult education seems to align very closely to—and, to some, replicates—the status quo. That was his path to Social Reform. Freire, however, takes a different path and aspires to rupture the status quo.

FREIRE'S PERSPECTIVE

Without the democratic intervention of the educator, there is no progressive education. (Freire, 1998, p. 57)

While Knowles wrote within the context of an established liberal democracy, Paulo Freire wrote from a context of dictatorship in post-World War II Brazil.

Knowles and Freire both advocated for transforming society through adult education, but with different orientations to the mechanisms for that transformation. Knowles espoused principles and strategies that promoted individual autonomy and agency as a means of changing society. Freire proposed almost the opposite: espousing principles and strategies for transforming society as a means of changing the lives of individuals and communities. The principles espoused in Knowles' early work align better with Freire's than many would admit, but context was a major influence in the approach each took toward revolutionizing society. Their goals were similar; the strategic means were different.

Adult educators working in a context where the principles of democracy are either not entrenched or do not represent the interests of their community often seem to find Freire's work more resonant than Knowles. I certainly did for a time. But my story is not unique. The African American activist and adult educator, bell hooks, has a story that very much resembles my own history:

> *I signed up for my masters program in adult education so I could make more money as a contract adult educator: getting my masters would increase my hourly rate quite a lot. I had hoped to learn a few things about pedagogy, but after a couple of years having to figure things out on my own I was doing OK. Mostly I wanted to get the degree to get the pay raise: teaching part-time almost paid enough for me to continue my activism full-time. Almost. But I was coming back to university under duress (and with a rather cynical bent): my undergraduate experience was one of busy work, cramming for exams, and cranking out papers at the 11th hour.*

The conversations about "social justice" in my first adult education seminars amused me initially. I encountered a room of middle-class, very comfortable, mostly white people nattering about how important social justice was, how adult education could transform society, blah blah blah: theoretical garbage. Few of my classmates (or professors) had got their hands dirty doing social justice work like my activist peers and I had. Poverty, addiction, homelessness were abstractions for most of them. They were life to me. My "adult ed. job" was what paid the bills so I could do what really mattered to me: fight homophobia, help people battling addiction, and give back as others had given back to me. Social justice was my life's work—my life's unpaid work.

By the end of the program my outlook had been transformed. My professors had, for the most part, accepted, celebrated and challenged me. I was mentored to better articulate my experiences—so I could focus on solutions, or at least, mitigation strategies. The "theoretical garbage" from the seminars helped me do something I had been unable to do before: make sense of how my life unfolded. For me, studying adult education became "the practice of freedom." (hooks, 1994)

Education, democracy, revolution, literacy, and critical citizenship are some of the key themes from over 40 years of Paulo Freire's adult education scholarship . Freire's work remains arguably the key global literature for adult education beginning with his description of teaching basic literacy and critical consciousness in Recifé, Brazil, through his work with non-governmental organizations and universities around the world. This work fundamentally aligns with the Social Reform perspective.

As I began to immerse myself in the canon of adult education literature, Freire captivated me. Reading his work (reading the world by reading his word, in fact) had a significant impact. To varying degrees and in different ways, my professors integrated many of the principles espoused by Freire about transformative adult education into their practice. It was uncomfortable at times, and certainly rather untidy in moments. But the practice of adult education was modeled as one where principles and ideals or values could (should) be at the centre of one's practice.

In mid-20th century Brazil, teaching people who were living in extreme poverty to read and write and concurrently teaching them to analyze and understand their world and its power relations was a political and revolutionary act. For Freire (1970) "to exist, humanly, is to *name* the world, to change it. Once named, the world in its turn reappears to the namers as a problem and requires of them a new *naming*" (p. 69, emphasis original). Freire viewed the purpose of literacy as a means to understand one's world, including its political dimensions. The goal of learning is Social Reform, i.e., to transform society. When authentically and effectively enacted, the Social Reform process transforms the educator as much as the student, since "the more educators and the people investigate the people's thinking, and are thus jointly educated, the more they continue to investigate" (p. 90).

Freire's early work was situated in the practice of literacy education, however his perspective on education more broadly is what interests Social Reform educators. Its greatest power resided in the potential of education to transform. For Freire:

> *Education is a political act. It's non-neutrality demands from educators that they take it on as a political act and that they consistently live their progressive and democratic or authoritarian and reactionary past.* (Freire, 1998, p. 63)

Throughout his writings Freire critiques traditional pedagogy's focus on content. He argues the "education of answers" does not foster creativity, which he sees as "indispensable in the cognitive process" (Freire, 1997, p. 31). Traditional pedagogy's emphasis on "the mechanical memorization of content" limits, rather than enhances, learning (p. 31). For Freire—and for many Social Reform educators, "only an education of questions can trigger, motivate and reinforce curiosity" (p. 31)—and therefore learning.

In his later works Freire (1997) wrote of what he called the "progressive perspective" (p. 75) on education and democracy. He describes this as "the process of teaching—where the teaching challenges learners to *apprehend* the object, to then learn it in their relations with the world—implies the exercise of critical perception, perception of the object's reason for being" (p. 75, emphasis original). This broadens the role of the teacher to that of a person whose responsibilities include "the sharpening of the learner's *epistemo-*

logical curiosity, which cannot be satisfied with mere description of the object's concept" (p. 75, emphasis original).

For many adult educators, Freire's work resonates because of his ability to address challenging, often disheartening or despairing circumstances (poverty, racism, sexism, and dictatorship) substantively and forthrightly, while remaining resolutely hopeful. In fact, for Freire "unhopeful educators contradict their practice" (Freire, 1997, p. 107). In helping learners develop critical consciousness, Social Reform educators must inspire thoughtful analysis and action to change that which must be changed. Freire rejected deterministic or fatalistic analyses in favour of "history (as) possibility" (p. 37). For him it was "impossible to understand history as possibility if we do not recognize human beings as beings who make free decisions" (p. 37, emphasis original).

Freire's writings continue to inspire me. His analyses of the practice of adult education, the social structures that impede democratic education, and his articulation of a philosophy about a pedagogy of hope still resonate years later. From a research perspective, however, Freire's work is sometimes seen as less valuable because it is not empirical; it is conceptual and largely reflective, based on moral principles. Perhaps because of its moral position and principled argument, Freire's work has given me a clearer sense of what adult education could be—its potential to do the right thing for the right reasons.

From my own context, having lived at various stages in my life in Canada, the United States, Australia and now New Zealand, what I also needed to understand was how the experience of people (citizens, if you will) within ostensibly democratic societies could have divergent educational outcomes. During my secondary education I was given educational opportunities that few of my working class peers were. I attended a public secondary school with a program for "gifted" students, where I was encouraged and expected, in fact, to perform well. I integrated those messages uncritically. I had no critical consciousness through which to do otherwise.

During my Bachelor of Arts, the superior calibre of my secondary education compared to my peers was evident. We had read more widely and learned to write better, in particular. And yet still, I struggled to remain motivated and engaged. For a long time I assumed the problems were my own. Many years later, in the work of Pierre Bourdieu, I began find answers.

BOURDIEU'S PERSPECTIVE

French sociologist Pierre Bourdieu used the concept of social capital to explain educational attainment and social stratification in the modern democratic state. Rather than focusing solely on educational attainment as a wholly individuated and cognitive experience (where individual learners perform and progress through various forms of formal education), Bourdieu links "*what* you know to *who* you know, and in whose circle you exercise genuine membership" (Butterwick and Egan, 2011, p. 117, emphasis original). Understanding how social forces larger than the individual impact education, in particular, speaks well to the ethos behind the Social Reform teaching perspective.

For Bourdieu (1997), social capital consists of networks made up of social obligations, relationships and interactions beyond the mere incidental or impersonal. Social capital, therefore, resides not wholly with an individual. It exists only where there are substantive, persistent social or cultural connections with others. For social capital to work—for it to have currency (or fungeability, as Bourdieu describes it)—one must bring something to a social network that is of value to other network members.

It is in the exchanges among network members that one's social capital demonstrates its value. Therefore, genuine, substantive, engaged membership in a network is key: merely signing up or showing up does not constitute genuine membership. One must participate in, contribute to, and draw upon the network's social resources. Passive participation is of little currency. Participation in different social networks means differing levels of social capital.

The implications of Bourdieu's work are multiple with regards to education, e.g., network access, network participation, and the inability of public education alone to disrupt social stratification. On a fundamental level, access to education is often driven by network access, for example, through family wealth or connections to better schools. But Bourdieu's analysis examines how some of the strategies for mitigating social stratification (such as scholarships or bursaries, or other opportunity programs for economically disadvantaged students to attend elite institutions, the purposeful mixing of students from different social classes, or creating wholly public university systems) are only somewhat successful in disrupting social stratification. Nor do increases in economic capital (income) sufficiently mitigate inequities in educational attainment. Highly waged unionized workers may be able to send their children to an elite, private university, but this does not ensure their children will have access to that university's network of social capital as 'legitimate' or genuine members.

An important aspect of genuine membership is one's ability to fully participate in network life. According to Bourdieu, knowing and being known by other members is merely the starting point. If one cannot muster the economic resources needed for full participation in elite networks, genuine membership is impossible. Among those who can fully participate, genuine membership yields both material and social benefits. In fact, according to Bourdieu, "the profits which accrue . . . are the basis of the solidarity which makes them possible" (p. 51). This reciprocity is an important part of elite network cohesion, even if some of this work might not seem transparently purposeful. "From a narrowly economic standpoint, this effort [socializing among the elite] is bound to be seen as pure wastage, but in terms of the logic of social exchanges, it is a solid investment, the profits of which will appear, in the long run" (p. 54).

Bourdieu allows that social capital can be acquired or lost. But he rejects the liberal notion that high quality public education alone is sufficient to disrupt social stratification, since public education cannot wholly revolutionize the ways in which social capital is transmitted. Public education can only, at times mitigate or lessen (rather than eliminate) the significantly complex system of social capital dissemination. This explains why parental income and access to elite institutions alone does not predict educational attainment. It also explains why my participation in a secondary school "gifted" program, where most of my peers were the children of university-educated professionals, only partially mitigated the disadvantages conferred by my working class background.

Ironically, understanding my own experiences (which confounded me until I explored Bourdieu's work) was no longer about me. I had found my métier as a learner. But I was driven to understand how education reproduces society's inequities to ensure my own practice did not. By this point I was back in the classroom, teaching at university for the first time. Gradually, I began to feel more confident not just as a teacher, but as an adult educator committed to unlocking the transformative potential of education. I was convinced this would not endear me to everyone in my classes. I was right.

JOHN EGAN'S PERSPECTIVE

John,

I wanted to say thank you. And to apologize. When I found out that our course would focus only on gender I was pissed off. I thought you were going to force feed us a bunch of feminist crap and we would have to spew out the answers you wanted.

But you didn't do that, or expect us to either. Instead you created a space where we could talk about our educational experiences—men and women—and how gender may have played a role in what was going on in our classrooms.

Learning that gender matters is going to make me a different teacher. Hopefully a better one. That wouldn't have happened if we weren't allowed to be honest in your class. Respectful, but honest. I hope I can do half as good a job as you when I start teaching.

One of the challenges of the Social Reform Perspective, particularly for new teachers, is to avoid proselytizing/preaching. Actively working towards creating a "better society" requires more than ideas of what would make it "better". It also requires advocating for a particular change in ways that do not result in students becoming entrenched in their existing views rather than opening themselves out to new perspectives—this quoted letter is getting at that tension.

The critical part of his letter is the middle paragraph, where he says that I (actually we) *created a space to talk about our educational experiences—men and women—and how gender may have played a role in what was going on in our (own) classrooms.* As with any complimentary letter from a student, this felt good. But more than that, it acknowledged something I've tried hard to do, that is, to remain open to the fact that people come to my classes with their own beliefs and values. And those are to be respected, even when challenging them.

One way of achieving that is to be guided in teaching by principles that also hold for the kind of change you want to see and achieve with students.

The following principles inform my Social Reform Perspective.

1. *The goal of all education is the betterment of society, individually and collectively.*

2. *My practice as an educator must align with my view of the world. It must be principled.*

3. *Each learner is equally important, therefore so too is my relationship with her/him.*

4. *Alignment between my beliefs, intentions, strategies, and forms of assessment is central to effective teaching. And those alignments are often very deeply rooted with little scope to change. Any tensions between beliefs, intentions, strategies, and assessment are particularly painful and disruptive to my goals.*

5. *Power exists in teaching and learning relationships regardless of one's dominant teaching perspective. How power is acknowledged, deployed, and harnessed is particularly important in Social Reform teaching.*

Embracing and sharing power with learners is important and requires vulnerability as a teacher. Lave and Wenger (1991) describe this as "*decentering* common notions of mastery and pedagogy" (p. 94, emphasis original). Challenging learners towards reflexivity requires that a teacher demonstrate such reflexivity. Surprisingly to some, so too is setting high expectations. This helps learners transcend limitations imposed by themselves, others, and society at-large. Knowles articulated this very clearly:

> *A democratic philosophy is characterized by a concern for the development of persons, a deep conviction as to the worth of every individual and faith that people will make the right decisions for themselves if given the necessary information and support. It gives precedence to the growth of people over the*

accomplishment of things when these two values are in conflict. It emphasizes the release of human potential over the control of human behavior. (p. 60, emphasis original)

Students who are perceived to be disadvantaged in educational contexts are not served by measuring their performance to a different (usually lower) standard of performance. Instead, identifying deficiencies in their prior learning or study skills, helping them develop strategies to mitigate such gaps, and working with them to manage and integrate these into their workload, better serves their interests and society's.

SOCIAL REFORM PERSPECTIVE IN PRACTICE

I joined the fight for queer rights in 1983. There were two "fights" going on: one with society (external) and one within myself (internal). For me, advocating for my human rights was also a process of unlearning homophobia and heterocentrism. In educating others I was educating myself. A decade later I was also working with people with mental illness and persons with addictions. The ways in which stigmatization and marginalization were operationalized against each of these communities varied. But the societal messaging received by each was consistent: *you are not important, you are not valuable or valued, you are, in fact, a problem.* Thus the internal and external fights remained, though my position as educator changed, since my own status in relation to each community was different.

A common challenge to all three communities is vulnerability to HIV/AIDS. Queer men, drug users and persons with mental illness are all much more likely to be living with HIV in western liberal democracies. My role in community education, university-based HIV/AIDS social research and community-based HIV/AIDS social research evolved as my understanding of the dynamics of oppression deepened. At the same time I began teaching at university, and I encountered normative practices and structural requirements wholly foreign to my community-educator self.

My educational practice has included classrooms, street corners, conferences, mass media, telephones and websites. My "students" have been peers, colleagues, family, strangers, even adversaries. My beliefs and intentions about the transformative potential of education have evolved over time. I have become more committed to this potentiality, rather than less. My frustration with aligning my actions along these principles has also increased. I have been that "unhopeful educator" that Freire (1997, p. 75) described. Paradoxically it is in more formal learning contexts that I find this lack of hopefulness particularly challenging.

My experience as an educator, a learner, and a student reflects Lave and Wenger's (1991) "historical production, transformation and change of persons" (p. 51). My participation in this historical production began when I became a learner, at home with my parents, siblings and extended family. As I moved into the formal realm of primary education the nature of my participation was shaped very much by the structure created to "educate" me. In general terms, these systems served me well for many years. It is difficult to make a claim they have not, given the levels of educational attainment I have achieved.

Except that, to a significant extent, these achievements were *in spite of* the limitations of the enterprise of public education. The inconsistent and at times poor alignment of educational systems with my own educational and social needs led me to question the purpose of (my) education. It would take me several years and my development of critical consciousness through community education and activism (and post-graduate study) for me to understand these dynamics. Without the informal, community-based learning, my formal education would have been insufficient. Each was enhanced (and complemented) by the other. Sadly this is a *post hoc* analysis: were these sorts of perspectives integrated into my secondary and post-secondary educational experiences, perhaps I would have identified a different tack to take than withdrawal and disengagement. Perhaps.

Paradoxically, it was the cynicism with the educational enterprise that motivated me to return to the university for post-graduate study. In a sort of pedagogical triangulation, I was able to take my understanding of the historical production of persons through education and reframe it as opportunity: initially an opportunity for me, but eventually as opportunity for society, through my educational practice.

Education is not the issue; how educational systems shape us and our society is. The challenge is to create spaces—within systems or external to them, as necessary—where educational achievement aligns with the principles of the Social Reform perspective. For me, this is very much a work in progress.

REFERENCES

Arthur, J., Davies, I., & Hahn, C. (2008). Introduction to the Sage handbook of education for citizenship and democracy. In J. Arthur, I. Davies & C. Hahn (Eds.) *The Sage handbook of education for citizenship and democracy* (pp. 1-10). Los Angeles: Sage Publications.

Bourdieu, Pierre (1997). The forms of capital. In A. H. Halsey, H. Lauder, P. Brown & A. Stuart Wells (Eds.) *Education: Culture, economy, society* (pp. 46-58). New York: Oxford University Press.

Butterwick, S., & Egan, J. P. (2010). Sociology of adult and continuing education: Some key understandings for the field of practice. In A. D. Rose, C. E. Kasworm & J. M. Ross-Gordon (Eds.) *Handbook of adult and continuing education* (pp. 113-122). San Francisco: Jossey-Bass.

Freire, P. (1997). *Pedagogy of the heart* (D. Macedo & A. Oliveira, Trans.). New York: Continuum.

Freire, P. (1970). *Pedagogy of the Oppressed*. D. Macedo & A. Oliveira, Trans.) New York: Continuum.

Freire, P. (1998). *Teachers as Cultural Worker: Letters to Those Who Dare to Teach* (D. Macedo, D. Koike & A. Oliveira, Trans). Boulder USA: Westview Press.

Groener, Z. (2006). Adult education and social transformation. In S. B. Merriam, B. C. Courtenay and R.M Cervero (Eds.) *Global issues and adult education: Perspectives from Latin America, Southern Africa and the United States* (pp. 5-14). San Francisco: Jossey-Bass, Inc.

Hall, B. L., Clover, D. E., Crowther, J., & Scandrett, E. (2012). Introduction. In B. L. Hall, D. E. Clover, J. Crowther and E. Scandrett (Eds.) *Learning and Education for a Better World: The Role of Social Movements (pp. ix-xvi).* Boston: Sense Publishers.

hooks, b. (1994). *Teaching to transgress: Education as the practice of freedom.* New York: Routledge.

Knowles, M. S. (1980) *The modern practice of adult education: From andragogy to pedagogy.* Englewood Cliffs: Prentice Hall/Cambridge.

Lave, J. & Wenger, E. (1991). *Situated learning: Legitimate peripheral participation.* New York: Cambridge University Press.

Pratt, D. D. (1993). Andragogy after twenty-five years. In Sharan
    Merriam (Ed.), *Adult learning theory: An update* (pp. 15-25).
    San Francisco: Jossey-Bass, Ina.

SECTION III

Section II provided a personal description of each perspective on teaching. This Section will explore deeper, often hidden, aspects of those same perspectives. Chapter 9 introduces tools to analyse, compare and contrast perspectives. Chapter 10 applies those tools to map the differences between perspectives. Chapter 11 introduces the *Teaching Perspectives Inventory* (TPI) as a means of profiling individual and collective orientations to teaching. Finally, Chapter 12 addresses the evaluation of teaching in ways that are equitable and scholarly while respecting the plurality of good teaching represented in this book.

Section III should persuade you that teachers cannot simply choose among perspectives any more than they can choose among personalities.

CHAPTER 9
Analytical Tools
Tactical Knowledge, Strategic & Normative Beliefs, and Types of Power

Daniel D. Pratt

INTRODUCTION

The chapters in Section II, each in a unique way, answer the question, "What is it like to think about teaching from these different perspectives?" Presented as they are, in different voices and using different types of descriptions, the chapters may have sparked a variety of reactions in you. Did you, for example, see an image of yourself in the "mirror" of one or more chapters? Did you find yourself rejecting one or more of the perspectives? Or, did you find yourself strongly reacting to parts of each? This chapter takes us further and provides tools to compare and contrast perspectives. But first I want to address some potential misunderstandings; after that, we will consider a set of belief structures and types of power that form the foundation for teaching perspectives.

As you read Chapters 4 through 8 you may have felt there was some overlap between perspectives. Indeed, there is, due to the fact that similar (even identical) actions, intentions, and beliefs can be found in more than one perspective. We may, for example, have similar intentions about helping people reflect or think critically about something. As a result, we may have similar beliefs about the importance of higher-level questions in promoting effective learning. However, the kinds of questions we ask, the way in which we ask those questions, and the way we listen and respond when people respond to our questions is directly related to our beliefs about learning, knowledge, and what would be most effective in helping people achieve those ends.

Similarly, every perspective shares a regard for the dignity of learners and the need to respect that dignity in all aspects of teaching. Yet, the way in which it manifests may vary across perspectives, depending on other beliefs that interact with this view of personal dignity and its relationship to learning. Any belief, in isolation from other beliefs, is not a reliable indicator of one's perspective on teaching.

`Two points are important to emphasize here: First, perspectives are not defined by any one belief; nor is any belief the exclusive property of one perspective. Perspectives share individual beliefs but are characterized by a unique belief structure, that is, a cluster of interrelated beliefs. The cluster of beliefs, in turn, interacts in such a way as to not only define the perspective but to influence the nuance of meaning for each of the beliefs. Thus, an affiliation with two or three perspectives is to be expected. Although perspectives represent philosophical orientations to teaching, they are not mutually exclusive orientations.

This overlap of perspectives leads to two common misunderstandings. First, because many instructional actions (e.g., techniques or methods) are common across perspectives, many people mistakenly confuse perspectives with teaching methods. I have had people say to me, "I use all five of these, depending on who I'm teaching and what we're trying to accomplish." To these people, the perspectives seem more like techniques that they can choose among as teaching conditions change.

Because actions are the most visible (and reinforcing) aspect of perspectives, it is quite understandable that perspectives can be mistakenly confused with teaching methods. But, as discussed in detail in Section I, methods are the visible "tip" of teaching; beliefs and intentions, the core of the perspectives, are invisible.

The second misunderstanding also relates to common aspects. People often say, "More than one of these perspectives 'fits' who I am and what I do as an instructor." These people have, quite correctly, identified overlapping beliefs shared by two or three perspectives. As a result, they resist any hint of being adequately described by just a single perspective and want to claim two or three as their orientation to teaching. This is entirely in keeping with the original research that yielded these perspectives on teaching. As I've said elsewhere (Pratt, 1992a; 2002; 2004; 2005; Collins & Pratt, 2011; Pratt, Boll, & Collins, 2007; Pratt, et al., 2012), most teachers hold not just one, but often two and sometimes three perspectives. Their fundamental philosophical orientation to teaching might be more accurately seen as a combination of perspectives. However, one perspective is usually more dominant while the others act as auxiliary or backup perspectives. That is, there is usually something about one perspective that is more central to people's values and personal philosophies than other perspectives. No teacher we studied held all five perspectives as dominant views of teaching.

In every case, the teachers we studied, through interviews and observations, were attempting to match pedagogical means (actions) to educational ends (intentions). Unfortunately, too often the emphasis was on the means, i.e., the actions of teaching, without due consideration of the ends. Yet more rare was any mention of the underlying belief structures that gave meaning, direction, and justification to both the means and ends of teaching. Even activities that were assumed to be neutral, such as lectures and discussions, wittingly or not, were infused with intentionality and justified by tacit beliefs related to knowledge, learning, and the assumed or expected role of a teacher.

This chapter provides four analytical tools for probing those deeper aspects of our teaching: tactical knowledge; strategic beliefs; normative beliefs; and types of power that characterize each perspective. **Tactical knowledge** is visible in the actions and routines that characterize someone's teaching and in the moments of adjusting intentions and actions to evolving circumstances. **Strategic beliefs** refer to the underlying epistemic and legitimating beliefs that support those routines, e.g., understanding and explaining why adjustments in intent and action may be necessary or justified. **Normative beliefs** are the social and cultural norms we enact and inhabit as educators. They are often unconsciously expressed in the roles, responsibilities, and relationships we develop with learners. The chapter ends with a brief discussion of **types of power** that resolve into four forms of control and authority within each perspective.

TACTICAL KNOWLEDGE (AND SKILLS)

Certainly, all teachers develop routines—actions they engage in with some regularity—that represent their 'style' of teaching. It may be the way in which an instructor begins a class or session, reviews an assigned reading, asks questions, bridges from one session to an-

other, leads discussions, or responds to people's questions. Whatever the routine, it becomes a relatively stable and predictable way
in which the person finds his or her style as a teacher.

Effective teachers use a variety of tactics to achieve desired
intentions. More experienced teachers tend to have a well-devel-
oped repertoire of activities and adjust their tactical knowledge to
evolving circumstances. They move easily between activities such
as:

- planning one or more sessions
- beginning and ending instructional sessions
- bridging between sessions
- adjusting explanations or lectures to the audience
- guiding or facilitating discussions
- transitioning between topics
- asking different kinds of questions
- clarifying misunderstandings
- providing feedback to learners

Routines, procedures, and instructional techniques are not difficult to learn; they are essentially actions that can be performed in
various ways, serving a host of different purposes or intentions. They
are necessary, but not sufficient, for effective teaching. Indeed, one
of the features that distinguishes novices from veteran teachers is
the ability to be flexible and adaptive, even creative, with common
routines, procedures, and techniques: deciding when to involve quiet
members, how to correct someone, how to move a discussion to a
new level of analysis, what to do when attention is waning, how to
deal with resistance to learning, knowing when people are ready for
a change in direction, and so forth. This is tactical knowledge because it goes beyond enacting scripts and cookbook recipes of technique or routine to incorporate decision-making and judgment gained
from experience.

However, even tactical knowledge must have ground upon
which to justify itself if challenged. Whether under the press of evaluation or the quiet of reflection, a teacher's ability to know 'why'
provides justification for both teaching actions and intentions. To
know when and how to adjust routines, procedures, and/or techniques may separate beginners from experienced teachers; but such

tactical knowledge must ultimately be answerable to 'Why?' for one to move beyond accumulated experience to reflective expertise. This is the role of strategic beliefs. Strategic beliefs provide the basis for justifying tactical decisions.

STRATEGIC BELIEFS

Epistemic Beliefs

Everyone has a personal epistemology, that is, a way of deciding when something (or someone) is true or believable. Some base their views on what they can see, hear, touch, or otherwise empirically observe in the world about them. Some base their belief on the credibility or authority of the source, e.g., doctors, lawyers, minsters, parents, and even teachers. Others may find truth in their personal experience of living and interpreting the world. Still others may believe that the only 'truth' is that which is divine.

Although the topic is important, it is beyond the scope of this chapter to go into detail about the nature of epistemic beliefs more generally. Rather, the focus here is on beliefs that govern someone's teaching. Those epistemic beliefs fall into three categories:

- beliefs about the content that is to be taught and learned;
- beliefs about the nature of learning; and
- beliefs about assessment, in particular, what would suffice as evidence that someone has learned that content.

Collectively, these epistemic beliefs constitute a personal epistemology that, consciously or not, guides our teaching and the assessment of learning. Therefore, epistemic beliefs form the heart of each perspective on teaching.

As a way of explaining epistemic beliefs, think of a course or topic you taught and ask yourself the following questions:

Content

- Within the field or subject area you teach, identify something that is essential for people to learn. Then explain why that is that essential.

Learning

- What is an effective way for people to learn that which you have identified as essential?
- What problems do they have learning it? Why do you think they have those problems?

Assessment

- What is a good or valid indicator that people have learned that essential aspect(s) of your field or subject area?
- What distinguishes between levels of achievement or performance of that essential aspect of what you want them to learn?

We don't usually talk about content, learning, and assessment using the term epistemology, but it is appropriate in this case because I am trying to emphasize that perspectives on teaching are not just preferences; they are contrasting philosophical orientations to teaching, learning, and assessment. Each perspective is built upon a foundation of epistemic beliefs that forms the basis for **deciding** what to teach, how to teach, and how to assess whether or not our 'content' has been learned. Epistemic beliefs also form the basis for **justifying** what we do and why we do it. Thus, our epistemic beliefs guide us to notions of truth, sources of authority, and forms of evidence that we do not easily surrender (e.g., see: Chapter 3 for epistemic beliefs related to learning and knowing).

When our notions of truth, authority, and evidence come into conflict with others, especially in matters where we hold strong conviction or values, the clash can have serious consequences. As an example, consider the story of a friend and her experience with conflicting sources of authority and forms of evidence.

Several years ago, my 9-year-old daughter was recommended for a special class for youngsters who were emotionally or mentally handicapped. When I first learned of the school's decision I was shocked and asked to meet with her principal and teacher to discuss the matter. Sometime in late October I was invited to attend a meeting to discuss their recommendation. When I arrived at the school the staff was already meeting and

I was asked to wait outside the conference room for 15 minutes before joining the meeting.

When invited in I was introduced to eight people, many of whom I knew from previous events at the school—the principal, vice-principal, area counselor, nurse, learning assistance teacher, district psychologist, special needs teacher, and, of course, my daughter's fourth-grade teacher. The principal began by expressing his confidence in the wisdom of the group to come to the best decision for my daughter. They had, of course, carefully considered the matter and reached a consensus that she should be transferred immediately to the special needs class.

When I asked the basis for their decision all eyes turned to the district psychologist. It seems she had "evidence" which was irrefutable. She had administered a standardized intelligence test and was quite confident that it was a "true" indicator of my daughter's ability. Even though others in the room had challenged the assessment, based on classroom observations, their evidence was considered less valid than standardized intelligence test scores.

Again I was shocked, and raised objections, looking to the class room teacher for support, commenting on the social and academic achievements I had witnessed at home and in her classroom. While I talked about my observations at home, and tried in vain to enlist the classroom teacher's support, my evidence was not convincing. It was, as someone in the room said, necessary to be as 'objective' as possible in this matter, and not let our personal wishes interfere with our good judgment. Besides, there was more reliable evidence: intelligence test scores.

While I argued with personal anecdotes the psychologist countered with data that were considered more 'objective'. It was, the psychologist said, a matter of trying not to be 'subjective' in this matter but, rather, to trust the best evidence available— the intelligence test scores. Most in the room agreed, the psychologist's data was the most trustworthy evidence. Nothing I could say or offer carried sufficient 'truth' to counter stan-

*dardized intelligence tests. Their evidence was simply irrefut-
able; my daughter should be placed in the special needs class.*

What my friend experienced was a clash of epistemologies, that is, beliefs about what kinds of evidence and authority are the best indicators of some 'truth.' In this case, her evidence was not sufficient to argue against the more 'objective' evidence of intelligence tests. As a result, she withdrew her daughter from the school and enrolled her in a small, private school where they discovered she had a learning disability that interfered with her reading and concentration.

In teaching, we are constantly making decisions based on our personal epistemology, decisions about how to represent our content, decisions about how to help people learn, and how to assess that learning. In essence, we are deciding whether or not people have learned something based on implicit or explicit understandings of what it means 'to learn' and 'to know'. From that we trust some kind of evidence (performance, writing, tests, learners' testimony, experience, etc.) as the basis for judging the effects of our teaching and the extent of people's learning. It is the nature of that evidence and our confidence in it that points toward the epistemic dimensions of our perspective. Epistemic beliefs also give support and meaning to the ways in which teachers explain why they teach the way they do, that is, to their strategic *legitimating beliefs*.

Legitimating Beliefs

Legitimating beliefs help teachers explain (to themselves or to others) why something works or does not work. They are used strategically when reflecting on teaching or justifying it to someone— students, colleagues, or even parents of students.

Teachers often reveal their legitimating beliefs in the form of conditional statements, as in—*when I do this, here's what happens.* Such statements give voice and reason to decision-making as teachers adjust to changing circumstances. Here's an example of what a physics teacher told me as she explained her intentional use of something called 'productive failure' when teaching students:

*If I intentionally have students working in small groups on a
problem that I know they cannot answer in the allotted time,
they will experience 'productive failure'. After they experience*

this 'failure' they will be better prepared to understand my explanation of how to solve the problem. And they will learn that 'failure' is an expected part of doing science.

She was quite clear about the rationale and the effect of having students intentionally fail an assignment. As it turns out, she has a lot of evidence to support this decision and her belief in the appropriateness of this 'technique' (Holmes et al., 2014; Singer et al., 2005). Thus, her legitimating beliefs are supported by evidence and form a basis for predicting that this pedagogical move is strategic and likely to succeed in helping students be prepared for her explanation of complex problem solving. It had the added bonus of helping students learn that 'failure' is to be expected when doing physics.

Legitimating beliefs, then, are statements of conviction or commitment that justify actions or intentions. They are most obvious and necessary when teachers are challenged about what they teach or how they teach. For example, here's a statement of someone explaining (legitimating) how and why he teaches ethics in professional practice the way he does:

Nothing is value-free or politically neutral to the lives of my students and their students. This has significant implications for my teaching. It means that I teach by my comportment as much as by my words. If I wish to teach compassion, I must be compassionate; if I wish to teach ethically appropriate behavior, I can only do so by being ethically sound in my own actions. This means, of course, there is always a hidden curriculum at play, one that is hidden from my view, but not from the view of those who are watching me teach—my students. Thus, it means that I must not only espouse these things, I must live them, especially when under the watchful eyes of learners.

Strategic beliefs—both epistemic and legitimating—are clarified and reinforced through reflection on experience, that is, through enacting our tactical knowledge and reflecting on its effect, both intended and unintended. They are rooted in personal epistemologies and commitments, and, like other beliefs, are held with different degrees of clarity, confidence, and centrality. Most teachers eventually develop a set of beliefs that explain and legitimate what they do. However, strategic beliefs are just one part of the inter-connected web of belief structures that make up perspectives on teaching. Next we look at another part of that web of belief structures: Normative beliefs.

Normative Beliefs: Roles, Responsibilities, and Relationships

The second set of beliefs is related to an educator's role, responsibility, and relationship with learners (Pratt, 1991; 1992a; 1992b; Pratt & Nesbit, 2000). These are the social norms of a teacher's perspective, much like the social norms that govern the interactions within other social groups, for example, a family, work unit, congregation, or club. Every social group develops a set of norms related to roles, responsibilities, and relationships. In families, for example, the roles of mother, father, children, grandparents, cousins, etc. revolve around individual responsibilities and acceptable (and unacceptable) ways of relating to each other.

Although they vary from culture to culture and across historical periods, it is usually clear to the members of a group how their roles, responsibilities, and relationships define appropriate ways of interacting. Teachers routinely assume well-defined roles within their field, their discipline, their culture, or some combination of all three. From those roles they enact appropriate responsibilities and relationships with their learners. For example, several of the teachers we studied saw their primary role to be that of content expert, responsible for accurately representing and delivering the content to the learners. These teachers, most often, characterized their relationship with learners as friendly, but impersonal (at arms length or business-like); and their relationship with learners was not to influence evaluation or assessment of learning. Others described their role as a combination of friend and counselor, primarily concerned with developing a sense of personal agency in their learners. Their primary responsibilities were the provision of support and challenge. They set high standards but provided sufficient support and encouragement to ensure people's success. As you can imagine, their relationship with learners was more personal, occasionally developing into a friendship that extended beyond the boundaries of teacher and learner.

The literature on teaching adults suggests a number of different roles for teachers: tutor, facilitator, instructor, preceptor, guide, or even professor. However, as much as we might choose a role for ourselves, those roles are all social, cultural, and historical productions, more than the creation of individual teachers. The way in which each is enacted, and the extent to which it conforms to the expectations of a community, determine whether or not someone's teaching is seen as 'legitimate' or worthy. In other words, the role of teacher we occupy is a normative role and must be 'performed' in accordance with the norms of a community of practice. Normative, by definition, means considered normal within social and cultural expectations.

Whatever role a teacher occupies, normative beliefs define patterns of authority, communication, and relationship. It may be easiest to explain this through a series of questions about your experience teaching. If you haven't had any teaching experience, think of what you would like to teach, the learners that you would teach, and a possible setting or context for your hypothetical teaching. Then explain what you see as your role. How would you describe your role as a teacher?

For some of you this will be easy to answer; others might want to check the list of possible roles below and select the name(s) that best describes their role. It is not unusual to think of more than one role, so don't limit yourself. However, if you choose several, try to look for the underlying or central meaning that links the roles you identified. What is the essence of those roles for you as teacher?

Instructor	Co-inquirer
Co-traveler	Mentor
Presenter	Co-learner
Interrogator	Expert
Change-agent	Role model
Explorer	Coach
Guide	Provocateur
Facilitator	Resource
Planner	Friend

Each role suggests a set of responsibilities and a particular kind of relationship with learners. Some suggest responsibilities that are tied to content (e.g., clear presentation, ability to clarify, organizing, and pacing of content). Other roles such as friend, co-traveler, and co-learner suggest more about the relationship you want to have with your learners, as well as an educational posture you might take with regards to the content.

Given the role(s) you have selected, what does that entail? What responsibilities are associated with the role or roles you identified? What distinguishes your role(s) from the others in terms of your responsibilities? What does it suggest about the relationship you have (or try to have) with learners? Try to go beyond the name of the role and specify what it means in terms of responsibility and relationship.

Then, take it one step further. Can you see any relationship between roles and views about knowledge, learning, and/or the assessment of learning? As you may have already guessed, the roles we assume as instructors are a product of the beliefs we hold about knowledge, learning, and the assessment of learning (e.g., Pratt, 1992a; 1992b; Tweed & Lehman, 2002). What we believe about knowledge affects our role and responsibilities as a teacher; and what we believe to be our responsibilities affects how we assess people's learning. No other aspect of teaching is more indicative of someone's perspective than his or her preferred means of assessing learning.

In turn, beliefs about one's role and authority, in relation to content, have a powerful influence on what might be considered believable evidence that learners have mastered our content. Thus, normative and strategic beliefs are reciprocally determinate of each other.

This complex web of beliefs – epistemic, legitimating, and normative – provides the foundation for perspectives on teaching. It also provides the basis for four types of power evident within perspectives.

TYPES OF POWER

Beliefs are not benign; they are substantial precursors to privilege and power in every teaching perspective. Just as beliefs and ideals are present, though not necessarily acknowledged, in each perspective, power is also present in every teaching session, and in every perspective on teaching (Brookfield, 2013). For some, it is hidden, kept out of the conversation, assumed not to be an issue. For others, it is a part of the explicit agenda of teaching and directly related to the goals of teaching.

Within the five perspectives we found four types of power related to beliefs. Each type of power is a slightly different reflection of epistemic, strategic, and normative beliefs. The four types of power are:

1. *Social or institutional title and role:* Some teachers establish patterns of communication and relationships with learners by calling attention to their official titles or role designations. This intensifies their power and authority in relation to learners and to the discourse of learning. While it is diminishing in many institutions, it is still quite common in some situations, for example in the military, where it is justified on the basis of normative structures of rank and authority. Where training mirrors professional or vocational practice, the normative structures of practice are replicated in the normative structures of training.

2. *Language or symbol system of content:* There are teachers who do nothing, or very little, to translate their expertise and knowledge into language that is accessible to learners. This slows the process of learning and perpetuates an imbalance of power and dependency in relation to the content. This is often justified on the basis of the need to uphold standards regarding the need for a body of 'foundational knowledge' in its authorized form, deemed necessary for further training or for practice.

3. *Gatekeeper to practice:* Teachers are often expected to make judgments about learners' readiness to move ahead in their careers. For example, when they write letters of reference for students, teachers hold a form of covert power over the students' future. This type of power comes from normative beliefs related to the teacher's status and authority within a community of practice, an acknowledged expertise related to that status, and an officially recognized responsibility for judging when (and if) learners are ready to enter practice.

4. *Assessment of learning:* When teachers have authority over the assessment of learning, they shape and direct peoples' learn-

ing and establish what counts as legitimate knowledge. This is the most taken for granted yet prevalent form of power held by teachers. It accrues from authority over decisions related to what will be learned and judgments as to when people have learned it. The combination of epistemic beliefs about the role of teacher in relation to knowledge (e.g., whether the teacher dispenses knowledge or encourages the construction of knowledge) is significantly related to the exercise of power over the assessment of learning.

I am not suggesting these are the only types of power manifest in teaching; clearly, there are important issues of power based on class, race, gender, age, culture, etc. However, among the 253 teachers studied, these forms of power were most readily observed and associated with epistemic, strategic, and normative beliefs. In our interviews, for example, we found that teachers holding a dominant Transmission or Apprenticeship Perspective made no mention of power; nor was it openly addressed in the teaching we observed. Although most certainly present, it was not a part of their focus or agenda. Thus, although not necessarily by intent, power remained 'under-the-table' in their teaching.

On the other hand, power was 'on-the-table' as an important issue with many whose dominant perspective was Developmental or Nurturing. Indeed, those teachers often talked of empowering learners, or of trying to reduce the effects of the power differential between themselves and learners. For these teachers, power was made explicit and became, for many, an important aspect of their teaching.

Social Reform teachers took a variety of positions regarding power, but the most vocal and visible position was similar to that shown by the radical educators described in Chapter 8. For Social Reform teachers, power was an important part of their ideals and central to all aspects of their work. For these teachers, power was not just on the table, 'it was the table.'

Brookfield (2013) clarifies how even the most non-directive and low key facilitator is exercising power. He provides a thoughtful and articulate explication of power and reminds us to be more mindful of the insidious nature of power in educational settings—the small acts of exclusion, stereotyping, and marginalization that are daily acts of 'micro-aggression.' Such a mindfulness can only be activated once we are aware of the omnipresence of power. Thus, while power is a fact of life in every teaching situation, it is acknowledged and represented quite differently across perspectives.

SUMMARY

Perspectives are not defined by, nor can they be recognized by, isolated actions, intentions, or beliefs. They are a complex web of interdependent beliefs and commitments. Like a spider's web, each belief and commitment is a necessary and integral part of the whole structure; tug on one belief and the entire web responds. Each belief is dependent on other beliefs for its meaning and place within the structure of the perspective. Chapter 10 explores those in more detail.

Because perspectives do overlap, it is necessary to be as specific as possible about their essential and unique character. Yet, it would be wrong to suggest that each perspective can be definitively drawn by listing beliefs, intentions, and actions. That would miss the central point thus far: that perspectives are based on complex, interrelated belief structures. Therefore, the next chapter will provide a portrait of each perspective, and identify the most essential attributes and relationships among its defining belief structures.

REFERENCES

Brookfield, S. D. (2013). *Powerful techniques for teaching in life-long learning*. Milton Keyes: Open University Press.

Collins, J. B., & Pratt, D. D. (2011). The Teaching Perspectives Inventory at ten years and 100,000 respondents: Reliability and validity of a teacher self-report inventory. *Adult Education Quarterly*, 61(4), 358-375.

Holmes, N. G., Day, J., Park, A. H. K, Bonn, D. A., & Roll, I. (2014). Making the failure more productive: Scaffolding the invention process to improve inquiry behaviors and outcomes in invention activities. *Instructional Science*. 42(4), 523-538.

Pratt, D. D. (1991). Conceptions of self within China and the United States. *International Journal of Intercultural Relations* (USA) 15(3), 285-310.

Pratt, D. D. (1992a). Conceptions of teaching. *Adult Education Quarterly*, 42(4), 203-220.

Pratt, D. D. (1992b). Chinese conceptions of learning and teaching: A Westerner's attempt at understanding. *International Journal of Lifelong Education* (UK) 1b (4), 301-319.

Pratt, D.D. & Nesbit, T. (2000). Cultures and discourses of teaching. In Arthur Wilson & Elizabeth Hayes (Eds.). *Handbook of Adult and Continuing Education.* San Francisco: Jossey-Bass.

Pratt, D. D. (2002). Good teaching: one size fits all? In Jovita Ross-Gordon (Ed.) *An update on teaching theory*, San Francisco: Jossey-Bass, 93, 5-16.

Pratt, D. D. (2004). Ethical reasoning in teaching adults. In M. Galbraith (Ed.) *Adult education methods.* (3rd ed.). Malabar, Florida: Krieger Publishing.

Pratt, D. D. (2005). Teaching. In L.M. English (Ed.), *International Encyclopedia of Adult Education.* New York: Palgrave Macmillan, 610-615.

Pratt, D. D., Boll, S. L., & Collins, J. B. (2007). Towards a plurality of perspectives for nurse educators. *Nursing Philosophy*, 8, 49-59.

Pratt, D. D., Sadownik, L., Jarvis-Selinger, S. (2012). *Pedagogical BIASes and clinical teaching in medicine.* English, L. M. (Ed.), *Health and Adult Learning.* University of Toronto Press, pp. 273-296.

Singer, S. R., Hilton, M. L., & Schweingruber, H. A. (2005). *America's lab report: Investigations in high school science.* Available on-line from the National Academies Press at: http://www.nap.edu/catalog/11311.html

Tweed, R. G., & Lehman, D. R. (2002). Learning considered within a cultural context: Confucian and Socratic approaches, *American Psychologist*, 57(2), 89-99.

CHAPTER 10
Analyzing Perspectives

Daniel D. Pratt and Dave Smulders

IDENTIFYING COMMITMENTS AND
BELIEF STRUCTURES

By now you will have gathered that perspectives are like multiple types of intelligence, evident and yet elusive entities. As through a lens, we look through our perspectives at what is visible (e.g., teachers' actions) and do not see the properties of the lens itself—commitments and belief structures. However, captured within the "lens" of perspectives, teachers' notions of learners, content, context, ideals, and what it means to teach are interpreted and held in place by their commitments and belief structures. These notions both enable and limit what teachers think about their own teaching and the teaching of others. Only by excavating these underlying structural properties can we begin to understand the full range of perspectives on teaching.

Chapter 9 spelled out the analytical tools for digging deeper into perspectives on teaching. This chapter uses those tools to reveal the underlying structure of each perspective, specifically: key beliefs, specific focus within the General Model of Teaching, primary role and commitment, and power issues. In addition, some of the most common teaching difficulties associated with each perspective will be discussed.

Each perspective will be introduced with a snapshot—a skeletal outline of the most essential features of that perspective. The snapshots sketch out only a superficial map of the underlying structures; they are meant to serve as a guide to the more detailed narrative analysis that follows. Because they do not portray the interactive nature of the beliefs and commitments, they are not an adequate or sufficient representation of each perspective. They are offered here as a way of summarizing the essential structures that define and differentiate perspectives.

Introduction

It would be difficult to imagine that anyone has not experienced a Transmission teacher. Virtually every study of teaching has recognized an orientation much like this one. It is safe to assume, therefore, that most readers can recognize this perspective and its central tenets within their own experience, as learner if not as teacher; but not, perhaps, as articulated using the analytical tools just introduced. What, then, do they tell us about this perspective?

Key Belief Structures

Effective Transmission teaching depends, first of all, on an objectivist orientation to knowledge as something that exists independent of the learner and can be manipulated and structured for transfer to learners. Teachers are expected to possess the knowledge that learners need. Indeed, it would be impossible, from this perspective, to be an effective teacher without having considerably more knowledge and skill than one's learners.

Individual differences and difficulties in learning are accommodated through adjustments in the delivery of content (breaking the content into smaller pieces, changing the sequence of presentation, or using different media and methods for delivery). For example, if people are having difficulty with a particular section or content, teachers proceed in smaller steps, slow down the presentation, review more frequently, adjust the content or modify the learning environment. More often than not, however, such teachers assume that learners must adjust to the methods of delivery and presentation, and do the best they can.

Effective teachers must be able to manipulate their content in ways that can help people learn it with as little distortion as possible. Learning, then, is viewed as something that can be controlled by the teacher through manipulating the content and/or its delivery. This means teachers must find effective and efficient ways of organizing the content into manageable pieces or chunks that can be learned within a specific time frame.

Portrait of the Transmission Perspective

The Transmission Perspective: A Snapshot	
General Model	
Key Beliefs	• What is learned should closely resemble what was taught. • The instructional process is shaped and guided by the content and it is the teacher's job to accurately represent that content and productively manage learning. • Teaching is, primarily, a matter of effective delivery of content.
Focus within the General Model	• Connection between teacher and content (Line Z) • Teacher's efficient and effective delivery of content and demonstration of expertise
Primary Role	• Presenter, expert, authority
Primary Responsibilities	• Set standards for achievement • Specify learning objectives • Select and sequence readings and assignments • Make efficient use of instructional time • Give clear and well-organized presentations • Provide answers, directions, clarifications, reviews and summaries • Engage learners at appropriate level and pace

Primary Commitment	• Deep respect for the content, expressed through:
	  - Accurate representation of content
	  - Enthusiasm for the content
	  - Encouraging people to go on in the subject`

Power Issues	• "Under the table" [i.e., assumed not to exist] • Located in knowledge/expertise of teacher and in mastery of language, symbol systems, and tools of the field/profession.

	• Expressed as authority over decisions related to content and assessment of learning
Assessment Strategies	• Developing objective means of assessment • Concerned with reproducing information or procedures according to established standards
Common Difficulties	• Adjusting to individual differences among learners • Empathizing with people who cannot understand the content • Providing effective opportunities for engagement with the content • Anticipating where (in content) and why learners will have difficulty • Shifting roles, e.g., from teaching advanced learners to teaching novice learners. • Thinking about teaching as more than lecturing or talking

It also means learning outcomes must be both observable and predictable. It is expected, for example, that content should be represented and taught in ways that allow for accurate assessment of learning. Consequently, it is common among those who have a strong commitment to content also to emphasize behavioral objectives and specific competencies which learners are to achieve. Vagueness in terms of what is to be learned is seen as a hindrance to learning, teaching, and assessment.

Primary Role

More often than not, the popular media portray teachers as coming from this perspective, where teachers are passionate and articulate presenters with a lifetime of devotion to their discipline. It would be interesting to know how deeply embedded and influential this image is within the psyche of teachers in adult and higher education. While most readers can probably think of memorable teachers that were some approximation of those movie images, we are certain that you also have examples of teachers that were considerably less than articulate or passionate; perhaps they were not even particularly skilled presenters. The truth is, whether animated or boring, passionate or stolid, adept or inept, Transmission teachers are devoted to their content. As such, their primary role is to dispense and defend that content as accurately, efficiently, and completely as possible. To be good at this they have to be able to plan, conduct, and evaluate learning in an objective, rational, technical manner.

When this happens, the process of teaching is often characterized using a language of production and control, referring to modules, delivery systems, input and output, minimal competencies, and referring to learners as the target audience. While the raw materials (learners) may vary when they begin the process, it is assumed that it is the responsibility of the teacher to bring all learners to some minimum level of competence at the point of exit.

Failure to learn is usually then attributed to the learner's lack of motivation. It is not unusual, for example, to hear teachers talk about a lack of motivation and/or native ability in their learners. They suggest learners don't try hard enough, or are lazy, unmotivated, or going through the motions. Perhaps they are trying to get by without really being committed to the content, without applying themselves. In other words, when Transmission teachers are faced with students' failure to learn, it is easy for them to assume it is the learners who are at fault.

Primary Commitment

As mentioned above, people holding this as their dominant perspective tend to have a deep respect for, and commitment to, the content they are teaching. They are enthusiastic, even excited, about the content and sometimes disappointed when students don't show the same enthusiasm (respect) for the material. Consequently, they may set high standards and expectations for their learners, just as they have for themselves, regarding learning and mastery of the subject matter.

Sometimes their respect and commitment go a bit too far when individuals ascribe qualities to their discipline that are, to say the least, contentious. Some teachers, for example, see themselves and/ or their content as a guardian of academic or professional standards. Failure is then interpreted as a necessary effect or by-product of screening out those who are not up to the standards of the field, discipline, or profession.

Power Issues

Power, within this perspective, is located in the knowledge and expertise of the teacher. It is embodied in the person of the teacher, which means that learners often come willingly to encounter this expertise, thus perpetuating an imbalance of power between teacher and learners.

As mentioned in Chapter 9, in the studies that led to this book, we found that teachers predominantly aligned with the Transmission Perspective made little or no reference to power as part of their personal belief structure or goals for teaching. It was not explicitly mentioned by them as something important in their teaching. It very likely never occurred to them that power might be part of their relationship to learners, content, or society. The process of teaching was understood to be more technical than personal, more objective than subjective, and more neutral than political.

Of course, power exists, even when not acknowledged; one or more of the four types of power mentioned in Chapter 9 is always present and influential in the process and outcomes of learning. Within the Transmission Perspective power is particularly evident in the tools—the language and symbol systems that are representative of the content and/or skills to be learned. Every trade, field, discipline, and profession has its own language for efficiently and effectively communicating between members. Participation on a work site, in a classroom, or in a professional gathering is dependent upon having some fluency with the language or symbol system of the trade or discipline (Wenger 1998). Language and symbol represent powerful means of control and, if not used carefully, can create substantial barriers to effective engagement for learning. Transmission Perspective teachers are usually not aware of this and, therefore, can easily use the discursive tools of their trade as a means of reinforcing existing power relations.

Assessment Strategies

When teachers have authority over the assessment of learning, in fact they have power over both learners and the curriculum; not only do they determine what is to be learned, and how it will be learned, they also determine the outcomes of a program. In effect, teachers become privileged actors in the discourse of education. Regardless of what the goals or objectives say, students will study and reproduce that which they think is going to be assessed. Thus, through this type of power, teachers determine what people will learn, what approaches they will take, and what will count as legitimate knowledge or skill at the end of a program.

It is not too difficult to understand why many teachers from this perspective use assessment as an extension of their authority. Consider the combination of epistemic and normative beliefs that are central to this perspective: objectivist orientation to knowledge, primary role as presenter of content, and a sense of responsibility and loyalty to the content. Transmission teachers sometimes espouse goals of developing critical thinking and problem solving. Yet as much as they may aspire to that intention, it is undermined as soon as they revert to requiring people to reproduce a body of knowledge. Thus, there is an unresolvable tension between the goal of developing critical thinking and the Transmission Perspective on teaching.

Common Difficulties

Our experience suggests there are many teaching from this perspective that are not entertaining or engaging. Very likely you too have experienced teachers that showed too many slides, talked in monotone, lectured to the chalkboard, never knew your name, were disorganized, or trivialized the content and tested on matters that seemed arbitrary and disconnected to life. When teaching is reduced to covering a body of content, or achieving a set of predetermined, irrelevant, or unproblematic goals, the result can be dull and tedious, regardless of perspective.

Many who teach from this perspective pride themselves on their expertise, knowledge, proficiency, and skill, much of which has become automatic to them. One of the most difficult aspects of teaching, for such people, is to empathize with learners who don't understand the content.

For many teachers, this may be the only perspective they have ever known. It might have been the dominant perspective governing their own learning, or it may now be the dominant way of thinking about teaching within their place of employment. In either case, they may have adopted it without question. If this is the case, they have only fleetingly reflected on issues of power or teaching effectiveness. They may never have questioned the power that is inherent in their content expertise or the language of their instruction. They may not have thought about effectiveness in teaching beyond the expansion and refinement of a repertoire of techniques. Indeed, they may not have even thought about whether there is any particular relationship between teaching and learning, and what that might mean for their roles and responsibilities. In other words, if this is the only perspective a teacher has ever known it is very likely to be a difficult shift to consider other perspectives as legitimate views of teaching.

Yet, at its best, teaching from this perspective can be compelling and engaging because the content itself is gripping, or because the teacher is entertaining. Such teaching is evident in organized and enthusiastic lecturers that animate their subject, or individuals that are so committed to their craft or profession that we cannot but embrace and consider that commitment and the subject matter. Effective Transmission teachers are truly dedicated and committed to that which they teach; there is never a sense that they are going through the motions of teaching to simply get to the end of the day.

Introduction

For some readers, Chapter 5 may have given voice to familiar experiences, especially if you have been fortunate enough to learn from a "master," or to apprentice under the tutelage of an experienced mentor within a trade, profession, or community. For others, this may be a somewhat distant portrayal of their experience as an apprentice, a romanticized view of the servitude endured as part of becoming a journey tradesperson or professional. As we mention throughout this book, perspectives encompass both good and bad practice. However, the Apprenticeship Perspective is re-emerging as a dominant force in professional and vocational education, and it is the basis for much exciting work on mentoring.

Key Belief Structures

For Apprenticeship teachers, what is to be learned is often equated with experience and characterized as "craft" knowledge, or knowledge which is embedded in, and derived from, contextually authentic action. Knowledge is believed to be distorted and diminished when abstracted or separated from situations of its applica-

Portrait of the Apprenticeship Perspective

The Apprenticeship Perspective: A Snapshot	
General Model	
Key Beliefs	• This perspective is based on the belief that expert knowledge is best learned in contexts of application and practice. • To abstract the knowledge and wisdom from practice is to drain it of its most essential qualities.
Focus within the General Model	• Dominant elements: context, content, and teacher • Knowledge, skill, and attitudes best learned using authentic tasks • Impossible to separate content from the expert practitioner
Primary Role	• Role model and coach
Primary Responsibilities	• Teach content in authentic, relevant tasks • Provide for observation of expert practitioners • Allow for legitimate participation in authentic practice • Provide coaching and scaffolding . . . what can they handle right now? • Fading of direction and feedback . . . relative to progress and maturity • Make expert thinking, decision-making, and strategies accessible to learners • Teach both domain and strategic content • Domain content: Facts, concepts, procedures, theories • Strategic content: Problem-solving heuristics
Primary Commitmen	• To role and identity as practitioner • To the shared values and standards of the community
Power Issues	• "Craft" knowledge (skill) is power • Role in community determines authority

	• Teachers are gatekeepers to practice
Assessment Strategies	• Linked to authentic tasks • Assessing within the Zone of Proximal Development • Setting contextual standards for achievement
Common Difficulties	• Articulating craft knowledge • Finding relevant and authentic tasks for classroom settings • Teaching those who want quick access to practice • Matching learner capability with authentic tasks

tion. Indeed, to remove knowledge from social contexts of practice is to drain it of its most essential qualities.

On the continuum of personal epistemologies (Chapter 2), this perspective is located midway between objectivism and subjectivism. Unlike the Transmission Perspective, here knowledge is not a discrete body of skills, ideas, facts, procedures, and so forth, which can be learned in one context and applied in another. Instead, it is a set of competencies, skills, and way of relating, as well as performing, within the community. Knowledge is inseparable from the contexts in which it is practiced or applied. It reflects a commitment to its community's values and to acting with competence in the performance of community roles.

Therefore, learning is best done within simulated or real contexts of application where competence, identity, community, and context are inseparably entwined.

Primary Role

Teachers holding this as their dominant perspective are, first and foremost, expert practitioners. Individuals are given the responsibility for teaching others about their expertise, whether in kitchens, physics labs, automotive shops or operating rooms. Experts are the role models and learners the observers of their expertise in action. As learners spend more time observing, and gradually participating, the instructor continues to model more of what is to be learned, while also coaching learners and bringing them into more active roles as members of the community of practice. Coaching is a combination of demonstrating, scaffolding, giving feedback, and gradually fading support and direction as learners mature in their knowledge and expertise.

Primary Commitment

Modeling and coaching constitute a means of enculturating learners into a specific community, that is, into a social grouping with a common sense of purpose and clearly differentiated roles and authority. Remember we defined enculturation in Chapter 3 as "internalizing propositions of meaning and value as appropriate, significant, and true for you". Whether the community is a family, a trade or vocation, a profession, or cultural grouping, the process of learning (enculturation) results from intensive, diversified, and prolonged participation in the work and social relations of the community. The primary commitment of Apprenticeship teachers is to the enculturation of novices into a proper understanding of the relationship between embodied knowledge and the community. This manifests as commitment to a craft, that is, a specialized form of expertise that represents acceptable standards of practice within the community. This knowledge can only be learned in authentic contexts of practice, among the community of workers that make up one's colleagues. Thus, there is a profound respect for the context of practice as the only legitimate site for learning and teaching.

Nonetheless, effective teaching, for Apprenticeship teachers, involves much more than mere demonstration before a willing audience of novices. It means knowing how and when to give learners more responsibility and more diverse roles, so as to push them toward their potential but not exceed it and how to engage with those learners further and further in authentic activity and communication.

Through this process, learners are expected to acquire not just the skills and knowledge of their community, but the commitment and confidence that come with an identity of mastery. That is, they are not just learning *about* something but, more profoundly, learning *to be* something (Jarvis-Selinger, et al., 2012). This unique quality of the Apprenticeship Perspective highlights some interesting points about the learning process and the role of the learner within this perspective.

Some time ago, a friend working as a junior resident in orthopaedics offered his story of starting on the periphery and gradually becoming an accepted and legitimate member of a community of medical professionals:

The journey from "recently graduated medical student" to "fully qualified surgeon" consists of at least 5 years of rotating through various surgical services. The rotations typically last 3 months and each rotation progresses in a similar manner. Entering the surgical changing room at the start of a rotation is a bit like entering a foreign country. The surgeons and anesthetist that I meet will occasionally utter a suspicious greeting, but more often I am simply ignored. I am a foreigner in their world. During the first few weeks the nurses and surgeons that I work with watch me like a hawk. The simplest act, such as putting on my surgical gown, is intensely scrutinized to ensure that I do it correctly. The nurses do not hesitate to inform me when my actions are incorrect. The surgeon has me watch him perform case after case. As a reward for my patience I am allowed to put the dressing on the patient's wound, an act which requires essentially no skill, but one which is nevertheless observed carefully. Throughout this period of indoctrination I remain silent. Day after day conversations flow easily between the nurses and the surgeon as if I am not even in the room. My job is to watch and learn. If I pass these early tests I am given more responsibility. Soon it is my job to close the wound. Gradually the nursing staff becomes more comfortable with my presence. After a month I am no longer an unfamiliar face and some nurses have even learned my name. Occasionally the conversation during surgery will be directed toward me. I now partake in the conversations which occur, although I am very cautious of what I say. In a similar manner I am accepted in the surgical changing room. No longer a complete stranger, I am free to engage in superficial conversation with the surgeons and anesthetists I meet there. Just as the extent of my interaction with the surgical staff increases, so too does my involvement in the operations. If all has gone well, after 2 months I am doing significant portions of many of the operations. Occasionally the surgeon will even leave me to do a very simple case on my own.

During the last month of my rotation I am no longer an outsider, I am one of them. I am included in the conversations and treated as a colleague by the staff. Operations are now more of a team effort between the surgeon and me. We work together to achieve a common goal. Although clearly the junior partner, I am not afraid to offer my own suggestions. At this stage, just as the 3 months are up, the training becomes enjoyable. But then, after saying my good-byes I am off to another service, at another hospital, where the process starts all over again. (Steve Pinney, personal communication).

Doctor Pinney's story is typical of many in apprenticeships, whether in professional schools, vocational or trade schools, or families. Even after four years of undergraduate work at Harvard, four more years of medical school at McGill University, and two years of specialization, he started on the periphery, observing and waiting for the community (particularly the staff surgeon) to decide he was capable of being given meaningful work. Dr. Pinney is now a highly respected orthopaedic surgeon practicing and teaching residents in San Francisco.

Assessment Strategies

Because learning is understood to be a process of socialization into the normative beliefs and values of the community, the evaluation of learning necessarily involves more than the recall of key information. As Hopkins notes in Chapter 5, "just because I am able to perform a task that is demonstrated to me doesn't mean I know how to properly engage and work with my peers." Effective assessment emerges from this concept.

Learners are expected to work alongside their teachers, taking on different roles and experiencing different kinds of engagement in the work and business of a community. Eventually, learners must spend time in real, rather than simulated, situations of practice if their knowledge and skill is to be credible. Thus, the dominant conception of learning, within this perspective, is similar to the third conception of learning described in Chapter 2: *Learning is the acquisition of information and procedures to be used or applied in practice.* The difference between this view of learning and a Transmission view, however, is in the process and the product of learning. Within the Transmission Perspective the process of learning focuses on 'acquisition'; here the focus is on 'participation' (Sfard, 1998). The product of learning in the Transmission Perspective is a change in sufficiency and accuracy of knowledge. Here the product is a change in competence and identity. Consequently, learners must dwell in situations of authentic practice if they are to learn the knowledge that typifies that practice. Learning is not merely a condition for membership, but is itself an evolving form of membership and identity within a community (Lave & Wenger, 1991; Wenger, 1998; 2000; 2006). As a result, assessment often takes into account the learners' Zone of Proximal Development and seeks to provide opportunities for learners to demonstrate their capacity to advance from the periphery to the center of their practice. Experienced practitioners first place learners alongside more seasoned practitioners somewhere on the periphery of practice, and then decide what learners will do, when they will do it, and to what standards. These teachers, in effect, set the standards against which learners are judged when they want to move from one role or level to another.

For more advanced learners it's not enough to work within their Zone of Proximal Development; instructors need to work with learners at the leading edge of their competence to help them move from experienced practitioner to expert practitioner. That's one of the characteristics of an expert—they work at the leading edge of their competence, continuing to improve rather than staying within the comfort of easy and familiar routines (Ericsson et al., 1993).

Progress in learning, therefore, is based upon achievement and experience, not only prior knowledge. Learners are often referred to by their role, title, rank, or place within the hierarchy of experience, for example, child, adolescent, and adult; *chef de par tie*, sous chef, and executive chef; medical student, resident, and attending physician; colored belts and degrees of black belt; and so on. Thus, proficiency (and authority) is often equated with experience or time within the community.

Finally, it is useful to remember that 'apprenticeship' in this perspective is not an invisible phenomenon. It has key elements: a particular way of viewing learning, specific roles and strategies for teachers and learners, and clear stages of development, whether for traditional or cognitive apprenticeship. But it is important to remember that in this perspective, one cannot learn from afar. Instead, one learns amid the engagement of participating in the authentic, dynamic and unique swirl of genuine practice.

Power Issues

Power, within this perspective, is housed in the accumulation of craft knowledge that is exercised in two forms: social role differentiation and gatekeeping. Each form plays out in the relations between teacher and learner; they are borne of the nature of communities of practice and the status and authority accorded teachers as masters within those communities. Learners who have worked in legitimate roles and sites of practice are assumed to have learned relevant knowledge and proficiency. If they have worked in specialized or higher status sites of the community's practice, they are also assumed to have taken on a different quality of knowledge and proficiency. As a result, they are accorded greater responsibility and status. For example, Bingham (1995) described an occupational first aid instructor's way of differentiating between students in his classes:

> [T]here are basically three kinds of students: newcomers with no experience; returning students that have no legitimate field experience (this category includes attendants in low risk, office environments where trauma calls are practically unheard of and those that have never had any field first aid duties); and legitimate field attendants . . . [they have experience not only in real settings but with trauma situations]. (pp. 5-6).

Bingham emphasizes that the "newcomers knew nothing, and the mistrained—those trained by someone else—knew wrong" (p. 6). Those that had trauma experience had a different quality of experience and knowledge. Equally important, because the instructor represented the community of occupational first aid practitioners, his own level of expertise was the benchmark for assessing student achievement. Therefore, individual differences among learners was a matter of how close or distant they were to the teacher's expertise. Given that, the teacher could decide in which ways to allow particular learners to assume legitimate and peripheral roles within the community of practitioners.

Teachers working within this perspective also occupy a gatekeeping position for others wanting entry to practice. Entry is often closely guarded by those already inside the community. Withholding of expert knowledge is one strategy for maintaining power and reinforcing a sense of being irreplaceable. When this happens, expertize is parceled out as a means of controlling access to practice and positions within communities. Expert power, which is the power that comes from possessing specialized expertise, is eroded quickly if others can obtain access to the expert's information. Similarly, power deriving from the ability to solve critical organizational problems will disappear if others can acquire the capacity to cope with these contingencies

Consequently, such teachers are in a position of "power over" (Currey, 1996) their learners as they determine who passes through and progresses toward full and legitimate participation in the work of the community.

Common Difficulties

As with any view of teaching, this perspective has its heroes and villains. Again, readers will have their own horror stories of "masters" who held absolute power over their learning and their future progress and also made life generally difficult. Yet, there are probably many stories of "masters" who were extraordinary role models and who put their work on the line for people to observe, critique, and use as a benchmark for learning. From the teacher's point of view there are some aspects of teaching from this perspective that are more than a little difficult. First, many are frustrated by their inability to put that which they know and do into words; they find it difficult to articulate their craft knowledge. Ask an experienced professional or tradesperson how they know what to do under difficult or complex circumstances, and most will fumble for words and ideas to represent actions and thinking that long ago became routine. They could easily justify what they do; it just isn't easy saying how they know that, or do what they do.

For those teaching in classrooms it is equally difficult to find authentic tasks for learners. Replicating the world of work within classrooms is one of the most difficult aspects of teaching from this perspective. Through simulations, case studies, problem-based learning, and role plays, they attempt to bring more reality into the relatively sterile environment of a classroom. Yet, even that is deficient, devoid of the whirl and pace of authentic working environments.

Finally, teaching from a dominant perspective of Apprenticeship requires an ability to scaffold or parcel out the work in ways that permit any learner to legitimately participate in the work to be done. For example, parents might teach their children to tie their shoes by starting with the pull of the bow, that is, the final act of tightening the bow. Each subsequent step is then added in reverse order so that, when they can tie the shoe unassisted, they will have worked backwards through many trials to the beginning. This backward chaining allows the learner to participate in the successful completion of the act while also seeing the completed tie each time they participate. Lave and Wenger (1991) have some additional examples in their book showing, for example, how apprentices in tailoring are first given the final task of sewing on buttons, because they can see the finished product and not cause any serious harm if they make a mistake. Yet, this is not easy; even when teaching in authentic contexts, it is difficult to dismantle the complex structure of one's knowledge and then scaffold it in ways that allow learners to participate at points of entry that are both meaningful and achievable. Many Apprenticeship teachers choose the easier, and less successful, strategy of simply allowing learners to observe and find their own points of entry.

Introduction

Within North America this perspective is the most prevalent view of teaching and learning in any curriculum or program concerned with critical thinking and problem or team-based learning. In science education it is the dominant perspective in both public and private secondary schools.

You may have noticed that the narrative structure of Chapter 6 looks very much the way an effective teacher would teach in the Transmission Perspective (Chapter 4). Arseneau has systematically structured the content in a clear and well-organized manner. The content is presented in manageable pieces or chunks, organized around two key ideas and seven principles, with an occasional review; the examples and language are familiar and easily understood. Yet, while the surface structure, or narrative, of Chapter 6 does resemble the advice of Chapter 4, it is in the deeper structures of beliefs and commitments that the Developmental Perspective departs from a Transmission orientation to teaching and learning.

`We make this point to illustrate the parallel between a well-written chapter (e.g., Chapter 6) and effective teaching within the

Portrait of the Developmental Perspective

The Developmental Perspective: A Snapshot	
General Model	
Key Beliefs	• The key to learning and teaching lies in discovering what the learner already knows or believes (prior knowledge) and building effective "bridges" between present and desired ways of thinking.
Focus within the General Model	• Learners' prior knowledge or conceptions of content • Use of content as means of developing thinking • Line X as "conversational inquiry"
Primary Role	• Guide and co-inquirer
Primary Responsibilities	• Assess or diagnose learners' prior knowledge • Adapt content to learners' prior knowledge • Challenge students' understanding of content • Provide more questions than answers • Encourage new ways of thinking and reasoning • Foster deep approaches to learning • Focus evaluation on ways of thinking and reasoning
Primary Commitmen	• To learners' prior knowledge as starting point • To desired ways of thinking as end point
Power Issues	• Allowing teaching processes to be influenced by learners' prior knowledge
Assessment Strategies	• Avoiding a surface approach to assessment (i.e., mere recall of information) • Looking beyond answers for underlying reasoning • Looking for use of different forms reasoning
Common Difficulties	• Letting go of being the "expert" • Asking good questions • Refraining from giving answers

	• Developing assignments and tests that are consistent with this agenda

Transmission Perspective. But we also use this to differentiate surface structure from deeper structures within perspectives. We go there next within the Developmental Perspective.

Key Belief Structures

Fundamental to this perspective are two beliefs about learning. The first is that people perceive the world (and therefore any content they study) through personal frames of reference that they have constructed from prior experience (Illeris, 2007). When confronting new content, learners project these ways of understanding upon the new content, attempting to find a reasonable "fit" between what they already know and that which confronts them. The fit is not always very good. However, even a poor fit is better than none. For, without our existing frames of reference, all learning would be like rote memorization of nonsense syllables.

This first belief about learning has direct consequences for a principle that is the platform for much of Chapter 6: prior knowledge is key to learning. In contrast to the Transmission Perspective, where learning is an "outside-in" process, in the Developmental Perspective learning is an "inside-out" process (Zehm & Kottler, 1993). Learners perceive and interpret new content in terms of their personal frames of reference for understanding the world. If the content "fits" those personal rules and ways of understanding, it is assimilated into existing cognitive structures and schemes. If it doesn't, the learner has two choices: either accommodate a different frame of reference or dismiss the new information and retain the original ways of understanding the world. Either way, prior knowledge and ways of thinking form the basis of each learner's approach to any new content and provide a window into current ways of reasoning.

The second belief is that the most important form of learning is a change in the QUALITY of thinking and reasoning within a specific content, discipline, or practice. Individuals come to education with different conceptions of content, and with different levels of sophistication in their thinking about that content. However, they are not irrevocably captive of their prior conceptions and ways of thinking. Indeed, as comfortable as those prior conceptions might be, the primary role of a teacher is to challenge, develop and then refine people's understanding and ways of thinking. To do this, teachers must find ways to engage learners' current understanding of content as the starting place for developing more sophisticated levels of thinking and reasoning.

The product of learning is new or enhanced understanding and cognitive structures that allow learners to move beyond their previous ways of thinking. Learning is a change in the quality of one's thinking rather than a change in the quantity of one's knowledge. Thus, learning is not simply a process of adding more to what is already there; it is, initially, a search for meaning and an attempt to link the new with the familiar. Ultimately, it is a qualitative change in both understanding and thinking. Thus, the dominant view of learning is similar to conceptions five and six in Chapter 2, both of which represent knowing differently, rather than knowing more.

Primary Role

Effective Developmental teachers act as guides or co-inquirers, building bridges between learners' present ways of thinking and more "desirable" ways of thinking within a discipline or area of practice. Bridging between these two forms of knowledge means teachers must be able to identify and then reconstruct essential concepts in language and at levels of meaning that can be understood by learners. In addition, learners' conceptions of knowledge and ways of thinking must be respected as the starting point for knowing or thinking differently. Thus, instead of working to pass along information or get information across, these teachers introduce learners to the essence of their content in ways that engage what people already know and challenge their ways of knowing. Arseneau (Chapter 6) presents a clear set of principles that delineate the teacher's role and responsibility. Beginning with learners' prior knowledge, teachers are to make explicit the relationship between what people already know (or ways in which they understand) and what teachers want them to know.

For the past thirty years, Michaelsen and colleagues (1994; 1996; 2004; 2007) have documented the power of team-based learning as one means for challenging, developing and refining people's problem-solving and reasoning skills. In that corpus of work one can see how learners' prior conceptions are elicited, negotiated among peers, and reconciled to more sophisticated understanding of content and use in problem-solving. Michaelsen explains how team-based learning can build enthusiasm for teaching by incorporating a fundamental shift in teaching:

> *Another reason that team-based learning builds enthusiasm for teaching is that most of the necessary changes are structural in nature. Instead of trying to make one's presentations more interesting and exciting, the major emphasis with team-based learning is on designing courses to give students opportunities and incentives to accept more responsibility for ensuring that learning occurs. Thus, the focus of the instructor shifts from "How should I teach?' to 'How can students best learn?' and the challenge for instructors has to do with designing courses and group activities with that new and different perspective in mind.* (Michaelsen, 2004, p. 49).

The shift from teaching to learning is central to the primary role of a teacher within the Developmental Perspective. Additionally, team-based learning represents a powerful form of the 'flipped classroom' repertoire of teaching and learning, which also repositions the role of a teacher from presenter of content to facilitator of learning.

Primary Commitment

Developmental teachers have a profound respect for learners' thinking and prior knowledge. Indeed, as can be seen in Arseneau's chapter, they take that as the starting point for their work, proceeding from the known (learners' prior knowledge) to the unknown (more sophisticated forms of understanding and thinking). Effective teaching takes its direction from the learners' knowledge, not the teacher's: bridges are built from the learner's point of view. This is a significant shift from the more traditional Transmission and Apprenticeship Perspectives on teaching, even though it is still the teacher's perception of desired ways of thinking that determines goals.

Power Issues

The Developmental Perspective holds significant implications for the nature and distribution of power within teaching-learning relationships. In the Transmission and Apprenticeship Perspectives, power was located in the relationship between teachers, knowledge, and membership within communities of practice, respectively. Through this power, teachers could exercise control over both the process and product of learning.

Within the Developmental Perspective, the locus of power begins to shift from being predominantly with the teacher, to a sharing of power with learners in two ways. First, the process of learning (and teaching) is assumed to start with what the learner already knows, that is, prior knowledge or conceptions of the content. Therefore, learners may have some authority and voice in deciding how teaching should proceed and whether teaching is/was effective. (Note: this is not entirely unique to the Developmental Perspective; e.g., the Apprenticeship Perspective also has regard for what learners know or can do, as is evident when teaching to a learner's zone of proximal development).

Second, because learning is assumed to be a change in understanding, learners must feel safe as they experiment and try out new ways of thinking. Thinking (out loud) in ways that are new, can be a risky business. It can be embarrassing, fearful, or just uncomfortable, depending on how people react. In particular, it can be risky if the person is confronted too quickly with errors or inadequacies, or if the person's thinking is contrasted with more sophisticated or complex ways of thinking. New ways of thinking, and ideas about the world, are in a very tender state when they are being born. Consequently, learners are at risk when they first try out their fledgling thoughts. This means Developmental teachers must be cautious not to use the power of their own knowledge or ways of thinking in ways that would damage or curtail students' willingness to experiment. Teachers who are in the midst of a role transition, perhaps as part of a curriculum change, may see this as a particularly important power issue as they change from content expert to facilitator of ways of thinking. This is, in part, why Arseneau stresses the need for an ancillary Nurturing Perspective.

Assessment Strategies

The Socratic dialogue that Arseneau describes as a teaching strategy in Chapter 6 might easily be mistaken for an assessment strategy. If teaching involves asking questions, then certainly a good way to determine how well students are learning is to continue and/

or modify a similar progress of questioning. However, this approach creates two significant problems: 1) the misperception of teaching for evaluation may create unnecessary anxiety in learners to fully participate in the question/answer dialogue and so they may miss the point of the exercise, and 2) questioning as a teaching strategy is meant to facilitate a dialogue, not become a test of the learners' existing knowledge.

Teachers from the Developmental Perspective, then, need to be careful to assure learners that posing questions as a form of teaching and repositioning the teacher's knowledge (in response to their comments) is not meant to put learners on the spot. As Arseneau points out in Chapter 6, a key aspect of the instructor's role is to create an environment that enables learners to develop their self-efficacy, to feel comfortable with questioning and approaches that 'flip' the instructor from presenter to inquirer and co-investigator, and then ultimately to create clear expectations for evaluation as it relates to learning.

This can have an added benefit of helping learners become more courageous in their discussions with peers and with the teacher. As Popovsky reports about his own teaching, students learn to challenge not only their own ideas, but also the dominant personalities in the room when they discover that those who dominate are not always right (Popovsky, 2004).

As Chapter 6 makes very clear, a challenge is not to give in to the temptation of providing recall-based assessments like multiple-choice tests. Rather, it is important to go beyond surface approaches to learning by incorporating higher order tasks with which learners can more ably demonstrate their learning not only of new information but also of new ways of thinking about their subject matter. If teaching from the Developmental Perspective involves guiding learners across a bridge of knowledge, then assessment invites the learners to cross that bridge independently. Therefore, any form of assessment must be congruent with the intentions of this perspective. It must assess forms of reasoning, rather than simply correct answers. This form of assessment is common in many of the humanities, where the answer may be less important than the reasoning that brought someone to that answer.

The same holds true in many technical or professional education occupations. Assessment must focus on authentic tasks that require learners to use two modes of reasoning: pattern recognition (Have I seen this kind of problem before; and would previous solutions apply here?); and analytical reasoning (What doesn't fit the picture of what I've seen before?) (Kahneman, 2011). While alternating between those two forms of reasoning, assessment might look for hypothesis generation (What's this about?), what kind of information learners think they need to better understand the problem or situation, how learners translate information gathered into a reasonable statement or understanding of the problem or issue, their consideration of possible solutions, and finally the prioritizing of solutions or diagnoses.

Readers may think this is about making a medical diagnosis. And it could be. However, it is also about auto mechanics. National Public Radio in the United States has hosted one of the finest displays of reasoning available in the public media and it's about diagnosing automotive problems. Here's how a medical doctor from Stanford University describes the work of two brothers from Boston—both experienced auto mechanics:

> *This weekly show spotlights two master clinicians. They are presented every conceivable problem related to their specialty. They solve cases by history alone. They laugh a lot and clearly enjoy what they are doing. And not only do they demonstrate superb diagnostic acumen, but they also model many of the core competencies (required of physicians). This is not a medi cal program, but rather National Public Radio's Car Talk.*

> *This weekly radio broadcast is hosted by two experienced mechanics and comical brothers, Tom and Ray Magliozzi. Listeners from across the United States call in to ask about car-related problems that a mechanic could reasonably be expected to solve ("The sound when I go downhill is kind of like two rocks being ground inside a Cuisinart.") to issues that are more tangential ("Can I drive in the car pool lane if I'm alone in my car but pregnant?"). Occasionally, the hosts have to act as mediators in car-related disputes, eg, "My husband is teaching the kids to hot-wire the family minivan; I think it's a bad idea. Who's right?"*

> *The cognitive task of the mechanic is virtually identical to that of the physician: both use history, examination, and reasoning that serve both the mechanic and the physician. Based on an*

admittedly unsystematic qualitative analysis of years of Car Talk programs, I will share some of the key elements of clinical reasoning that students can observe (and teachers can highlight). (Dhaliwal, 2011).

Dhaliwal presents an eight-step rubric for assessing clinical or mechanical reasoning, from building rapport to getting feedback on one's judgment. The article is well worth reading, for the humor as well as the striking parallel between automotive and medical diagnosis. But the take-home message from a Developmental Perspective is that we must know what reasoning in our field looks like before we can develop appropriate means of assessment.

Common Difficulties

Within this perspective, it is necessary for teachers to explore people's current conceptions of content and then challenge those conceptions as a means of helping learners move to more sophisticated levels of thinking and reasoning. This is not always easy. A common tendency for beginning teachers within this perspective is to fall back into the role of "expert" and provide more answers than challenging questions, instead of letting students explain, clarify, or even defend their current position in relation to what an instructor or text has explained.

Three common difficulties that are easily 'corrected' include:

- Remembering to question 'up-the-ladder' when multiple learners are present so as to avoid embarrassing senior learners in front of their more junior colleagues or peers.
- Giving learners time to think and construct meaning. When asking a question, the amount of 'wait-time' is critical if learners are to actually think before speaking. What seems like 10 seconds of wait-time is often only 1 or 2 seconds. The better the question, the more important a teacher wait and give people time to think before responding. And then, there's a 'second wait-time'—waiting after the first response to hear a second response. Both are important for helping people learn new ways of thinking, reasoning, and decision-making.
- 'Parking' answers and ramblings. This may be the most com-

mon difficulty, especially among novice teachers. Again, the tendency is too often to give the answer or tell a story, rather than let people think before responding. Giving answers not only disrupts their thinking, it teaches learners that they can wait and the instructor will give them the answer.

But perhaps the most difficult challenge for teachers in this perspective is to develop means of assessing learning that are congruent with the beliefs and intentions of this perspective. While they may be able to bridge from the learner's prior knowledge to more desirable ways of understanding and thinking, they may not be able to develop critical questions, assignments, tests, and other means of assessment that allow learners to demonstrate how their thinking has changed, or how they can now think and reason like a professional.

Introduction

Readers who are familiar with adult education practice in less formal and traditional settings such as adult basic education, nursing education, self-help groups, parenting education, and a host of other "caring" occupations, such as primary and elementary education, may recognize the Nurturing Perspective. More than any other perspective, it resembles the andragogical image of an adult educator as portrayed in North America by Malcolm Knowles (1980, 1984, 1986). But perhaps more than others, the Nurturing Perspective reveals a much closer view of learners as well. It is impossible to analyze this perspective without constant reference to learners, their needs, capabilities, and influence. For those who have suffered negative experiences with more traditional approaches to teaching and learning and who may have lost faith in education and its impersonal systems, this perspective offers hope.

Key Belief Structures

When teachers from this perspective look at learners, they see a whole person who brings an emotional, as well as intellectual, past to the existential moments of learning. Every learner has his or her own story to bring to the teaching and learning environment. It

Portrait of the Nurturing Perspective

The Nurturing Perspective: A Snapshot	
General Model	
Key Beliefs	• Learning is related to a learner's self-efficacy. • The learning environment should be safe, trusting and comfortable enough for learners to take risks, make mistakes, celebrate success.
Focus within the General Model	• Establishing a strong connection between teacher and learners (Line Y)
Primary Role	• Facilitator, supporter, guide
Primary Responsibilities	• Fostering a climate of trust and respect • Engaging empathically with individual needs • Promoting and supporting learners' self-efficacy while enabling greater responsibility for learning • Reinforcing the bridge between effort and achievement
Primary Commitmen	• Respecting and nurturing dignity and self-esteem of learner • Attending to learner needs • Pursuing self-efficacy as the goal, achievement as the means
Power Issues	• Striving towards a greater balance of responsibility between teacher and learner • Eliminating barriers associated with social and institutional roles and titles • Avoiding dependency, encouraging greater self-determination
Assessment Strategies	• Emphasizing frequent, low-stakes feedback, rather than high-stakes (e.g., grades), to encourage and support further learning.

	• Allowing learners to share in the responsibility for and development of assessment of their learning.
Common Difficulties	• Assessing learning according to institutional expectations • Dealing with set backs in a learner's progress • Setting appropriate boundaries in a teacher-learner relationship • Avoiding burnout from too much concern for learners. • Managing an effective balance between challenge and caring • Wanting (too much) to be liked

is this view of prior knowledge—about self *and* about self as learner—that is the focal point of this perspective.

Because learning is believed to be an emotional, as well as cognitive, engagement, the environment must be a place where people can express emotions as well as thoughts, fear as well as joy, uncertainty and confusion as well as insight. Consequently, there are three principles related to the learning environment. First, in moral terms, the individual should be treated as an end, not a means. Everything that is done should be with the dignity and security of the learner in mind. That means the learning environment must be a trusting and safe place where learners can take risks and not be humiliated or diminished for mistakes. Second, it must be a place where learners can attribute success to their own effort and ability, rather than luck or the sympathetic kindness of a teacher. Finally, it must be a place where the relationship between learner and teacher is both caring and challenging. Collectively, these beliefs bring the emotional aspects of the learner into sharp relief for the first time.

In our research, teachers expressing these beliefs talked about learners who came to them with a history of educational abuse, where teachers taught through intimidation, where challenge was perceived as more threatening than rewarding, and where students felt more diminished than nurtured. These perceptions were not limited to adult basic education students or "early leavers" from schools. Even "successful" graduate students talked about learning environments that left permanent scars and taught them how to pretend they knew when they really didn't, for fear of being embarrassed or marginalized.

Primary Role

Nurturing educators, as Smulders points out in Chapter 7, acknowledge the influence of personal relationships between teachers and learners. As friend and facilitator, teachers have a delicate balancing act—they must be both caring and challenging toward learners. However, because acts that are caring and challenging can be related to moral and ethical issues, the centrality of the learner-teacher relationship can be both a strength and a liability within the Nurturing Perspective. It is a strength when the relationship fosters growth in confidence and self-efficacy; it is a liability when it breaches personal values or boundaries. As such, it occupies a dominant position in the thinking of the teacher and opens one to greater risk. Whereas other perspectives may feel some justification in a relationship that is "at arms length," nurturing teachers see this as abrogating a central responsibility.

Primary Commitment

Within this perspective, teachers reveal a sense of personal regard for the welfare of learners, both inside and outside the formal learning environment. It is not derived from a sense of duty or obligation, nor from professional or institutional roles. Rather, it is derived from an ethic of caring, a form of commitment, a genuine regard for the other, and a belief that success depends on the readiness and well being of learners.

Such teachers are clearly committed to the whole person that has come to them as learner and certainly not just the intellect of the person. Indeed, unlike the Apprenticeship Perspective, where content and practitioner are merged, in the Nurturing Perspective, content serves as the vehicle for learner self-efficacy; the emotional wholeness of the learner is primary. This has significant implications for how teachers interact with learners, what they consider legitimate conversation and discourse, and how they address power issues in their roles, responsibilities, and relationships with learners.

Power Issues

As with the Developmental Perspective, this orientation to teaching and learning seeks to empower the learner, both in the process and the product of learning. The process of teaching must maintain a genuine concern for the dignity and psychological well-being of the learner; neither self-esteem or self-efficacy is to be sacrificed on the alter of achievement. Effective teaching environments must be, therefore, places where people feel safety and trust. As a result, the process of teaching can only be judged effective if achievement is the means and self-efficacy is the end.

Consequently, there is a shift from "power-over" based on the teacher's expertise (Transmission and Apprenticeship Perspectives), to "power-with," based on a sincere relationship between teacher and learner (Bates et al., 2013; Currey, 1996). Nurturing teachers make every attempt to reduce the tendencies for their positions or expertise to imply or engender power that might undermine the growth and attribution of success to learners. An example of these efforts is an expectation that learners can participate in setting the agenda for their learning, including content selection or assessment design.

Language (or symbol systems), as mentioned in discussing the Transmission Perspective, is a powerful means of controlling access to content. Within the Nurturing Perspective that power is diminished and shared by demystifying and decoding the ideas into language and concepts that are already familiar to learners. However, even within this more egalitarian relationship, it would be wrong to assume there is an equality of power. To ignore the differences in responsibility and authority between teacher and learners is naive, especially as they relate to the assessment of learners and the responsibility of assuring safe practice.

Assessment Strategies

Supporting and guiding learners to develop self-efficacy is one of the primary intentions of teaching from the Nurturing Perspective. This means that a teacher expects such self-efficacy will result in stronger, longer-lasting results, in much the same way that the Developmental instructor seeks to promote effective habits of learning for students. Part of the teacher's task, therefore, is to encourage and support the development of that capability. As Smulders shows in Chapter 7, developing an effective strategy for delivering feedback, particularly for assessments, is a critical responsibility of the teacher.

But should effort count? And if so, how should it be counted and how much should it count? Drawing on the work of Swinton (2010) and colleagues at a small college in the US, Weiman answers 'yes', if done strategically:

> *Students got two grades in each of these courses: one for content knowledge (measured in the traditional ways with exams, papers, projects, etc.) and one for effort (measured by things like attendance, meeting deadlines, participating in class, etc.). Content knowledge was weighted at 40% of the course grade and effort at 60% for first-year courses. Those amounts were reversed for second-year courses and no effort grades after that. Professors were allowed to define effort so long as the definitions were clear and communicated directly to students. The paper reporting on the system analyzed the effort-learning-grade relationship differently than previous research (more robustly, according to the researcher who offers justification for that claim). The finding is as we'd expect: "the effort grade affects the knowledge grade positively and significantly. This is strong evidence that more student effort does lead to increased learning." (Swinton, p. 1182) That's not surprising to faculty, but it probably was to these low-achieving students who discovered that effort did make a difference. When they tried hard, they got results. (Weiman, 2014).*

As a result, assessments designed by the Nurturing instructor need not be any less demanding than by other teachers. More importantly, however, effectively delivered feedback on effort and achievement can work not only to boost confidence and alleviate anxiety, but also to improve learning and performance. Without sensitivity to a learner's level of confidence, the intended effects of feedback and its learning potential are lost. Such confidence comes not from praising the individual, but from feedback that acknowledges good work and links that to effort (Dweck 2007; 2009).

Common Difficulties

There are several difficulties associated with this balancing act, but three in particular are common to this perspective:

Implementing assessments that run counter to nurturing commitments and beliefs.

As with most of the perspectives, the evaluation of learning and learners can be problematic. Many teachers work in situations that measure learning according to pre-set standards, such as departmentally set tests or assignments, grade point averages, licensing or certification requirements, and so forth. Because these standards are often tied to socio-economic status and opportunity, learners (and teachers) tend to equate achievement with self-worth. As a result, teachers who care deeply about their learners struggle to meet external requirements, perhaps as a condition of keeping their job, while trying to ease the wounding that can come from yet another low achievement score on an important test.

Maintaining the boundaries between teaching and counseling.

Because these teachers focus on the emotional wholeness of the person, they often slip into the role of counselor. In fact, the lines between teacher and counselor often are blurred in this perspective, which means some Nurturing teachers succumb to exhaustion and burnout from trying to be all things to all people.

Finding a balance between caring and challenging.

Perhaps the most difficult aspect of being an effective Nurturing teacher is that of reconciling the apparent (though not true) contradiction between caring about learners while also holding them to reasonable expectations of work and achievement.

It is easy to misinterpret the name of this perspective and assume that nurturing means making things easy for learners, or crediting them for effort regardless of accomplishment. For example, novice Nurturing teachers tend to assume that by reducing expectations or standards, whether in assignments or evaluation (challenges), they are showing that they care for their students. When discussing assignments or requirements, they may give in to requests to lighten the load or raise someone's mark, or give credit for time on task, rather than what was accomplished. However, more experienced

Nurturing teachers do not confuse caring with rescuing learners from difficult situations or tasks. To do so could easily be perceived as a vote of "no confidence" in the learners' ability to do what they know they must eventually do.

Nurturing teachers cannot ignore external standards; they simply don't accept that those standards are the most important indicator of dignity, worth, or even personal achievement. They also realize that self-efficacy is not raised through the gift of kindness but, rather, through personal effort and a sense of pride in one's accomplishment. Thus, effective Nurturing teachers help learners set realistic and achievable goals, plan and work systematically toward those goals, acknowledge personal abilities and limitations that pertain to the achievement of those goals, and in doing this, constantly attribute success to the effort and good work of the learner rather than their own benevolence.

Effective Nurturing teaching is, therefore, dependent upon a particular kind of relationship—one that is both challenging and caring. The crucial point here is that both must be present for either to be potent. Teachers that only challenge and demand without caring are usually perceived as insensitive; those that care but easily weaken in their resolve to challenge, are perceived to be "nice" but not helpful, and certainly not memorable (Pratt, 1987).

Introduction

This is the most difficult perspective to analyze; it has no single, uniform characteristic set of strategic or normative beliefs. The "radical educator" described in Chapter 8 is a good example of teaching within this perspective. Yet, it is not completely representative of the range and diversity of Social Reform educators. For example, Social Reform teachers can be found in community development, women's health, Aboriginal education, AIDs awareness, Mothers Against Drunk Driving, the civil rights movement, environmental education, labor union education, religious education, and even within such established occupations and professions as automotive repair and medical education. Those who are Social Reform teachers have a unique sense of mission that directs and defines their teaching. Their personal "mission" is the implementation of a well-articulated ideal, which Social Reform teachers assume is necessary

Portrait of the Social Reform Perspective

The Social Reform Perspective: A Snapshot	
General Model	
Key Beliefs	• The most salient and dominant feature of this perspective is an explicit, well-articulated ideal. Although every perspective on teaching is an expression of an ideal, or an ideology, it is usually implicit, operating unconsciously to direct teaching. In this perspective, the ideals and ideology have emerged to a position of dominance and centrality.
Focus within the General Model	• Focus on ideal as social, political, or moral imperative • Ideal deemed appropriate for all and necessary for a better society
Primary Role	• Advocate for an ideal • A model for challenging authoritative positions

Primary Responsibilities	• Authentically represent the ideal, in words and actions
	• Clarify relevance of ideal in:
	  - classroom
	  - discipline
	  - work/practice
	  - society
	• Demonstrate relationship and connection between ideal and content
	• Justify and defend ideal against challenges
	• Move individuals toward commitment and action
	• Focus on the collective rather than the individual

Primary Commitmen	• To ideal and/or ideology • To collective social change rather than individual learning

Power Issues	• Pressure to conform to ideal or ideology • Positional authority and expertise vs. democratic facilitation
Assessment Strategies	• Emphasis on critical thinking • Recognizing conventional standards of evaluation while seeking to transcend externally imposed limits
Common Difficulties	• Including those who enrolled for 'content' • Responding to those who object to the ideal • Having patience with learners who assume content to be value-neutral • Assessing according to externally imposed criteria for course content

for a better world. It is the clarity of a specific ideal and a missionary sense of purpose that gives rise to each form of the Social Reform perspective.

Virtually all Social Reform teachers make three assumptions: first, that their ideals are appropriate for all; second, that they are necessary for a better society; and third, that the ultimate goal of teaching is to bring about social reform, not simply individual change. It is the collective, not the individual, that is the object of change—thus, the name Social Reform Perspective. Apart from this, effective Social Reform teachers have much in common with effective teachers in other perspectives. They are clear and organized in their delivery of content; they gradually and appropriately bring learners along with them as they perform complex duties in a community of practice; they ask probing questions and use powerful metaphors that help learners bridge between prior knowledge and new concepts; and, many work hard to respect and promote the dignity and self-efficacy of their learners.

However, these are not indicators of the essential belief structures of Social Reform teachers; they are the means by which they work toward a particular set of ideals. It is the ideals that are central to their commitment and ultimately the basis on which they judge the effects of their teaching. Effective Social Reform teachers articulate and integrate their ideals and content in ways that illuminate both, while making clear the place of each within the social order. Thus, it is essential to clarify first, the specific ideals, and second, the belief structures related to those ideals, if we wish to accurately interpret and understand a particular Social Reform teacher's intentions and actions. To illustrate, we will analyze the ideals and belief structures of radical educators as an example of the Social Reform Perspective. In doing this, we will draw upon the material in Chapter 8 and the work of Ira Shor and Paulo Freire, two of the most renowned radical educators in adult education.

Key Belief Structures

First, radical educators generally hold to at least three key beliefs:

- no education is ideologically neutral
- educational systems reflect the views and interests of those in possession of social, economic, and political power
- all knowledge is socially-constructed

Radical educators use education as a means of creating a more just and humane society. Whatever the nature of an injustice, a central belief is that power lies at the heart of much of what is unjust in society today. Thus, if education is to redress injustices, based on issues of power, radical educators must always be conscious of the role and significance of power: who has it and who does not. Thus, to the initial three beliefs, we add three more:

- all education is infused with issues of power
- injustice is intimately linked to issues of power
- education can only redress injustice if it addresses issues of power

By drawing attention to power within the classroom and society, radical educators use education as a means of changing society. However, while education may be a means toward that end, radical educators believe that the individual learner is only an instrument of change, not the object of change. It is social change—not individual growth, development, empowerment, or learning—that is the ultimate measure of success. Thus, goals and concepts such as "individual empowerment" and the development of "personal autonomy" are not usually representative of this perspective. They assume a hierarchy of power that places the teacher in a higher position, as dispenser of power. They also suggest that independence and autonomy are not the ultimate destination of learning and education. From a radical education perspective, independence and autonomy may be viewed as useful intermediate goals, but they are not enough to catalyze the necessary political transformations within a society.

Radical educators operate from positions of inclusion and recognize forms of knowledge independent of the usual hierarchies of expertise and authority. For example, in organizations with several layers of positional authority radical educators don't assume that someone in a superior position has more knowledge. Indeed, it may be just the opposite; depending upon what knowledge is needed, it may be the workers on the line that have more knowledge to change things. Thus, the epistemic beliefs that buttress this perspective are firmly rooted in a subjectivist, egalitarian view of knowledge; it is a view that assumes experience is as good a teacher as texts, and that participants are rather well educated in matters pertaining to their future needs.

You might ask, "Are we still talking about content that is part of a program? Can this really be a legitimate view of knowledge in a college, university, or even a hospital ward? What about curricula or subjects we are required to teach?" Radical educators agree there must be a curriculum. They are not anti-curriculum, per se, only opposed to the authoritarian and elitist ways in which it reproduces injustices in society. The challenge, for radical educators, is one of clarifying the underlying values embedded within the content and curriculum that serve to perpetuate injustices. As noted by Egan in Chapter 8, within any curriculum there are issues of power, control, and elitism which act as gatekeepers to much of the formal educational system, and silence learners into passivity and a sense that they have no right to challenge preexisting forms of knowledge and learning.

Rather, radical educators believe the curriculum, as a body of knowledge, is both received and reconstructed within the bounds of language, culture, and historical time and place. Learners are understood to be situated within a set of values that influence both the process and product of learning. The emphasis is on the interdependence and co-determination of individual, social, historical, and cultural knowledge. Consequently, radical educators know they are neither the owner nor the sole author of any content they are teaching.

The type of learning that parallels this personal epistemology is similar to the fifth conception of learning in Chapter 2: a complex interpretive process aimed at understanding reality and self as co-determinant. Starting with problems or issues within learners' lives, radical educators use content as a means of exploring and challenging problems and the "givens" in their lives. Math, English, art, physics, nursing, or economics are (re)located in the problematic and social contexts of people's lives.

In contrast, recall that the Apprenticeship Perspective places learners in real settings, occupying legitimate roles so as to learn the tangible and intangible aspects of work, interaction, and relationship. From this point of view, learning is understood to be a process of enculturation into the norms and practices of a particular role, group, setting, and set of relationships. From a radical educator's point of view, learning must critically examine those norms and practices, entering the lives of learners at the nexus of injustice, if it is to be meaningful.

Primary Role

Radical education's agenda may be social change, but its immediate goal is to get people to look more closely at their assumptions and examine more carefully their common sense understandings about the content. Within this process the primary role of the educator is to first draw out what learners know. However, the agenda that drives this perspective is linked to collective social structures, not just an individual. Thus, it goes further than the "bridging" that is a feature of the Developmental Perspective. For example, teachers within the Developmental Perspective might begin an encounter with new content by exploring learners' conceptions of the content as a means of gauging a starting point, and then build bridges to more sophisticated forms of understanding, reasoning, and application of that content.

In contrast, radical educators who are committed to bringing about social change through developing learners' cognitive and political insights, are interested in what kinds of political, as well as conceptual, ideas are operating, and how those are related to larger social structures. Thus, an activity starting with students' experiences and/or conceptions initiated by a radical educator would be:

> . . . *directed toward the learner, not as an individual, but as a representative of social structures and networks of power and privilege, class and gender, economy and ethnicity, and so forth. Instructional content and processes are not abstracted from peoples' lives.* (Freire & Shore, 1986, p. 106).

The primary strategy, then, of the radical educator is to locate a dialogue about any content in the experience, language, and culture of the learner. Learning and teaching begin with the experience and knowledge of participants, and highlight the ways in which content interacts with social structures in the lives of participants. In this perspective the teacher is trying to, first, discover with the students that which is most problematic about their perception or understanding. As Freire says, we don't only look at the familiar, we try to understand it—socially and historically. The global context for the concrete and the general setting for the particular are what provides a critical view on reality. In this way, situating pedagogy in culture does not merely exploit or endorse the given, but seeks to transcend it. That is, the themes familiar to students are not thrown in as a manipulative technique, simply to confirm the status quo or to motivate students (Freire & Shore, 1986, p. 104).

From the vantage of the ideals espoused by a Social Reform teacher, his or her primary role is to pose problems or, in the language of radical educators, to make problematic that which is taken for granted. By posing problems educators expect learners to eventually interrogate their own assumptions and beliefs and to learn how to ask deeper questions and research thoughtful answers as a means to action. Therefore, the role of the teacher is one of "democratic facilitator" wherein the teacher is concerned about developing critically aware people equipped to recognize and actively, thoughtfully resist injustices.

Primary Commitment

Radical educators, like most Social Reform teachers, announce their ideological partisanship as an integral part of their teaching agenda. It is up front and acknowledged to learners and colleagues alike as an expression of commitment. In the early sessions of teaching, they make clear their political, moral, or social commitments and their relationships to the process and outcomes of teaching and learning. This clarity may be verbalized; most often it is revealed through teachers' actions. In any case, these teachers are not only clear, but very often unyielding in their commitment to their ideals, which are an essential aspect of who they are as people and teachers.

Power Issues

As you might have guessed, radical education is about power, and making explicit that which is usually implicit—people's values and ideals. It is also about challenging the status quo and changing social structures that perpetuate injustices in society. Therefore, it should not be surprising that its teaching is often in conflict with other established (and often nonexplicit or assumed) values or ideals. As learners are invited to peer behind the hegemonic veils of power, they discover their own unconscious submission to the status quo; they also unveil the values and ideals of others whose "good life" depends on maintaining the status quo. This is fertile ground for at least two kinds of conflict that are rooted in issues of power: how to use a teacher's expertise, and how to manage competing values and vested interests.

First, learners may see the teacher as the expert, but may eventually resent and challenge the very status (power) they have accorded him or her. This is both a power issue and a common difficulty for radical educators. In order to build the educational agenda from the lives of their learners, expressed in their language, and from their point of view, radical educators must neutralize, but not abandon, their own expertise. Again, as evident in Egan's chapter, the transition from teacher to "democratic facilitator" is not an easy one, as it requires a delicate dance of making available, but not imposing, legitimate "expert knowledge."

Second, most educational groups contain competing values and vested interests based on power. Some of those differences may be based on gender, as in the power to shape the informal rules for a group discussion; others may be based on positional authority and role, for example, when different levels of a hospital staff meet in the same instructional setting. Indeed, they are so common that mainstream adult education literature abounds with ideas for handling "difficult situations" or "troublesome learners." However, radical education reframes both the difficult situation and troublesome learner as natural and necessary occurrences in the life of a working group (Brookfield 2013). Instead of finding ways to avoid or resolve these power struggles, so as to get on with the agenda, radical educators try to have participants focus on the nature of the conflict as it relates to issues of power and privilege in the group. Instead of seeing conflict as a stumble along the path to the content, it is experienced and examined as part of the destination. It affirms conflict in groups, rather than avoiding it, as something that is natural and necessary for working collectively toward common goals.

Assessment Strategies

Given the ideal-based goals of Social Reform educators, the assessment of learning is best seen as taking place along a continuum of change—change in perceptions about the status quo and change in the application of critical thinking to any subject.

Because radical educators believe that learning is a process of transformation, a fundamental change in perceiving the world, and . . . "discovering vulnerable points for breaking through, an evaluation of that learning necessarily involves checkpoints along that process. Simply recognizing that we are surrounded by political membranes is an advance. Then, finding means to go beyond its limits is a social action goal [of this perspective]" (Freire & Shore, 1986, p. 105).

As suggested above, Social Reform educators cannot ignore the issue of knowledge acquisition in their own evaluation of learning and in how they assess learners, but along with this goes the idea that knowledge should be subjected to some critical analysis about its origins, as well as its relations to power and people's lives.

Common Difficulties

Most readers will know if they have experienced the missionary zeal of a radical reform educator. To the extent that we have agreed with their ideals we may have been more tolerant of their approaches to teaching. If, however, we have been presented with a teacher advocating an ideal that we oppose, we are likely to have had a different impression of the quality of teaching. For this reason, Social Reform educators often have 'bifurcated' student evaluations of their teaching, that is, students either give them high ratings or very low ratings. There is little middle ground when students are judging the quality of Social Reform teaching.

In addition, if the most important goal is to change society, and not just the individual, then evaluation of learning and/or teaching is more than a little difficult for several reasons. First, the most relevant test of student learning and teacher effectiveness lies beyond the bounds of the immediate teacher-learner relationship and context for learning; second, the most important evidence of social change will, very likely, be delayed in occurrence beyond the boundaries of course or program time limitations; and third, many of the reforms sought by radical education teachers would require changes in the organization that hired the teacher and may now be asking for evidence of effective teaching. For these reasons, most radical educators accept evidence of their effectiveness that is more closely aligned with individual changes in awareness, belief, and commitment.

Perhaps the most serious difficulty within this perspective is for radical educators to maintain a high degree of consistency and congruity between their espoused ideals and teaching behavior. It is one thing to champion an ideal; quite another to live that ideal. Teaching is in grave trouble when there is a disparity between the teacher's words and actions. It is all the more unsettling when the words advocate a moral or principled high ground and the actions are not so virtuous. Here too, many readers will have experienced someone's teaching that seemed at odds with an espoused set of convictions or values.

CONCLUSION

This chapter has taken you into the heart of each perspective, revealing the essential belief structures that define and differentiate perspectives on teaching. At this point you should have a clearer picture of five qualitatively different ways of thinking about, and enacting, what is simply called "teaching." In closing this chapter, we want to leave you with an important point about perspectives on teaching: Perspectives are not inert; nor are they benign. They influence what we see, how we interpret what we see, what we then decide to do, and how we justify our decisions and actions. The power of perspectives becomes obvious when teaching is being evaluated or when attending a workshop that introduces different ways of thinking about teaching and learning.

The next chapter will introduce the *Teaching Perspectives Inventory* and what it tells us about ourselves as teachers, and what it tells us about large cohorts of teachers at different levels and from different professions and disciplines.

REFERENCES

Bates, J., Konkin, J., Suddards, C., Dobson, S., Pratt, D. D. (2013). Student perceptions of assessment and feedback in longitudinal integrated clerkships, *Medical Education*, 47(4): 362-374.

Bingham, W. (1995). *Adult Education Term Paper*—ADED 519, The University of British Columbia, Vancouver, Canada

Brookfield, S. (2013). *Powerful techniques for teaching adults*. San Francisco: Jossey-Bass.

Currey, I. (1996). *Teaching, power, and curriculum change.* A major paper submitted for the masters of education, The University of British Columbia, Vancouver, Canada.

Dhaliwal, G. (2011). The mechanics of reasoning. *Journal of the American Medical Association (JAMA)*, 306(9); 917-918.

Ericsson, K. A., Krampe, R. T., & Tesch-Romer, C. (1993). The role of deliberate practice in the acquisition of expert performance. *Psych Review,* 100(3): 363-406.

Freire, P., & Shore, I. (1986). *A pedegogy for liberation: Dialogues on transforming education*. South Hadley, MA: Bergin and Garvey.

Illeris, K. (2007). *How we learn: Learning and non-learning in school and beyond.* New York: Routledge.

Jarvis-Selinger, S., Pratt, D. D., & Regeh, G. (2012). Competency is not enough: Integrating identity formation into the medical education discourse. *Academic Medicine.* 87(9), 1149-1305, Septembe.r

Kahneman, D. (2011). *Thinking fast and slow.* Toronto: Doubleday.

Knowles, M. S. (1980). *The modern practice of adult education: From pedagogy to andragogy.* Chicago: Association Press, Follett Publishing Co.

Knowles, M. S. (1986). *Using Learning Contracts: Practical approaches to individualizing and structuring learning.* San Francisco: Jossey-Bass.

Knowles, M. S., & Associates. (1984). *Andragogy in action.* San Francisco: Jossey-Bass.

Lave, J., & Wenger, E. (1991). *Situated learning: Legitimate peripheral participation.* Cambridge: Cambridge University Press.

Michaelsen, L. K. (2004). Getting started with team-based learning, In Michaelsen, L. K., Bauman Knight, A., and Fink, L. D. (Eds.) (2004). *Team-based Learning: A transformative use of small groups in college teaching.* Sterling, VA: Stylus Publishing, 27-50.

Michaelsen, L. K., & Black, R. H. (1994). Building learning teams: The key to harnessing the power of small groups in higher education. In Kadel, S & Keehner, J. (Eds.). *Collaborative learning: A Sourcebook for higher education,* 2, 65-81. State College, PA: National Center for Teaching, Learning and Assessment.

Michaelsen, L. K., Black, R. H., & Fink, L. D. (1996). What every faculty developer needs to know about learning groups. In Richlin, L. (Ed.). *To improve the Academy: Resources for faculty, instructional, and organizational development,* 31-58, Stillwater, OK: New Forums Press Co.

Michaelsen, L. K., Knight, A., and Fink, L. D. (Eds.) (2004). *Team-based Learning: A transformative use of small groups in college teaching.* Sterling, VA: Stylus Publishing.

Michaelsen, L. K., & Sweet, M. (2007). Creating effective team assignments. In Michaelsen, L. K., Parmelee, D. X, McMahon, K. K., & Levin, R.E. (Eds.). *Team-based learning for health professions education,* 35-59. Sterling, VA: Stylus Press.

Pinney, S. (1995, September). Electronic message, Vancouver-Hong Kong.

Popovsky, J. (2004). Using team-based learning in a very traditional, cultural, and institutional context, In Michaelsen, L. K., Knight, A., and Fink, L. D. (Eds.) (2004). *Team-based learning: A transformative use of small groups in college teaching.* Sterling, VA: Stylus Publishing, pp. 169-172.

Pratt, D. D. (1987, May). *A study of memorable teachers.* Address given to the annual meeting of the Newfoundland and Labrador Association for Adult Education.

Sfard, A. (1998). On two metaphors for learning and the dangers of choosing just one. *Educational Researcher*, 27(2), 4-13.

Swinton, O. H., (2010). The effect of effort grading on learning. *Economics of Education Review*, 29, 1176-1182.

Vygotsky, L. S. (1978). *Mind in society: The development of higher psychological processes.* Cambridge, MA: Harvard University Press.

Wenger, E. (1998). *Communities of practice: Learning, meaning and identity.* Cambridge, University of Cambridge Press.

Wenger, E. (2000). Communities of practice and social learning systems. *Organization, 7*(2), 225-246.

Wenger, E. (2006). *Communities of practice: A brief introduction.* Retrieved January 16, 2012, from http://ewenger.com/theory/index.htm

Weiman, M. (2014). Motivating students: Should effort count? *Faculty Focus*, Magna Publications, August 13.

Zehm, S. J., & Kottler, J. A. (1993). *On being a teacher.* Newbury Park, CA: Corwin Press, Inc.

CHAPTER 11
Profiling Your Teaching
The Teaching Perspectives Inventory

John B. Collins and Daniel D. Pratt

INTRODUCTION

Teachers at every level and in many contexts are being asked to articulate and reflect on their approach to teaching. They do so for many reasons, some more benign (as part of a workshop) and others more critical (as part of an evaluation). Within the education community, whether educating youth or adults, few would argue against these activities. Most teachers simply presume it is a worthy and appropriate task, perhaps assuming that it will provide better understanding and more equitable judgment of teaching.

At the same time, there is a move to adopt a single, dominant view of effective teaching. In other words, teachers are asked to reflect on who they are and how they teach but with an implied message that that reflection should conform to some preconceived notion of a "good" teacher. As mentioned in Chapter 4, the argument for this move is, in part, a reaction against teacher-centered instruction which has dominated much of education, particularly adult and higher education, for much of the past century. Yet to argue for a singularity of good in teaching while also asking people to reflect on their teaching implies a false promise of opportunity to be different from the dominant view of teaching (Pratt, 2005a). It also contradicts a mounting body of evidence that effective teaching depends on context (Pratt, Sadownik, & Jarvis-Selinger, 2012), discipline or field of practice (Shulman, 2005), and culture (Tweed & Lehman, 2002). Clearly, one size does not fit all. (Pratt, 2002)

RESEARCHING PERSPECTIVES ON TEACHING[1]

Nearly three decades ago, observations and interviews were used to assemble the evidence that is presented in this book as five perspectives on teaching. In essence and substance, these perspectives are echoed in the work of Kember (1997), Apps (1996), Brookfield (2006), and others, although sometimes by different names and descriptions. Furthermore, we soon learned that, in addition to variations in teaching perspectives, there were also differences in how commitment to teaching was expressed; different teachers held different *Beliefs* about teaching, set themselves different *Intentions* to accomplish, or undertook different *Actions* in their instructional settings (see Chapter 2). From that work emerged a powerful heuristic for simplifying the myriad things that can occur during any instructional event, a general model of teaching (Figure 11.1) that abstracts a teaching session into five elements (teacher, learners, content, context, and ideals) and three relationships (teacher–learner, teacher–content, and learner–content). Collectively, these eight features help researchers and practitioners organize and classify narratives about how teachers differ in approach and justification of their teaching.

Importantly, the general model of teaching and its constituent elements and relationships presumes nothing about "effective teaching." Nor does it suggest a causal relationship between teaching and learning. Rather, it respects teaching as a personal activity that is socially mediated, culturally authorized, and historically situated. The general model respects adult and higher education practices wherever they occur by describing a set of elements and relationships that are neutral with respect to the form and context of practice as well as the ends to be achieved through teaching.

INSTRUMENTING PERSPECTIVES ON TEACHING

However, to arrive at such "thick descriptions" of how instructors conceptualized their teaching required 2 to 3 hours of one-on-one

---

[1] Chapter 11 is a revised and updated version of an article first published in Adult Education Quarterly, November 2011 with permission. DOI: 0741713610392763v1 - Dec 15, 2010.

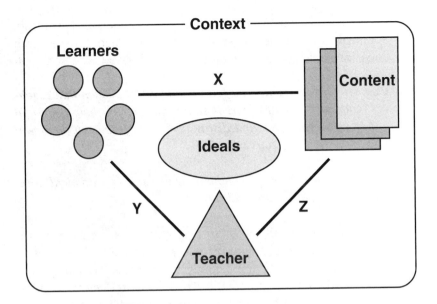

Figure 11.1 A general model of teaching

interviews, observation, and subsequent analysis for each teacher. The obvious question was whether there might be a more streamlined self-reporting option that could characterize teachers' perspectives faster and with less effort but with reasonable fidelity. Thus was born a decade-long effort to develop a self-administering inventory (eventually online, self-scoring, and with automated report-back) for respondents to describe their individual profiles as teachers. We had collected hundreds of pages of transcripts, observations, field notes, and other phenomenographic data during interviews with teachers in various academic, cultural, basic education, skills acquisition, religious/spiritual, and leisure learning settings. Embedded in this data set were thousands of utterances reflecting teachers' diversity of perspectives and commitments to teaching. These transcripts and field notes became the initial source of "I statements" reflecting each item's focus on certain perspectives while differentiating it from others.

Since the research team had first conjectured then ratified with each teacher what her or his dominant perspectives were, it was a straightforward task to abstract characteristic utterances from teachers in each perspective and to cluster them into categories believed to reflect Transmission, Apprenticeship, Developmental, Nurturing, and Social Reform. From these data, we developed two research questions for streamlining that process:

1. *Can selected utterances be refined and restated such that teachers' endorsements of different statements reflect their dominant teaching perspectives and distinguish them from non-dominant or recessive perspectives?*

2. *Can such an inventory demonstrate acceptable statistical standards of reliability and validity?*

From more than 200 of these original stems, items were reworded and refined to characterize one perspective more expressly and to distinguish it from the remaining perspectives. We pared these down to 155, then 120, and finally to 75 items reflecting simultaneously balanced representations of Beliefs, Intentions, Actions and learner–teacher, learner–content, and teacher–content relationships (Chan, 1994). One-week test–retest sorting into categories by 10 experienced judges demonstrated an 80% consistency. These 75 items yielded six clear factors (Apprenticeship initially emerged as a "practice vs. modeling" distinction), which Chan subsequently reworked as scale scores and tested against 471 adult night school teachers' socio-demographic characteristics and instructional practices.

After that initial analysis, we revised the 75 items once again and streamlined them into a 45-item version with nine defining statements per perspective, each represented by three Belief statements, three Intention items, and three Action declarations. This 45-item version was first tested in paper–pencil format on several hundred respondents (including almost the entire student cohort graduating with University of British Columbia elementary, secondary, and adult teaching certificates in 2000) and examined for scale consistency (a-reliability) and interpretable factor structure. These items, together with background information about socio-demographic attributes and professional histories, were placed online as a self-administering, self-scoring instrument in late 2000. Streamlining of web page layout, response formats, and background information questions continued into mid-2001. In its current format, each question is a 5-point agree/disagree statement or a 5-point frequency report (*never, rarely, sometimes, usually, always*).

IMPLEMENTATION AND STANDARDIZATION

Following its launch, the *Teaching Perspective Inventory* (TPI) quickly gathered momentum and an overall pattern of its respondents emerged. Part of its online appeal was its instant feedback, which provided respondents with an immediate profile of relative strengths of their perspectives as well as an abbreviated summary showing how their beliefs, intentions, and actions coalesced to differentiate among their perspectives. Early reports of the inventory's psychometric properties have been noted elsewhere (Pratt & Collins, 2002), but a more recent publication (Collins & Pratt, 2011) outlines much larger-scale results.

GOING LIVE ON THE WEB

In mid August of 2001, the current version of the TPI went online. The data bank's index (first) case (August 17, 2001) is a Puerto Rican teacher/researcher whose subject specialty was curriculum and instruction and whose learners were mature adults. By the end of that same day, 3 more people had completed the inventory; within a week, 54; by the end of the first month, 342; and by the end of 2001, there had been 1,066 respondents. The respondent count passed 50,000 in September 2006 and exceeded 100,000 in April 2009. By mid-2015, the count had passed 300,000.

In late 2011, the inventory's website was updated. A few respondent demographic questions that had been located toward the end of the inventory were repositioned in order to guide respondents to envision a specific teaching setting with particular learners, defined content, and explicit context. Thus the revised instructions guide respondents' mental imagery toward a particular context and setting rather than an ill-defined, less vivid, unfocused generic encounter. The revised website went live online late December 2011 and by early 2014 had accumulated more than 33,000 records from respondents—about 50 per day.

Although the largest fraction of respondents are located in the United States (42.5%) and Canada (22%), about 36% of the completed profiles come from more than 120 other countries around the world. Furthermore, although most people reported English as their first language (75%), substantial numbers also reported Spanish (10.3%), French (1.3%), Mandarin (1.7%), Cantonese (0.8%), and Hindi, Punjabi, and more than 100 other (9.9%) languages.

WHO TAKES THE TPI?

The TPI was designed principally with teachers in adult and higher education in mind, but respondents to the inventory span the spectrum of educational roles. Respondents report their primary role as teacher (47.1%), administrator/manager (8.9%), practitioner (11.9%), researcher (3.7%), student (17.8%), or "other" (10.6%). Their instructional responsibilities include learning groups ranging from young adults (44.6%) to mature adults (16.9%), youth (18.4%), children (18.4%), older adults (1.4%), and seniors (0.3%); thus, teachers of school-age children form about a third of the respondents. Overall, substantially more women have completed the TPI (65.6%) than men (34.4%). The largest fraction of respondents report that their "usual learners" are university undergraduates (22.9%); followed by graduate students (8.5%); community college, vocational, or adult night school learners (14.4%); secondary school learners (16.6%); elementary school learners (15.6%); and a variety of others (general public, workshops, conferences; 8.9%). Most teach in settings that grant university or college credit (35.7%), K-12 credit (21.2%), or certificate or diploma recognition (15.3%), whereas 27.8% teach in noncredit learning situations. Respondents' educational qualifications span the spectrum from high school diplomas (11.9%), through bachelor's (40.2%), master's (26.9%), to doctoral degrees (11.6%). "Other" designations in education (9.5%) often include specialty qualifications, current enrollment in masters or doctoral programs, or dual qualifications (MD, PhD). Although about 14% (mostly students) are at the beginning of their teaching careers, most respondents have substantial histories as educators (M 7.8 years) or practitioners (M 8.2 years) and report that teaching responsibilities consume a majority of their professional responsibilities (55.0%). The large majority report an employment home base in the educational sector (69.5%), whereas others are located in health (13.0%), government (4.5%), business (4.2%), volunteer (1.5%), and "other" (7.3%) sectors. Just more than half report that they were prompted to complete the TPI as a course requirement (54.9%). The next highest group took the TPI on recommendation from a colleague or friend (18.0%). The remaining respondents report that it was a discovery while searching the web (7.1%), a career search (7.5%), or some "other" (12.5%) reason for taking the TPI.

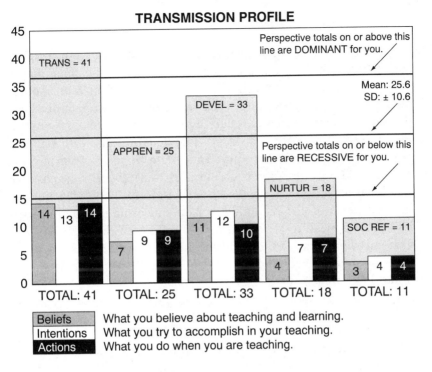

TRANSMISSION PROFILE

Perspective totals on or above this line are DOMINANT for you.

TRANS = 41

Mean: 25.6
SD: ± 10.6

DEVEL = 33

APPREN = 25

Perspective totals on or below this line are RECESSIVE for you.

NURTUR = 18

SOC REF = 11

TOTAL: 41   TOTAL: 25   TOTAL: 33   TOTAL: 18   TOTAL: 11

Beliefs	What you believe about teaching and learning.
Intentions	What you try to accomplish in your teaching.
Actions	What you do when you are teaching.

Figure 11.2 Sample profile

REPORTING RESULTS TO RESPONDENTS

The TPI website automatically scores each person's answer pattern and provides an immediate graphic profile of their scores (Figure 11.2), which they can print, along with five "Explanatory Paragraphs" describing the essence of each perspective as well as a 10-step interpretation guide. By following the guide, respondents should be able to read their TPI profile and interpret the results for themselves.

Respondents' results are also automatically emailed to the address they supply while completing the questions. The profile sheet consists of five vertical bars–one for each perspective—running from a theoretical minimum of 9 to a maximum of 45. Within each bar is printed each respondent's numerical totals as well as the three commitment subscore components (Beliefs, Intentions, and Actions) that constitute their total.

Teaching Perspectives

Although scores for each perspective can vary from 9 to 45, suggesting a midrange average of 27, in practice the scale means average around 34, suggesting an overall upward bias of about 7 points on the response scales (SD, D, N, A, SA [strongly disagree, disagree, neutral, agree, strongly agree] or N, R, S, O, A [never, rarely, some-times, often, always]). Individual means, with standard deviations in parentheses, vary from scale to scale. Transmission averaged 33.3 (4.6), Apprenticeship 36.4 (4.2), Developmental 34.6 (4.3), Nurturing 36.7 (5.0), and Social Reform 29.0 (6.0), indicating that items on the Nurturing or Apprenticeship scales are generally more appealing (or socially desirable) than Social Reform or Transmission items. Details of these means, standard deviations, and other commonly accepted parameters of scale performance can be found in Collins & Pratt, 2011.

Variations on Commitment

Each perspective comprises three manifestations of "commitment to teaching": *Beliefs, Intentions*, and *Actions*. In Pratt's foundational conversations with teachers, these expressions of commitment most often emerged early in the interviews ("Well, what I really believe about teaching is . . .," "What I'm actually trying to accomplish with my learners is . . .," or "What I usually do in the classroom is . . ."), followed later by further disclosures indicating preferences for a Transmission, Apprenticeship, Developmental, Nurturing, or Social Reform Perspective.

Each commitment score is a 15-item sum of five Belief items (one for each perspective), five Intention items, or five Action items. In theory, these Commitment scores could range from 15 to 75 and would suggest a midrange average of about 45. In practice, they average between 55 and 56; Beliefs 55.5 (6.2), Intentions 56.9 (6.9), and Actions 56.9 (6.7).

While overall averages are similar for large samples, individual respondents can show dramatic differences from Beliefs to Intentions to Actions. Inconsistencies between Beliefs and Intentions were comparatively rare, but when discrepancies did occur, they were most often between Beliefs and Actions or Intentions and Actions. Institutional policies that were at odds with personal beliefs explained a number of such instances. Neither workload nor length of experi-

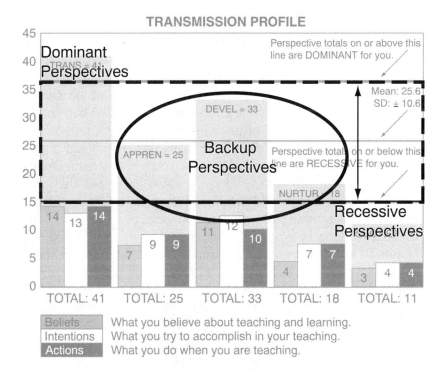

Figure 11.3 Transmission profile

ence were associated with such inconsistencies, but men reported them slightly more often than women.

Dominant, Backup, and Recessive Perspectives

In most instances, people's TPI profile charts (Figure 11.2) show a "'stepped" configuration with one (or sometimes two) perspective standing out notably higher than the remainder. These prominent perspectives are those that teachers often describe as "Where I'm most 'at-home'" or "How I most often see myself." These are labeled one's *Dominant* perspective. Similarly, one score is often notably lower than the remaining four and is termed *Recessive*.

Each respondent's profile has three horizontal lines (Figure 11.3). The middle line is that person's mean for all five perspective scores. The top line is the threshold for that person's 'Dominant Perspective'—any perspective score that reaches or exceeds that line is Dominant for that individual. The bottom line is the 'Recessive Perspective' threshold—any perspective score that is at or below that line is recessive for that individual. Numerically, these are computed as plus or minus one standard deviation around the mean (middle line) of each respondent's own five perspective scores, hence the spread separating dominant from recessive is individualized for each person. Between the two bars are one's *backup* perspectives— skills and strategies that can be called on when needed but that are not always at the forefront of one's instructional tool kit.

Because the TPI is brokered via many universities and organizations, such as Arizona State, Clemson, Columbia, Cornell, Dublin, Harvard, Hawaii, Minnesota, York, the Dental Hygiene Educators of Canada, and Education Resources Information Center (ERIC), there is a steady influx of data. Yet between 2008 and 2009 when respondent numbers increased from 60,000 to more than 100,000, the norms had not changed significantly, suggesting there is stability in what has been reported above. Among the 206,000+ respondents in this sample, Nurturing is the most common dominant perspective (50%), followed by Apprenticeship (38%), Developmental (18%), Transmission (14%), and Social Reform (3%).

For a video example of how to interpret a TPI profile, look for the link on the TPI web site. Alternatively, put the following into your browser: *Dan Pratt interpreting a TPI Profile*

The video, in four sections, shows Dan Pratt helping Tom McKenna interpret his profile. The running time is in parentheses after each section name.

Section 1 *The TPI as a conversational tool* (3:43)

Section 2 *Orienting an adult educator (Tom McKenna) to his pro file* (8:48)

Section 3 *Deconstructing a profile* (14:32)

Section 4 *'Next steps' for this particular teacher* (11:52)

USES OF THE TPI

A Framework for Understanding

Messick (1989) argues that there is no such thing as "validity in the abstract"; a measuring instrument is valid only if it accurately and helpfully informs decisions or actions. Thus, what can people gain from interpreting their TPI results? In workshops and debriefing sessions, teachers "see themselves" in their profiles and explanatory interpretations. They also recognize colleagues whose profiles are different from their own. From such activities they gain understanding and respect for a plurality of approaches to teaching, as well as an expanded vocabulary of concepts and terminology that frequently find their way into personal statements of teaching philosophy. The fact that different people have different profiles confirms that there is more than one acceptable way to think about teaching and that people's profiles and interpretational materials are powerful tools for faculty development exercises and group goal clarification (Pratt, 2002).

When respondents complete the TPI, they are invited to reflect on their results using a ten-step guide. With the guide, respondents review brief descriptions of the five perspectives in order to familiarize themselves with their philosophical orientations. They then examine their profile, looking at such aspects as their dominant, back-up and recessive perspectives, the height and range of their scores, any remarkable discrepancies between beliefs, intentions and actions. The information in their results should prompt some speculation about respondents' own views and confirm or challenge any existing assumptions on teaching and learning. Finally, respondents are encouraged to compare results with peers, colleagues, and others in their domain of practice and/or expertise. Respondents may want to take the TPI more than once and compare their results over time. In this way, the TPI is anything but the last word on a teacher's profile; rather, the results should contribute to ongoing reflection that can span an entire career.

Faculty Development

Self- and peer observations are more effective when observers recognize that good teaching is much more than "doing it the way I would do it" (Courneya, Pratt, & Collins, 2008). At the University of California, Davis School of Medicine, the TPI is a central before and after descriptor of perspective change in year-long programs of faculty development (Srinivasan et al., 2007). Similarly, the TPI is an instructional tool at the University of Toronto School of Medicine and the University of British Columbia Faculty Certificate Program on Teaching and Learning in Higher Education (Hubball, Collins, & Pratt, 2005).

At a more systemic level, the TPI is a faculty development requirement at Strayer University where (to date) nearly 1,000 faculty members from across their 42 multistate campuses have completed the TPI. At Republic Polytechnic, a problem-based tertiary technology training institution in Singapore, all incoming teaching staff are required to complete the TPI during their initial weeklong facilitation-training workshops. A year or two later, these new instructors assemble a portfolio of supportive materials to present at a certifying interview that includes a second, more recent, update of their TPI profile. Second profiles are significant predictors of who will gain certification on their first attempt and distinguishes them with respectable statistical accuracy (η^2=.31) from those whose certification will be delayed for a second or third year or who will ultimately leave the institution. More than 2000 TPI records exist for these instructors.

Workshop Training

Professional workshop training educational activities are often built around concepts and insights gained when attendees arrive at the training location with copies of their TPI profiles already in hand and ready for discussion. This allows time for self-study and reflection and for decisions about which aspects of the profile might be freely shared or maintained private. The task of workshop leader (or invited guest) in providing an overall framework of the teaching perspectives and what they mean is simplified greatly if most attendees bring along their own profiles and questions they wish to discuss.

Often in such professional education workshops, the question arises "precisely *whose* training and education are under consideration here?" If the continuing education of mid-career professionals is the educational objective, then workshop activities and discussion topics can be quite different from workshops focusing on novices or newly certified entrants into a discipline. Learning activities (hence teacher perspectives) should pay close regard to the differences between education of the next generation vs. continuing education of current professionals. Gibson (2013) has noted that workshops and training for instructors in vocational and trades schools need to pay particular attention to distinguishing between activities geared to instructors for their own career advancement vs.

instructional strategies intended to enhance their skills in managing knowledge and skill acquisition of their own trainees, most of whom are in the earliest phases of a new occupation.

A sample of professional groups that regularly use the Teaching Perspectives Inventory with their membership includes: The Harvard Macy Institute for Health Professionals, the American Association of Orthopaedic Surgeons' Annual Educators' Course, the Canadian Society for Medical Laboratory Science, and a wide variety of faculty development programs at colleges and universities.

Research Projects

The TPI has been the instrument of choice for dozens of master's theses, doctoral dissertations, and research projects in the United States and Canada and around the world. These works have investigated a range of issues, learners, and contexts, such as: student teachers' "journeys" toward becoming teachers (Jarvis-Selinger, 2002), conceptual equivalency of teaching perspectives across languages (Lu, 2006; Ruan, 2004), an exploration of the influence of context in educating medical technicians (Tiffin, 2008), discontinuities between occupational therapy instructors' beliefs, intentions, and actions (Kehres, 2008), teaching perspectives and supervisory practices of cooperating teachers (Clarke & Jarvis-Selinger, 2005), and contrasts of beliefs and intentions of teachers in online and face-to-face instructional settings (Panko, 2004). Similarly, Baynard (2012) examined international norms for nearly 4000 teachers in primary, middle, and diploma settings of the International Baccalaureate Organization. Perspectives differences for university faculty at risk for professional burn out were examined by Matofari (2014). Altschuler (2012) examined how clinical faculty in nursing, social work, and counseling with different dominant perspectives used reflective journaling in different ways. Loewen & Jelescu-Bodos (2013) compared pharmacy faculty and preceptors in terms of their TPI profile and their learning style, as indicated on a modified version of Kolb's Learning Style Inventory. While most faculty were dominant in Apprenticeship, as learners they were generally assimilators or convergers.

International contrasts among university instructors regarding translations and wording of the TPI itself have been examined by Misieng (2013) for Malaysian vs. North American professors. Rotidi

(2014) compared TPI profile differences between Greek university professors and a sample of international counterparts characterized by Biglan's taxonomy of teaching disciplines.

As well, the TPI is finding application in many countries and in a variety of languages and cultures. To date, it has been translated and tested in Spanish, French, Portuguese, German, Greek, Persian, Turkish, Chinese, Indonesian, Korean, Malay, and Japanese, although only the English, Spanish, and Chinese versions are currently online.

Reviews of Teaching

Awareness of one's perspective on teaching is useful, especially when teaching is under review. Peer reviewers are often selected because they fit within the culture and norms of teaching within an instructional unit. Thus, it is not uncommon for reviewers to look for some reflection of themselves as the measure of good teaching. In doing so, reviewers may project their own perspective on the teaching they are to review. This can put teachers at risk, particularly if they are being reviewed by someone whose approach to teaching is markedly different from their own. When a person's TPI profile is used as part of a pre-review discussion, conceptual differences about teaching can be clarified before judgments are made about the quality of someone's teaching. Whether in formal, non-formal, or informal educational contexts, this is of no small consequence for anyone whose teaching is being reviewed for continuing employment.

Student perceptions of instructors' teaching perspective are not common but do exist and highlight how students assess and value certain perspectives over others. Williams (2011) reports that 797 students reporting on 34 PBL facilitators "[t]aken as a whole . . . showed that the tutors rated themselves significantly higher on the Apprenticeship, Developmental, Nurturing, and Social Reform Perspectives as compared to the students" (p. 48).

Improving Teaching

Being aware of one's perspective is undoubtedly helpful to being mindful about teaching, but it is not a sufficient indicator of an effective teacher; and the TPI does not actually indicate whether one is doing a good job at teaching. Each perspective can represent both effective and ineffective teaching; no perspective is inherently or universally better than any other perspective. Perspectives are a blend of personal philosophy (beliefs and intentions) and contextual factors. Yet some perspectives are a better fit to some teaching contexts than others. For example, Apprenticeship Perspectives fit very well in workplace learning, but that does not mean that everyone teaching in workplace settings should adopt an Apprenticeship Perspective. There are many highly effective teachers in the workplace who hold views other than Apprenticeship. But our data suggest that more often than not, those who teach in workplace settings hold an Apprenticeship Perspective as their dominant view of teaching. Furthermore, there are strong "signature pedagogies" within the professions that make for a better fit between forms of training or education, eventual workplaces, and particular teaching perspectives (Shulman, 2005; Jarvis-Selinger, Pratt & Collins, 2007). However, what matters most is not which perspective fits in what setting. Rather, the question is whether we can help people improve their teaching by capitalizing on their perspectives on teaching.

Although we know a good deal about effective teaching of adults, we also know that no teacher embodies all the findings that characterize highly effective teaching. They do so in some cases because some findings fit their personal, situational, and cultural circumstances better than others (Pratt, 2005b, 2009, 2010; Pratt & Collins, 2000, 2002). Bain's (2004) work with teachers from North America, for example, shows that highly effective teachers know their content area very well and know the essential questions, debates, and issues that characterize their discipline or field of practice. They do not try to "cover" a lot of material. They try, instead, to help students address the big questions: the larger picture governing a body of knowledge and/or practice. Bain (2004) also found that highly effective teachers know how to engage their students in those questions, issues, and debates. Those two findings give direction for all who want to improve their teaching but they are particularly helpful for those who perhaps hold to that conventional idea of a singular best way to teach. Teaching within each perspective can be improved by focusing on findings from research that are consistent with that perspective.

MOVING FORWARD

The TPI offers opportunities well beyond a simple exercise in self-examination and values clarification among adults who hold varieties of teaching responsibilities. In systematic studies, it has shown itself to be a powerful tool in faculty development, teaching assessment, teaching improvement, peer reviews of teaching, and a variety of research investigations of adults teaching adults (and sometimes children) in learning settings around the world.

There is yet another important aspect of the TPI that speaks to its practical value and the necessity to acknowledge and respect a "plurality of the good" in teaching. It has to do with the very nature of teaching. Teaching is, of course, a dynamic and complex activity. But it is also an intellectual, relational, moral, and cultural activity. It is intellectual because it deals with claims to truth; it is relational because it places people in interdependent roles and responsibilities; it is moral because it makes judgments of propriety, value, and worth; and it is cultural because relationships and propriety are culturally and historically constituted. Therefore, by its nature, teaching is not an individual act but, rather, a social act that is situated in time and traditions that have intellectual, relational, moral, and cultural dimensions. Each of these is differentially respected and revealed through the constructs that make up the TPI.

However useful the TPI may be in helping teachers clarify their perspectives, it should not be viewed as a diagnostic tool for purposes of screening or remediation. Such use would presume that one (or more) of the perspectives is inherently better than another. As this book should make clear, we do not hold that view. Rather, the TPI should be used as a discussion tool to promote reflection, discussion, clarification, and, most important, respect for the intellectual, relational, moral, and cultural aspects that are essential to understanding what it means "to teach."

REFERENCES

Altschuler, M. (2012). *Teaching perspectives and usage of journal writing.* (Unpublished doctoral dissertation). Barry University. Miami Shores, FL.

Apps, J. (1996). *Teaching from the heart: Professional practices in adult education and human resource development series.* Malabar, FL: Krieger.

Bain, K. (2004). *What the Best College Teachers Do.* Cambridge: Harvard University Press.

Baynard, Elizabeth. (2012). *The IB teacher professional: identifying, measuring and characterizing pedagogical attributes, dispositions, perspectives and practices.* International Baccalau_ reate Organization. IB Global Center, Bethesda, MD.

Brookfield, S. D. (2006). *The skillful teacher* (2nd ed.). San Francisco, CA: Jossey-Bass.

Campbell, D. T., & Fiske, D. W. (1959). Convergent and discriminant validation by the multi-trait, multi-method matrix. *Psychological Bulletin, 56*, 81-105.

Chan, C. H. (1994). *Operationalization and prediction of conceptions of teaching in adult education* (Unpublished doctoral dissertation). University of British Columbia, Vancouver, British Columbia, Canada.?

Clarke, A., & Jarvis-Selinger, S. A. (2005). What the teaching per-| spectives of cooperating teachers tell us about their advisory practices. *Teaching and Teacher Education, 21*, 65-78.?

Courneya, C. A., Pratt, D. D., & Collins, J. B. (2008). Through what perspective do we judge the teaching of peers? *Teaching and Teacher Education, 24*, 69-79.?

Gibson, S. (2013). (Personal communication; Dissertation Committee Meeting, July 2013).

Hubball, H. T., Pratt, D. D., & Collins, J. B. (2005). Enhancing Reflective Teaching Practices: Implications for Faculty Development. *The Canadian Journal of Higher Education, 35*(3), 57-81.

Jarvis-Selinger, S. A. (2002). *Journeys from student to teaching: Charting the course of professional development* (Unpublished doctoral dissertation). University of British Columbia, Vancouver, British Columbia, Canada.?

Jarvis-Selinger, S. A., Pratt, D. D., & Collins, J. B. (2007). Do academic origins influence perspectives on teaching? *Teacher Education Quarterly, 34*(3), 67-81.

Kehres, E. (2008). *Faculty beliefs, intentions, and actions in occupational therapy education* (Unpublished doctoral dissertation). Ohio University, Athens.?

Kember, D. (1997). A reconceptualization of the research into university academics' conceptions of teaching. *Learning and Instruction, 7*, 255-275.

Loewen, P.S., & Jelescu-Bodos, A. (2013). Learning styles and teaching perspectives of Canadian pharmacy practice residents and faculty preceptors. *American J of Pharmacy Education*, Oct 14, 2013; 77(8): 163. doi: 10.5688/ajpe778163.

Lu, X. (2006). *Conceptual equivalence of teaching perspectives in Chinese and English.* (Unpublished master's thesis). University of British Columbia, Vancouver, British Columbia, Canada.

Matofari, F. (2014). *Path analysis of the influence of teaching perspectives and burn-out on instructors' turnover intentions.* (Unpublished doctoral dissertation). Oklahoma State University. Stillwater. OK.

Misieng, J. (2013). "Translation, Adaptation and Invariance Testing of the Teaching Perspectives Inventory: Comparing Faculty of Malaysia and the United States". *Graduate School Theses and Dissertations.* Retrieved from http://scholarcommons.usf.edu/etd/4921

Messick, S. (1989). Validity. In R. L. Linn (Ed.), *Educational measurement* (3rd ed., pp. 13-103). New York, NY: Macmillan.

Nunnally, J. C., & Bernstein, I. (1994). *Psychometric theory.* New York, NY: McGrawHill.

Panko, M. (2004). *The impact of teaching beliefs on the practice of e-moderators* (Unpublished doctoral dissertation). University of New England, Armidale, New South Wales, Australia.

Pratt, D. D. (2002). Good teaching: One size fits all? In J. Ross-Gordon (Ed.), *An up-date on teaching theory* (No. 93, pp. 5-16). San Francisco, CA: Jossey-Bass.?

Pratt, D. D. (2005a). Personal philosophies of teaching: A false promise? *ACADEME, 91*, 32-36.

Pratt, D. D. (2005b, April). *Teaching international students* (Grand rounds presentation). St. Michael's Hospital, University of Toronto Medical School, Toronto, Ontario, Canada.

Pratt, D. D. (2009, April). *Why can't everyone be like me: Variations on a theme of excellence.* (Thomas Q. Morris Invited Lecture). Columbia University Medical School, New York, NY.

Pratt, D. D. (2010, February). *The power of context and community in clinical teaching: How do Australians compare?* (Opening plenary for Education Week). Faculty of Medicine, University of Melbourne, Australia.

Pratt, D. D., & Associates. (1998). *Five perspectives on teaching in adult and higher education.* Malabar, FL: Krieger.

Pratt, D. D., & Collins, J. B. (2000, February). *Cultural variations on a theme of "good teaching"* (for Ritsumeiken/UBC students and faculty). University of British Columbia, Vancouver, British Columbia, Canada.

Pratt, D. D., & Collins, J. B. (2002, November). *International perspectives on teaching: Internationalizing education in the Asia-Pacific region.* Paper presented at the 30th Annual ANZ- CIES Conference, University of New England, Armidale, New South Wales, Australia.

Pratt, D. D., Sadownick, L., & Jarvis-Selinger, S. (2012). Pedagogical BIASes and clinical teaching in medicine. In L. M. English (Ed.), *Health and adult learning* (pp. 193-209). Toronto, Canada: University of Toronto Press.

Rotidi, G., Collins, J. B., Karalis, T. & Lavidas, K. (in press). *Using the Teaching Perspectives Inventory (TPI) to examine the relationship between teaching perspectives and disciplines in Higher Education. Studies in Higher Education.*

Ruan, X. (2004). *Conceptual equivalency in translating Teaching Perspectives Inventory (TPI): A Chinese perspective.* (Unpublished master's thesis). University of British Columbia, Vancouver, British Columbia, Canada.

Shulman, L. S. (2005). Signature pedagogies in the professions. *Daedalus, Summer,* 52-59.

Srinivasan, M., Pratt, D. D., Collins, J. B., Bowe, C., Stevenson, F., Pinney, S., & Wilkes, M. (2007). Developing the master educator: Cross-disciplinary teaching scholars program for human and veterinary medical faculty. *Academic Psychiatry, 31,* 452-464.?

Tiffin, S. (2008). *Effective clinical teaching for medical technologists in Canada: Five case studies.* (Unpublished master's thesis). University of British Columbia, Vancouver, British Columbia, Canada.?

Tweed, R. G., & Lehman, D. R. (2002). Learning considered within a cultural context: Confucian and Socratic approaches. *American Psychologist, 57*(2), 89-99.

Williams, J. (2011). *Beliefs, Behaviours, and Professional Development of Tutors in Problem-Based Learning.* Doctoral dissertation published by Erasmus University, Rotterdam. Printed by Ruby Printing Pte. Ltd, Singapore.

CHAPTER 12
Evaluating Teaching
Approaches That Are Equitable and Scholarly

Daniel D. Pratt

At the start of this book you were introduced to a General Model of Teaching and the commitments and defining attributes of five perspectives on teaching. These five perspectives were then illustrated by authors, each of whom holds one of the five as their dominant perspective. In order to detail the diverse belief structures and commitments that comprise these perspectives, several analytical tools were introduced and discussed. These led, in turn, to a summary "snapshot" and more detailed profile for each perspective. Now I want to address the problem of judging quality across that diversity. The purpose of this chapter, therefore, is to produce guidelines and principles for evaluating teaching.

There are three goals to designing effective evaluations that honour the perspectives illustrated in this text: First, the process of evaluation must be thrown open so as to reduce the anxiety and increase the dialogue about what constitutes effective teaching; second, evaluation procedures and criteria must go beyond generalized and superficial approaches to teaching; and finally, evaluations must be both scholarly and equitable—scholarly so as to make visible the substantive aspects of teaching, and equitable so as to not promote or impose one perspective over another when making judgments about the quality of teaching.

I begin this chapter with three questions that must be addressed if the process is to be more open and less anxious. Following that, surface and deep approaches to evaluating teaching are compared, and some specific and practical ideas will be given for making the evaluation process more equitable and scholarly. The chapter ends with seven principles for evaluating teaching.

OPENING THE PROCESS OF EVALUATION

Anyone whose employment or promotion has ever been dependent (even slightly) on the evaluation of his or her teaching knows the tension that accompanies that experience. Even when colleagues are a part of it, the process is often filled with anxiety. Why is this so and how might we reduce the anxiety while increasing the rigor? First, I think much of the anxiety comes from uncertainty. Evaluators seldom negotiate or even discuss the grounds for their evaluation. Nor are teachers reassured that their teaching will be patiently and deeply understood before it is judged.

Second, because the evaluation process and criteria are not usually open and negotiated, there can be a mismatch between the perspectives of those doing the evaluation and the person being evaluated. This causes incongruities to go unexamined and unspoken, as if they didn't exist, there is an increased risk that judgments are about differences of perspective rather than levels of effectiveness in teaching.

Third, evaluation is a process of judging—it sets the value and appraises the worth of something. However, the process is seldom impartial or balanced in power. It involves values and vested interests, with evaluators always in a more powerful position *vis-a-vis* those values and interests. Evaluators are not required to reveal anything about their own teaching, including their beliefs, intentions, or actions, or results of previous ratings and evaluations they might have had. They may be good teachers; or they may not be good teachers. Nevertheless, it is their opinion and judgment about the quality of teaching that counts.

If we are to reduce the anxiety, while also increasing the rigor of evaluations, we need to find ways to open the process and allow better communication between those being evaluated and those doing the evaluating. Assuming people know why an evaluation is being conducted (students, teacher, and evaluators alike), and how the information from the evaluation will be used, there remain three important questions that are seldom asked and which can form the basis for an open and collaborative process of evaluation:

- WHO is being evaluated?
- WHO are the evaluators?
- WHAT is to be evaluated?

Who Is Being Evaluated?

When evaluating teaching, we look through the lens of our own beliefs about teaching. If evaluation is to be open, we must try to step outside tha lens and ask, "Who is the person being evaluated? How do his or her beliefs differ from my own? And, how might that influence my evaluation of this person's teaching?" These questions highlight the central tenet of this chapter: Evaluation of teaching must have regard for the underlying beliefs of those involved in the process, particularly the person whose teaching is being evaluated.

Perspectives on teaching are an extension of individuals within their institutional, social, cultural, and political contexts. Too often the view of teaching held by those in positions of power and authority is accepted, uncritically and unconsciously, as the best or only view of teaching. Such hegemonic assumptions regarding correct or best ways of teaching violate the central premise of this book— that perspectives on teaching (and therefore evaluations of teaching) are inherently pluralistic rather than monolithic. To re-establish a more appropriate, thoughtful balance in evaluation, teachers that are being evaluated must have the opportunity to consider and reveal their beliefs and intentions.

Who Are the Evaluators?

Equally compelling is the question of who is evaluating, and therefore judging, a person's teaching. Again, it is necessary to see the evaluator as both an individual, possessing a dominant perspective on teaching, and an extension of the unit or institution that may have its own dominant view of effective teaching. Both the person and institution have commitments and values that will be played out in the evaluation process; both should be made clear in the evaluation process.

The most essential foundation for evaluation is that both the evaluator and person being evaluated clarify their commitment(s). It would be wrong to assume that only the person being evaluated need clarify commitment; to do that is to increase the imbalance of power that already exists by giving one party (evaluators) information which can be used in the process, but denying the other party (teacher) information to use in negotiating the meaning of what is observed, reported, and used in judgment.

Granted, it may not be realistic to expect that evaluators will be as thorough and revealing in expressing their perspectives on teaching as will the person being evaluated; most often, they have the choice of whether or not to even engage in this dialogue. However, there is room for the teacher being evaluated to probe these values and positions before the process begins so as to be in a position to speak about differences in perception, interpretation, and evaluation as they emerge.

What Is to Be Evaluated?

Most instruments and procedures for evaluating teaching in adult and higher education are designed for efficiency and breadth of application. They start from a conception of teaching as a generic set of skills and duties, not substantively influenced by one's beliefs about content, context, or the characteristics of the students taught. As a result, they most often take a surface approach to evaluating teaching by focusing on duty and/or technical skill.

Yet, if evaluation of teaching is to be scholarly, it must look beyond duty and beneath technique to examine the deeper belief structures associated with variations in what is taught, why it is important, and how it can best be taught to "these people, in this setting, and at this time." Evaluation must look at the substantive aspects, rather than just the most common attributes, of teaching. This is the focus for the next section of this chapter, where we will explore not only the differences between surface and deep approaches to evaluation, but also how to make the substantive aspects of teaching visible for evaluation while remaining fair to each of the perspectives in this book.

SURFACE APPROACHES TO EVALUATION

Focus on the Duties of a Teacher

In these times of educational accountability, one approach to evaluating teaching that has gained considerable attention is what Michael Scriven calls the "duties-based" approach. This approach cuts across perspectives (and styles) and suggests that the best we can do, in the midst of philosophical and cultural diversity, is ask whether or not teachers are fulfilling their duties. Duties, as prescribed by those who take this view, are concerned with fair treatment of students, preparation and management of instruction, and evidence that students learn what is in the objectives when they do the set activities. In response to a question about how to evaluate teaching while respecting and tolerating diversity, Scriven replied:

> *In the recent teacher evaluation literature, there is a point of view which can handle the problem you raise, namely the "style-free" approach. On this view, the only thing you can require of a teacher is the performance of duties, e.g., fairness in the treatment of students, effort in the preparation and management of instruction, and successful learning by students that do the prescribed activities. So the style [perspective] of teaching, e.g., didactic vs. inquiry, is totally irrelevant to teacher evaluation, and hence you can honor divergence while requiring success. The success is measured in the usual ways, with heavy but not exclusive use of student ratings at the pos-sec level.* (Michael Scriven, personal communication, May 2,1995)

He goes on to explain that he is the author of this duties-based approach and that the K-12 version has been through more than 40 revision cycles, using feedback from several thousand teachers and administrators. There is, he said, a less well worked out version for college-level teaching, though no source was given.

This approach seems to take the position that we cannot, in any morally and intellectually honest way, acknowledge all possible forms of good teaching; there are too many possible variations on the "good" of teaching. Thus, the only recourse for evaluators of teaching is to identify those who are negligent in the performance of duty.

Some may say this is one way to be fair to all five perspectives; yet, I doubt that we could get the authors of Chapters 4 through 8 to agree on what are the most essential duties for a teacher. In fact, this approach ignores the very essence of each perspective—the belief structures and commitments—and imposes a set of instrumental values that might be more amenable to one perspective than others. In addition, "duty" is a socially constructed notion. One's sense of duty is inextricably bound up with one's cultural heritage. In China, for example, one's sense of duty as teacher involves the establishment of a lifelong relationship with students and a responsibility to develop their moral character as well as their professional competence (Pratt, 1991, 1992; Watkins & Biggs, 2001; Wong, 1996). Many teachers in such societies would be insulted to have the notion of a teacher's duty circumscribed in such limited ways as spelled out by Scriven. Furthermore, while Scriven's notion of duty may seem expedient and even appropriate for some institutions in North America, it perpetuates the belief that the quality of teaching cannot, and therefore should not, be part of determining who is retained, promoted, or given merit increases. Unless we can rigorously and reliably differentiate between poor, adequate, and exemplary teaching, there is no way to reward people for the quality of their teaching.

Focus on Technical Aspects of Teaching

Another popular approach to evaluating teaching within adult and higher education is the assessment of the technical aspects that cut across disciplines, contexts, and philosophical perspectives of teaching. The workshop described at the beginning of Chapter 2 is an example of one type of faculty development activity popular in higher education. Because such approaches to the improvement and evaluation of teaching are campus-wide and conducted through a centralized office their focus is, primarily, on the technical aspects of teaching—planning, setting objectives, giving lectures, leading discussions, asking questions, communicating under difficult circumstances, and providing feedback to students.

These are important and, though not sufficient, they are a necessary part of what makes an effective teacher. This assumes that the role and responsibility of a teacher to represent and transform a particular body of knowledge to a particular group of learners are the same, despite the subject or the group of learners. This not only ignores the obvious differences between disciplines and professional fields of study, it also dismisses the differences between novices and advanced learners, laboratories and lecture halls, and teaching one student vs. one hundred students. Even the most generic of skills must bend to the conditions of who, what, and where the teaching is being done. Thus, we might have some difficulty reaching agreement on what should constitute *the* technical aspects against which all teachers should be judged.

Yet, their strength is also their weakness; in their generality they lose specificity and substance. When one looks only at the technical aspects of teaching, it matters little whether one is teaching English literature, mathematics, music, or automotive mechanics. For example, I watched a friend in China teach for two hours in a language I didn't understand. At the end of the lesson, she asked for feedback on her teaching. Though I understood neither the language nor the content, I was able to say some- thing about the technical aspects of her teaching. I could see how often she asked questions, to whom she directed them, and what patterns of response occurred. I could see how much the discussion passed through the teacher and how much of it spread horizontally to involve the students in the far corners and back of the room. I could comment on her use of the chalkboard and power point slides, e.g., that she seemed to talk to the board and screen more than to the students. In general, I could say something (apparently) useful to her about her class, without having understood a word of what was said.

As common as these technical aspects are to teaching across disciplines, contexts, and even cultures, there are problems with taking this approach to evaluating teaching. First, we must agree on what technical aspects are universal and necessary to be a good teacher. Squires (1999) highlights this dilemma when he contrasts teaching as rational activity, craft, or art. When teaching is seen as a rational activity, evaluation would focus on the achievement of pre-specified objectives. If seen as a craft, the evaluation of teaching would focus on design and implementation. However, when seen as an art, evaluation would focus on connoisseurship. In each case, the technical aspects should be consistent with the general notion of teaching; but we should not expect them to transfer well to other notions of teaching.

Both surface approaches—duties-based and technically focused—impose a particular set of values and yet, implicitly deny that values should be a part of the evaluation of teaching. In the duties-based approach, for example, the most essential responsibilities (duties) of teachers sound very similar to the primary responsibilities listed in the snapshot of the Transmission Perspective on teaching (Chapter 10). While this view of duties may be acceptable to some, it would be unacceptable to others. It would not, for example, be the most crucial duties for teachers holding the opinion that education is the foundation for a democratic society and must, therefore, challenge those aspects of society that reproduce injustice and inequality (Chapter 8). Those duties may be part of one's responsibilities, but for radical educators, among others, they are not the most essential duties.

Finally, both of these approaches skip over questions of commitment, and the relationship between beliefs about knowledge, learning, and instructional roles and responsibilities. When those questions are omitted, evaluation threatens to be an exercise in assessing what is easy, rather than a process of judging what is essential—what teachers think constitutes knowledge and learning.

Clearly, one cannot be a good or effective teacher without concern for duty and the technical aspects of teaching. These are necessary and important aspects of teaching. But, if teaching is more than duty and skilled performance of technical aspects, how can it be evaluated? We must shift from the generic to the specific, from universal to contextual, and from technical to substantial aspects of teaching.

DEEP APPROACHES TO EVALUATION

The essential ingredient left out of both surface approaches above is the very essence of most adult and higher educators' identity—their content. There can be no teaching without content; something (and someone) must be taught. Whether they teach in universities, colleges, trade schools, or evening adult education programs, most faculty think of themselves as a member of a profession, discipline, or trade, rather than as a teacher (Becher, 1989). More often than not, they introduce themselves in terms of those associations, as historians, chemists, nurses, librarians, carpenters, and so forth. Their subject area is a pivotal aspect of their identity as teachers. As a result, if evaluations are to be credible, the substantive aspects of what is taught must be considered. The decisions teachers make—what is included/excluded from a course, what is emphasized/minimized, and what is assessed as evidence of learning—give some indication of the deeper structures beneath their fulfillment of duty and performance of techniques. Without an evaluation of the substantive aspects of teaching, evaluators are likely to elevate duty and technique to a distorted sense of importance and omit that aspect of teaching upon which people build a lifetime of identity.

Where to Look

Any good teaching evaluation process must consider at least three substantive aspects of teaching, regardless of one's perspective: *planning, implementation, and results.* Within planning, teachers should be able to articulate their intentions and beliefs (commitment and/or justification) related to the subject and their teaching. Colleagues (within one's institution) and peers (external to one's institution) are the best judges of intentions and beliefs related to the content, including the history, purposes, and policies surrounding a course or someone's teaching.

Within the implementation of that planning, there should be evidence of a match between espoused beliefs and intentions, and the enactment of those beliefs and intentions. Colleagues and learners should provide evidence of implementation effectiveness (Bain, 2004). Colleagues can look for the match between espoused and enacted beliefs and intentions. However, learners are also an important source of data; they have a more complete picture of a person's teaching and can judge as to whether it was responsible and respectful as well as meaningful.

Results refer to learning outcomes. Alongside an evaluator's scrutiny of the results of formal evaluations of learning (tests, assignments, projects, etc.), there should be an assessment of progress on the stated goals, and the extent to which people learned things incidental to those goals, but important nonetheless. Good teaching very often reaches beyond assignments and tests for its impact. Indeed, for some of the perspectives presented in this text, evidence in the form of tests and assignments may be incidental to more important outcomes of teaching, e.g., an evolving sense of identity as a member of a community, or having developed more complex ways of understanding one's discipline, or feeling an increase in self-efficacy. These may be more significant kinds of learning than the formal results of examinations, yet they are virtually invisible in traditional means of learner assessment and teacher evaluation. Thus, for a broader, more encompassing estimate of the results of teaching, learners must be given the opportunity to assess their own learning as well as the relationship between their learning and someone's teaching.

In summary, then, effective teaching must have some evidence of clear and significant intentions, which are enacted or carried out in ways that are consistent with those intentions and respectful of learners. Teaching then results in learning outcomes which are related to the teacher's intentions and are evident to the learners. To illustrate how planning, implementation, and the results of teaching can be evaluated in substantive ways that are equitable and scholarly, a few specific examples are presented next.

SOME PRACTICAL EXAMPLES

Planning: Peer Evaluation of Intentions and Directions

There are, at least, four questions to be answered about a teacher's planning. They address a combination of intentions and beliefs that, if clarified, give insight and meaning to the teacher's actions. They also provide a foundation upon which the next two aspects of teaching can be judged—implementation and results.

- What is the teacher trying to accomplish? (Intentions)
- Why is that important? (Beliefs/Justification)
- What (and whose work) is included and excluded? (Intentions)
- Why? (Beliefs/Justification)

These are questions and evaluations that can only be addressed by those familiar with the content area of instruction—usually one's col- leagues (within the same institution) and/or peers (outside one's institution). One procedure for evaluation of a teacher's planning that holds promise to be both equitable and scholarly is what Shulman and Hutchings call the "reflective memo" (1995). Although it is intended for higher education, it could also be used in adult education.

The Reflective Memo

When someone's teaching is to be evaluated, that teacher is asked to select a course and the most important assignment for that course. With the course syllabus and assignment in mind, the teacher writes a reflective memo that discusses the instructional and intellectual goals for the course, and how the assignment will contribute to those goals. Prior to any observations of teaching, the instructor meets with the evaluators and discusses all three parts: syllabus, assignment, and reflective memo. The purpose is to address the questions raised at the outset of this chapter about "who" and "what" aare being evaluated. The documents are used to open the evaluation process by probing and revealing information about the deeper intentions and beliefs of the teacher and the evaluators, and clarify just what is being evaluated.

In preparation for this, teachers are given a set of questions to consider and use as prompts to guide them as they compose their reflective memo. They are not expected to respond to each question. Instead, they are to select questions that engage them in critical reflection on their planning. Because this is a reflective memo, it is recommended that instructors be given the questions well in advance, to allow time to think about them before composing the three to five page memo that elaborates upon underlying intentions and beliefs.

Neither the course syllabus/documents nor the reflective memo alone is as revealing as the combination of them. The teaching plan and assignment allow colleagues to review actual samples of teaching materials; the reflectivememo supplies underlying thinking, and provides a context and frame- work for interpreting and judging substantive aspects of planning.

The entire exercise is an example of how the evaluation of teaching can incorporate reflection on key commitments and belief structures. Incidentally, it also allows the evaluators to make explicit their own beliefs and commitments related to teaching and learning, providing a conversation among the peer evaluators and the teacher about what constitutes good teaching.

The questions below are a sample of what might be included in the directions to teachers. Because the original questions proposed by Shulman and Hutchings were biased toward one or two perspectives, I have replaced them with a more neutral set of questions. They are grouped according to tactical knowledge, normative beliefs, and epistemic beliefs (Chapter 9) to illustrate the link between substantive aspects of teaching and underlying legitimating belief structures. However, when using them it may not be appropriate to group or label them this way. For convenience, all questions are written in the language of a "course" but are appropriate for other forms of teaching as well.

Questions about Tactics and Strategies

•   How does the course begin? Why does it begin as it does?
•   How can you tell when things are going well?

- Think back to a recent episode that didn't go well. Describe it and explain why you think it didn't go well. What would you do differently next time? Why?
- What does it require to be really good at teaching your subject?
- What do you think is the relationship between teaching and learning?
- What do you plan to do next, to improve your teaching in this course?

Questions about Roles, Responsibilities, and Relationships

- What is your primary role in this course? Why?
- What do you and your students do as the course progresses?
- How has your teaching role been successful for you in the past?
- How has that role been difficult or less than successful?
- Why do you think your role has/has not been particularly successful for you?
- What is the role of students or learners in this course? Why?
- How do you know when you're successful as a teacher?
- What is the nature of your relationship with students?

Questions about Knowledge

- What do you want people to learn in this course? Why is that important?
- What crucial issues, key arguments, debates, and authors are to be considered?
- Whose work (authors, critics, practitioners, artists, etc.) is most central to the way you have developed this course and its content? Why?
- Whose work (authors) have you intentionally omitted? Why?
- How does your course link with or lay a foundation for other courses?
- How does it complement or contradict learning from other courses?

Questions about Learning

- What do learners find particularly fascinating about your course? Why?

- Where do they encounter their greatest difficulties in understanding or motivation? Why?
- Where do they do best in the assignments or examinations? Why?
- Where do they have the greatest difficulty in assignments or exams? Why?
- How does your course build on people's prior knowledge or experience?

Questions about Assessment of Learning

- What is the most important assignment in this course?
- Why is it important and how does it reflect your overall intentions?
- How does it reflect your notions of what learning means?
- How does it reveal differences in learners' thinking, acting, or believing?
- How does it get at the key concepts or skills in your course?
- What standards do you use in assessing peoples' work on this assignment?
- How would your standards change if you were teaching a more advanced or an introductory course on this topic?
- How have your standards for this course changed over time? Why?
- What have you learned about improving this assignment, your course, or your teaching as a result of learners' responses to this assignment?

As I said, it is not intended that all questions be used; they are offered as a range of possible and sample questions that will help teachers reflect and reveal the deeper structures of their beliefs and commitments related to teaching. Some kind of reflective activity is necessary if teachers wish to communicate their perspectives to evaluators. It is also necessary if teachers are to become critically aware of their own perspectives on teaching, and if the process of evaluation itself is to promote the improvement of teaching. In so far as the exercises invite reflection on tensions, questions, problems, and educational issues the teacher may be struggling with, they may also prompt a more convincing account of teaching excellence. Furthermore, these means can certainly supplement, and perhaps replace, existing sources of data that treat teaching as unproblematic, skilled performances.

Peer Review in Higher Education

Several institutions, my own among them, have recently instituted a parallel promotion track based on teaching and curricular leadership. In doing so, the evaluation of teaching has to meet the scholarly standards of peer review. Peer review of teaching has, therefore, become a pivotal aspect of scholarly scrutiny (Hubball, Clarke, & Pratt, 2013).

For some, this close scrutiny of teaching may run against assumptions and traditions of academic freedom, especially in higher education. Yet, it seems ironic that academics are willing (and expected) to go public with other kinds of scholarly work, but close the door on their teaching. Teaching is, even more than other forms of scholarship, a public act within a community of students and colleagues that affects all members of that community. To protect it from the same kind of scrutiny given to research or publication is to promote its continued marginalization within academic settings. Teaching must be accountable to the same standards of evaluation as other forms of scholarship, and this must involve colleague and peer review.

Because judgments about teaching often have regard for the history, purposes, policies, and articulation with other program requirements within a department or institution, colleagues are usually asked to assess the quality of planning documents (Centra, 1993). This is not an unusual occurrence. However, to increase their rigor and credibility, judgments must be perceived to be impartial and of high standards. One way to accomplish this is to have the same planning materials, and reflective memo, sent out for peer review by a respected academic, at arms length, involved in similar work/teaching at another institution, much as is done the review of academic writing.

The entire exercise is an example of how the evaluation of teaching can incorporate reflection on key commitments and belief structures. Incidentally, it also allows the evaluators to make explicit their own beliefs and commitments related to teaching and learning, providing a conversation among colleagues, peer evaluators, and the teacher about what constitutes good teaching.

Still, this exercise does not absolutely guard against unfair judgment of a teacher. To do that, evaluations of planning and intent must focus on the individual's representation of a perspective, not the perspective per se.

As part of this, evaluators must look beyond planning to the implementation of plans and intentions as another source of data on someone's teaching. The most common form of data gathering for this aspect is observations by colleagues and learners. The next section offers some practical guidelines for the conduct of teaching observations.

Implementation: Peer and Learner Observations

Classroom observations, as they are usually conducted by colleagues, take only a snapshot of teaching and tend to focus primarily on technical skills of presentation, questioning, responding, and so forth. As such, observations have a poor record and limited potential for the evaluation of teaching. As French-Lazovik reported in a review of literature on classroom observations in higher education:

> The general finding is that it does not provide a sound method of evaluating the teacher's in-class activities. A few classroom visits by one colleague cannot be expected to produce a reliable judgment . . . Even when the number of colleagues is in creased to three, and each makes at least two visits, the reliability of resulting evaluations is so low as to make them use0 less . . . (1975, p. 75).

This is not a surprising finding, given the usual way of conducting classroom observations, at least in higher education. As described in Chapter 3, this is what happened when my teaching was being observed for consideration of promotion at my university. An observer (a senior colleague) entered the room armed with his personal and private "yardstick" of good teaching against which this my teaching was to be assessed. During the visit the observer sat in the back of the room, alternating between sitting passively and scribbling the occasional note. Under the rules of engagement, neither the notes or the thoughts of the observer were presented to me as a way of explaining what was seen, what was considered important (or not), and what value was placed on the process and content observed. After the instructional session was completed, the observer offered a word or two of reassurance and even set a time to discuss the observation, before exiting. This is all too common an occurrence in higher or further education.

To make matters worse, classroom observations are too often driven by the perception that teaching need only be adequate, because it doesn't occupy an important place in the reward system. As a result, the usual process of observing a colleague is neither democratic nor compassionate; moreover, the product is often neither helpful to the teacher nor reliable to the process of making a judgment.

The American Association for Higher Education (AAHE) *Peer Review of Teaching Project* (1995) offers several guidelines for improving observations by colleagues. They are presented below, with some additions and modifications, as part of a strategy for reducing the anxiety and increasing the reliability associated with gathering implementation data.

- *Avoid "parachuting" into a class,* making your observations, and then exiting to make judgments without consulting with the teacher.
- *Make observations part of a consultation process that includes both a pre-visit and a post-visit meeting.* The pre-visit meeting should establish the purpose of the observation, the goals for the class, and how those goals fit within the overall agenda for the course. The post-visit meeting should be a debriefing to discuss what the observer saw. As well, the teacher's own assessment of the session should be included in the discussion.
- *Link observations to reviews of teaching materials, the reflective memo, and discussions of these materials.* Colleagues' observations and meetings with students should assess the internal consistency of a teacher's espoused and actual beliefs and intentions. Planning, implementation, and results should be complementary.
- *Conduct several observations,* distributed across the entire term of a course, rather than a single snapshot look at one session.
- *Combine observations with other information about the person's teaching,* including interviews with students, review of course materials, examination of assignments and samples of student work.

- *Use a team approach,* in which colleagues pair up or work in small groups to visit one another's classes over the term of a course.
- *As observers, be open to learning* about different approaches to teaching while judging the quality of another's teaching.
- *Let students know what is happening and why;* tell them the purpose of the evaluation and the role of observations in the process.

Notice that this method of peer observation is not the same as the glimpse one would get through one or two observations of someone's teaching; nor is it entirely dependent upon colleagues' opinion of teaching. Learners in this aspect of evaluation are an important source of data and opinion. By being clear in purpose and procedure to learners and teachers alike, this method offers a more open process of evaluation that can, potentially, reduce anxiety and increase the likelihood that observations will focus on substantive aspects of teaching. Most importantly, this approach is meant to complement the review of course materials and the teacher's reflections on plans and assignments.

Substantive approaches to evaluation of teaching also require assessment of a third aspect—the effects of teaching. For data on that, evaluators must turn to learners and *their* assessment of the effects of teaching on *their* learning.

Results: Assessment of Learning

Overall, there is no more widely used source of data for evaluating teaching than learner opinion. Learners are perceived by many to be the most reliable source of data about the relationship between teaching and learning on the grounds that they are witness to the teaching across time and the best judge of its effects on their achievements (Cashin, 1988; Kahn, 1993). Learner opinion is considered a necessary, and sometimes sufficient, source of evidence on which to judge the quality of teaching, even across diverse groups of learners, disciplines, and cultures (e.g., Marsh, 1986; Marsh, Touron, and Wheeler, 1985; Watkins, 1992; Watkins, Marsh, and Young, 1987; Watkins and Thomas, 1991).

Yet, most learner evaluations focus on the process rather than outcomes of teaching. For example, they often ask to what extent

the teacher clarified goals and objectives, was organized and prepared, used time wisely, emphasized key concepts, provided timely
feedback on assignments, was enthusiastic about the subject, and
treated learners with respect. While this may be useful information
for the improvement of teaching, it is not very useful for assessing
the effects of teaching. For example, it does not address what was
taught and what was learned, the value of that learning, or the effects of teaching upon student learning. If learner evaluations are to
be credible, the data must reflect issues clearly related to the effects
of teaching; and learners must be a logical source of that data.

In order to make learner evaluations equitable to all perspectives on teaching, they must be designed with a broad conception
of what effective means, including both intended and unintended
outcomes. Learners also bring perspectives to the task of evaluating
teaching; they know what is effective for their class and for their
learning. Therefore, unlike the evaluators, learners *should* be invited to judge the effectiveness of teaching from their point of view;
it is *their learning* that is a measure of the teacher's effectiveness.

In addition, while examinations, assignments, lab work, and
even portfolios of students' work are important evidence of learning, they may not be accurate or sufficient indications of the relationship between teaching and learning. We all know people and
circumstances where achievement was not due to the teacher but to
diligence and determination on the part of the learner. Thus, for
information about learning to be equitable and credible, it must be
related to the *perceived effects* of teaching, not the personal diligence or attributes of learners.

This requires another note of caution: opinions about a teacher
must not be confused with opinions about a subject or course. It is
possible to value a course or subject, but not the teacher; it is also
possible to appreciate an instructor but not the subject or course.
For example, learners may have taken a particularly critical course
that opened new vistas of thinking; yet, their teacher may have been
only marginally effective and not at all central to their awakening.
Conversely, a teacher may have been critical for an individual, or
even a group of students, but the subject or course may have been
only incidental to that impact. In both cases, if the evaluation of
teaching is to be scholarly and equitable it is important not to mix
the perceived value of a course with the effectiveness of a teacher.
For an evaluation to be credible, it should differentiate between evalu-

ations of courses and instructors, and between levels of effectiveness ranging from poor to exemplary teaching.

With these conditions and cautions in mind, the literature on *summative ratings* of teaching suggests that learners can provide reliable information on the following topics:

- An estimate of progress on course goals
- *Information on additional learning (beyond course goals)*
- *An overall assessment of the value of a course*
- *An overall rating of the instructor's effectiveness*

Each topic is presented below, as part of a *sample learner evaluation form* (Figure 12.1) with appropriate response scales and related open-ended questions. The order is important to this process—beginning with an assessment of personal learning, followed by an assessment of the course, and concluding with a rating of the effectiveness of the instructor.

By asking about the effectiveness of the teacher last, people have had a chance to vent any negative or positive feelings they might have that could confound the rating of the instructor (e.g., a required course or a favorite subject). Furthermore, this sequence allows them to consider their learning separate from the teacher's effectiveness.

In PART A, students are asked to rate their progress on a number of key goals related to the course/instructor under evaluation. The sample form allows for five goals; the number will vary, but probably shouldn't exceed ten. Goals that are rated should be the same as those given to learners at the beginning of a course. Prior to receiving the results of the evaluation the instructor gives a weighting to those same goals as an indication of intention and emphasis within his or her teaching. Student learning (progress) can then be compared with an instructor's intentions, as indicated in the weighing of his or her goals (Cashin & Downey, 1995).

Notice that the scaling for PARTS C and D is different than most rating forms, allowing for course and instructor to be evaluated in four categories: poor (0), marginal (1-2), adequate (3-4), and exemplary (5-6). This is to counter the tendency with most evaluation forms to rate the majority of teachers at the higher end of the scale, thus losing the ability to identify those who are "uncommonly" effective. If learners' evaluations are to be scholarly and credible, evaluators should be able to differentiate between poor, marginal,

Student Evaluation Form

This evaluation form asks you to provide information on the following:

PART A: An estimation of your **progress on course goals**
PART B: Additional **learning** (beyond course goals)
PART C: The overall **value of this course** to you
PART D: An evaluation of the **instructor's effectiveness**

Your responses will contribute to an evaluation of the instructor's teaching. In addition to your opinion, there will be an assessment of the course readings, assignments, and content by the instructor's peers. The instructor will also be asked to provide information related to the teaching of this and possibly other courses.

PART A: PROGRESS ON GOALS—Using the scales below, rate your progress on each of the goals listed. These should be the same goals you were given at the beginning of the course. Then, comment on what was helpful and what else would have facilitated your progress related to these goals.

1. *Rate your progress on each of the course goals listed below: (circle a number for each goal)*

Goal (a) _____
Rate your progress: 0) none 1) little 2) some 3) average 4) good 5) excellent 6) extraordinary

Goal (b) _____
Rate your progress: 0) none 1) little 2) some 3) average 4) good 5) excellent 6) extraordinary

Goal (c) _____
Rate your progress: 0) none 1) little 2) some 3) average 4) good 5) excellent 6) extraordinary

Goal (d) _____
Rate your progress: 0) none 1) little 2) some 3) average 4) good 5) excellent 6) extraordinary

Goal (e) _____
Rate your progress: 0) none 1) little 2) some 3) average 4) good 5) excellent 6) extraordinary

2. *What was particularly HELPFUL to your progress on these goals?*

3. *What else could have been done to FACILITATE your progress on these goals?*

PART B: ADDITIONAL LEARNING—If you can, identify any additional learning from this course or instructor that was particularly important to you. If you cannot think of any, leave this section blank and go on to PART C.

4. *Within this course, was there something else you learned (in addition to the goals above) that was particularly important to you?*

5.   *Why is that important to you?*

PART C: VALUE OF THE COURSEóOn the scale below, rate the value of the course. Then, comment on what was particularly valuable and what could be done to make the course more valuable.

6.   *Provide an overall rating of the VALUE of the COURSE: (circle one)*
     0) none 1)very little 2) some 3) average 4) more than most courses 5) far exceeded most courses 6) an exceptional courses

7.   *What was particularly VALUABLE?*

8.   *What could be done to make the course MORE VALUABLE?*

PART D: EFFECTIVENESS OF THE INSTRUCTORóUsing the scale below, provide an overall rating of your instructor. Then, comment on the ways in which your instructor could be more effective. Notice that the highest ratings are reserved for those instructors perceived to be among the most effective in your program or in your experience as an adult learner.

9.   *Provide an overall rating of the INSTRUCTOR: (circle one)*
     0) poor 1) marginally effective 2) sometimes effective 3) usually effective 4) always effective 5) one of my most effective 6) an exceptional teacher

10.   *What did the instructor do that was PARTICULARLY EFFECTIVE?*

11.   *What could the instructor do to be MORE EFFECTIVE?*

Figure 12.1 Sample Learner/Student Evaluation Form
(continued from previous page)

adequate, and truly exceptional teaching. Thus, as is mentioned in the instructions to learners in PART D, the highest ratings are reserved for teachers who are perceived to be among the most effective—in a program, an institution, or the learner's adult experience. In addition, there is allowance for comments that give more specific feedback about what was valuable, helpful, and effective, as well as how the learning, course, and teaching could be improved.

In summary, students are asked to tell evaluators to what extent their course is valuable, their instructor effective, and that they are making progress on goals that are deemed important by a faculty member and student peers. In terms of an evaluation's credibility, these are questions that must be addressed; they are also questions that only students can answer.

It would be difficult to reconcile a difference of opinion that said a teacher was uncommonly effective, yet people learned very little; or if people said a teacher was only marginally effective, yet they learned more than in most courses. Yet, evaluators must know what part the instructor played in the learning that resulted from a course. One would hope there is agreement between these questions; but if there isn't, it is a clear indication for the need to inquire as to why there isn't.

Self-evaluation: The Teaching Portfolio

Teachers are increasingly being asked to prepare documentation that substantiates their efforts and accomplishments in teaching. This approach is called the *teaching portfolio* and holds great promise. It had its start in Canada, under the sponsorship of the Canadian Association of University Teachers (CAUT) and was intended to expand the body of evidence administrators could consider when making personnel decisions. According to the original guide called *The Teaching Dossier,* it is a "summary of a professor's major teaching accomplishments and strengths. It is to a professor's teaching what lists of publications, grants, and academic honors are to research" (Shore, 1986, p. 1), a kind of "extended teaching resume . . . a brief but comprehensive account of teaching activity over a defined period of time." (AAHE, 1991, p. 3). A great deal has been written on the subject (e.g., Foster, Harrap, & Page, 1983; King, 1990; Seldin, 1991; Stark & McKeachie, 1991; Vavrus & Collins, 1991) and does not need to be repeated here. However, if teaching portfolios are to be taken seriously, they must be perceived as scholarly pieces of evidence about teaching. How can that be accomplished?

One way in which teaching portfolios can be more scholarly is to incorporate reflection as part of the substance upon which judgments are made. Rather than judging the volume of work submitted, or the sheen of its lamination, evaluators might ask teachers to provide evidence of growth and change, success and failures, plans and aspirations, with reflective comments/memos that take the reader/evaluator deep into the substance and reasoning of the teacher's evolving thinking and approaches.

As well, the Statement of Teaching Philosophy might be used more judiciously. My colleague, Gary Poole, suggests the following:

The Teaching Philosophy Statement is intended to orient reviewers to the dossier by providing a clear rationale for the elements and data found within and a framework for reflection on teaching. Though this purpose seems clear enough, it has been difficult for reviewers to know just what to look for when evaluating a statement of teaching philosophy. Fortunately, these statements have evolved through at least three distinct phases that indicate levels of development in scholarly teaching and make it easier to assess the quality of a statement.

The First Phase: A Statement of Valuing Teaching

Early versions of the Statement of Teaching Philosophy often described how important teaching is to the individual. I doubt anyone has ever read a statement in which a person states that teaching doesn't matter. Common phrases include such things as, "It is very important that we educate our students to be contributing citizens who can think critically." Or, "I take my teaching responsibilities very seriously, and I am always fully prepared before I enter the classroom." Or, "Students deserve the very best education we can provide for them."

While these statements might be reassuring or even inspirational, they provide no details or rationale that give justification or explanation for teaching in particular ways; nor do they constitute the basis for reflection on teaching. Consequently, they are often read cynically as simply a collection of platitudes.

The Second Phase: A Statement of Personal Theories of Teaching and Learning

The first phase says, in essence, "Teaching matters to me and so I work hard at it." The second phase says, "I teach the way I do because it is consistent with what I believe about learning." This phase represents a significant step forward for Statements of Teaching Philosophy. Statements are more focused on learning, with people actually thinking about how students learn and constructing teaching strategies that align with beliefs about what promotes learning.

Common phrases from this second phase include such things as, "Students today have shorter attention spans and so it is important to change topics and/or pace frequently". Or, "Students learn better when they receive feedback and have a chance to revise their work accordingly." Or, "Students as a rule do not like to do group projects, so I spend at least 30 minutes of class time explaining why group projects are important."

While such personal theories may provide an orientation to elements within the dossier, they are usually derived informally from personal observations and anecdotal examples. As such, reflection on teaching is prone to stereotypical thinking and "availability bias," or the tendency to overgeneralize from information that is most readily available.

The Third Phase: The Application of Scholarly Literature to Inform Practice

The second phase says, in essence, "My teaching is based on a few powerful ideas that have proven useful to me." In the third phase, statements evolve from personal theories to referencing widely disseminated, peer-reviewed literature and/or theory related to learning or teaching. While it is possible that a person may espouse a "pet theory" in such a statement, at least there is a connection between scholarship and practice that provides a rationale for what is contained within the dossier and a substantive basis for reflecting on teaching. This is not to say that a faculty member should write a 250-word statement that evaluates the relative merits of competing theories of learning. Rather, to be able to cite one that is used as a guiding light would be laudable.

Examples of phrases include, "My teaching is informed by Chickering and Gamson's (1987) Seven Principles of Good Practice for Undergraduate Education; in particular, their recommendation to use active learning techniques." Or, "In all my teaching, I try to be mindful of Pratt's (1998) notions of challenge and support, and the benefits of maximizing both together." Or, "I have been influenced considerably by Kuh's (2008) list of what he calls 'high-impact educational practices.'"

> *A good Statement of Teaching Philosophy will provide a brief and understandable explanation of the principles, theory, and/ or evidence that guides teaching practices and form the basis for reflection on those practices* (Poole, 2014).

In other words, much of what has been said thus far about scholarly evaluation of teaching applies as well to self-evaluations of teaching. They must be rigorous and go into substantive aspects of teaching if they are to be credible.

Being Strategic: Involving Key Individuals

Finally, we must consider the costs and benefits associated with this more elaborate approach to the evaluation of teaching. Clearly, the time and resources needed to assess and document the quality of teaching in the ways described here go well beyond the usual learner evaluations and colleague observations. In many institutions there will not be support for such an expenditure of diminishing resources on the evaluation of teaching. Yet, this is a catch-22. Until such time as the evaluation of teaching is rigorously and credibly documented, it will not be considered a legitimate scholarly activity; but, until it is valued alongside the more traditional scholarly activities, resources will not be spent in documenting its substantive nature. Therefore, we must be more strategic in the development and implementation of evaluation procedures.

One way in which to begin the process is by focusing on helping the person who writes the report that goes forward within the institution. Too often, the work of evaluation has been focused on helping the faculty member document his or her teaching, without giving enough thought to the person that must take the recommendations forward on behalf of the candidate who is up for review. For example, in most of higher education the key person responsible for making a case for reappointment, tenure, or promotion is the department or division head. He or she is responsible for taking the evidence (and possibly a personnel committee's recommendation) to the next level in the institution. In effect, this individual becomes the chief advocate for the person who is under review. Evaluation criteria, procedures, and evidence should facilitate this person's work. Indeed, without this strategic concern, evaluations are at risk of being ignored or dismissed, thus perpetuating the catch-22 of teaching not being valued because of the ways in which it is conceptualized and documented, yet not being rigorously documented because it is not highly valued.

SUMMARY

The challenge of this chapter has been to suggest guidelines and principles that honor the diversity of teaching perspectives while also increasing the rigor of evaluating teaching. It would be relatively easy to offer evaluation guidelines that are equitable but which do not concern themselves with rigor. Surface approaches based on duties and/or technical aspects of teaching do this. Yet, good teaching is scholarly; to be less than that in its evaluation is to be unfair, not in the sense of promoting one perspective over another, but in not seeing what lies at the core of that which is uncommonly good about truly effective teaching. To be scholarly in the evaluation of teaching requires a fundamental change in approach—one that shifts the focus of evaluation from surface features to deeper structures and one that asks, "why" more than "how." Without this crucial shift in approach, teaching will continue to be seen as a relatively mechanistic activity, devoid of the most essential ingredient—one's professional identity.

And yet, the very diversity of perspectives, coupled with the inherent structural imbalances in the process of teacher evaluation, seem to pre- sent a formidable barrier to changing evaluation. As such, this chapter began with some suggestions about how to open the process to perspectives on teaching that are different from those that predominate within a group or an institution. The use of reflective memos as an artifact around which to discuss and negotiate ideas about good teaching in a collaborative exchange of views allows the assessment of teaching to also become a means by which the community improves its teaching.

Indeed, the evaluation of teaching should not be an end in itself, but a vehicle for educational reform or improvement. To that end, I invite those who are charged with the evaluation of teaching to recognize and acknowledge the lens through which they view and interpret another's teaching. At the same time, I ask that evaluators not succumb to the entrapments of efficiency and anonymous representation of that which is intensely personal—one's teaching.

The benefits, therefore, from equitable, scholarly, and appropriately respectful evaluation processes are legion. It simply makes sense, from the learners', the teachers', and the institutions' points of view to embrace evaluation methods that attend to substantive rather than surface aspects of teaching. With that in mind, I close this chapter with a list of seven principles which, if used to guide evaluation, will respect a plurality of the good in teaching and promote its continuous thoughtful improvement.

Principles for Evaluating Teaching

Principle 1: *Evaluation should acknowledge and respect diversity in belief structures and commitments.*

Principle 2: *Evaluation should involve multiple and credible sources of data.*

Principle 3: Evaluation should assess substantive, as well as technical, aspects of teaching.

Principle 4: Evaluation should consider planning, implementation, and results of teaching.

Principle 5: Evaluation should be an open process.

Principle 6: Evaluation should be concerned with the improvement of teaching.

Principle 7: Evaluations should be done in consultation with key individuals responsible for taking data and recommendations forward within an institution.

CONCLUSION

If this book has persuaded you that the diversity of teaching is not accidental but is rather a manifestation of deeply held beliefs applied to a vast array of learners, subjects, and contexts, it will have partially succeeded in its intent. Acknowledging the legitimacy of multiple perspectives, comprehending how to analyze those perspectives, and relishing the different ways they approach teaching and learning, is, after all, still confined to mental exercises. But teaching is visceral. It changes and challenges each participant every time the class starts. It is full of thought provoking moments; indeed, it is one of those rare professions that can grow immensely more interesting over time. This book will have really succeeded when it not only comes off the shelf of your library, but off the shelf of your own self-expectations as a teacher. Once you find yourself practicing, observing, evaluating, and discussing teaching in full enjoyment of its many faces of excellence, then you will have made this text your own. I wish you well on that journey.

REFERENCES

American Association for Higher Education (AAHE) (1991). *The teaching portfolio: Capturing the scholarship in teaching.* Washington, DC: Author.

American Association for Higher Education (AAHE) (1995). *From idea* to prototype: The peer review of teaching—choosing from a menu of strategies *(pp. 4-5). Washington, DC: Author.*

Bain, K. (2004). *What the Best College Teachers Do.* Cambridge: Harvard University Press.

Becher, T. (1989). *Academic tribes and territories: Intellectual enquiry and the cultures of disciplines.* Milton Keynes: SRHE and Open University Press.

Brookfield, S. D. (2006). *The skillful teacher: On technique, trust, and responsiveness in the classroom (2nd ed.).* San Francisco: Jossey-Bass.

Cashin, W. E. (1988). *Student ratings of teaching: A summary of the research.* Idea Paper No. 20. Manhattan: Center for Faculty Evaluation & Development, Kansas State University.

Cashin, W. E., & Downey, R. G. (1995). Disciplinary differences in what is taught and in students' perceptions of what they learn and of how they are taught. In N. Hatva & M. Marincovich (Eds.), *Disciplinary differences in teaching and learning: Implications for practice* (pp. 81-92). New Directions for Teaching and Learning, No. 64, Winter, San Francisco: Jossey-Bass.

Centra, J. A. (1993). *Reflective faculty evaluation.* San Francisco: Jossey- Bass.

Foster, S. E, Harrap, T, & Page, G. C. (1983). The teaching dossier. *Higher Education in Europe, 8(2),* 45-53.

French-Lazovik, G. (1975). *Evaluation of college teaching: Guidelinesfor summative and formative procedures.* Washington, DC: Association of American Colleges.

Hubball, H., Clarke, A., Pratt, D. D. (2013). Fostering scholarly approaches to peer review of teaching in a research-intensive university. In D. J. Salter, (Ed.). *Cases on Quality Teaching Practices in Higher Education*, Chapter 12, pp. 191-211.

Kahn, S. (1993). Better teaching through better evaluation: A guide forfaculty and institutions. *To Improve the Academy, 12,* 111-126.

King, B. (1990). *Linking portfolios with standardized exercises: One example from the teacher assessment project* (Technical Report). Stan-ford, CA: Stanford University, School of Education, Teacher Assessment Project.

Marsh, H. W. (1986). Applicability paradigm: Students' evaluations ofteaching effectiveness in different countries. *Journal of EducationalPsychology, 78,* 465-473.

Marsh, H. W, Touron, J. & Wheeler, B. (1985). Students' evaluations ofuniversity instructors: The applicability of American instruments ina Spanish setting. *Teaching and Teacher Education, 1,* 123-138.

Poole, G. (2014). *The Evolution of the Statement of Teaching Philosophy*. University of British Columbia.

Pratt, D. D. (1991). Conceptions of self within China and the United States. *International Journal of Intercultural Relations* (USA), *15* (3), 285-310.

Pratt, D. D. (1992). Chinese conceptions of learning and teaching: A Westerner's attempt at understanding. *International Journal of Life-long Education* (UK), *11* (4), 301-319.

Seldin, P. (1991). *The teaching portfolio: A practical guide to improved performance and promotion/tenure decisions*. Boston, MA: Anker Publishing.

Shore, B. M. (1986). *The teaching dossier: A guide to its preparation and use* (Rev. ed.). Montreal: Canadian Association of University Teachers.

Squires, G. (1999) *Teaching as a Professional Discipline*. London: Falmer Press.

Stark, J. S., & McKeachie, W. (1991). *National center for research to improve postsecondary teaching and learning: Final report*. Ann Arbor, MI: NCRIPTAL.

Shulman, L., & Hutchings, P. (1995). Exercise I - teaching as scholarship: Reflections on a syllabus. In P. Hutchings (Ed.), *From idea to prototype: The peer review of teaching—a project work book.* Washington, DC: The American Association for Higher Education.

Vavrus, L., & Collins, A. (1991). Portfolio documentation and assessment center exercises: A marriage made for teacher assessment. *Teacher Education Quarterly, 18(3),* 13-39.

Watkins, D. (1992). Evaluating the effectiveness of tertiary teaching: A Filipino investigation. *Educational Research Journal, 7,* 60-67.

Watkins, D., & Biggs, J. B. (2001). Teaching the Chinese Learner: Psychological and pedagogical perspectives.

Watkins, D., Marsh, H. W., & Young, D. (1987). Evaluating tertiary teaching: A New Zealand perspective. *Teaching and Teacher Education, 3,* 41-53.

Watkins, D., & Thomas, B. (1991). Assessing teaching effectiveness: An Indian perspective. *Assessment and Evaluation in Higher Education, 16,* 185-198.

Wong, M. (1996). A study of traditional Chinese apprenticeship: A look at five Chinese masters. Unpublished master's thesis. The University of British Columbia, Vancouver, Canada.

Wong, W. (1995). Use of teaching portfolio to capture your scholarship in teaching. *Teaching-Learning Tips,* Issue 10/95. Educational Technology Centre. The Hong Kong University of Science and Technology: Clear Water Bay, Kowloon, Hong Kong.

Author Index

Akerlind, G. S., 50
Alet, A. L. 123
Alsardary, S., 194
Altschuler, M., 291
Ambrose, S. A., 56, 78, 98
American Association for Higher
  Education, 314, 320
Anderson, O. R., 131
Aoki, T., 161
Apps, J., 175, 280
Arseneau, R., 53
Arthur, J., 200
Ashton, P., 165
Ausubel, D. P., 85
Azer, S. A., 78
Bain, J. D., 50
Bain, K., 58, 77, 85, 88, 89, 97, 293,
  307
Bandura, A., 179
Bateman, W. L., 175
Bates, J., 61, 262
Baynard, E., 291
Becher, T., 306
Belluck, P., 79
Benassi, V.A., 98
Bender, J., 188
Biggs, J.B., 94, 304
Bingham, W., 247
Blumberg, P., 194
Boll, S. L., 218

Bonn, D. A., 225
Booth, S., 94
Bordage, G., 85
Bourdieu, P., 200, 207-209
Bowers, J., 114, 115
Bowman, S., 78
Bridges, M. W., 98
Brookfield, S. D., 144, 182, 184,
  185, 191, 229, 230, 273, 280
Brown, P. C., 79, 80, 97
Brown, S., 78
Burke, K., 43
Burkill, S., 78
Butler, A. C., 79, 80
Butterwick, S., 207
Calderhead, J., 165
Candy, P. C., 26, 131, 157, 158
Carraccio, C., 123
Caruseta, E., 194
Cashin, W. E., 315, 317
Cate, O. T., 123
Centra, J. A., 312
Chan, C. H., 282
Chapman, V., 188
Christensen, C. M., 79
Clark, B. R., 107, 110
Clarke, A., 291, 312
Clover, D. E., 199
Cobb, P., 114, 115
Coles, C., 144

Subject Index